SHAKESPEARE AS A
WAY OF LIFE

SHAKESPEARE AS A WAY OF LIFE

SKEPTICAL PRACTICE AND THE
POLITICS OF WEAKNESS

JAMES KUZNER

Fordham University Press New York 2016

Copyright © 2016 Fordham University Press

Fordham University Press has no responsibility for the persistence or accuracy of URLs for external or third-party Internet websites referred to in this publication and does not guarantee that any content on such websites is, or will remain, accurate or appropriate.

Fordham University Press also publishes its books in a variety of electronic formats. Some content that appears in print may not be available in electronic books.

Visit us online at www.fordhampress.com.

Library of Congress Cataloging-in-Publication Data

Kuzner, James.
Shakespeare as a way of life : skeptical practice and the politics of weakness / James Kuzner.
    pages cm
Includes bibliographical references and index.
ISBN 978-0-8232-6993-8 (hardback) — ISBN 978-0-8232-6994-5 (paper)
1. Shakespeare, William, 1564–1616—Criticism and interpretation.   I. Title.
PR2976.K85 2016
822.3'3—dc23

2015031054

Printed in the United States of America

18 17 16   5 4 3 2 1

First edition

Contents

SHAKESPEARE AS A
WAY OF LIFE

Introduction: Shakespeare's Skeptical Practice and the Politics of Weakness

Reading Shakespeare helps us to live with epistemological weakness and even to practice this weakness, to make it a way of life. In this book I show how his works offer a means for coming to terms with basic uncertainties: about how we can be free, about whether the world is abundant, about whether we have met the demands of love and social life. I also show how this offer of Shakespeare's implies a politics.

Despite its title, this book is not bardolatrous. Later I consider many measures of Shakespeare's worth, but I begin by dwelling on an unusually influential one, related to but distinct from my own, set out by Keats. What "Shakespeare possessed so enormously," Keats explains, is "*Negative Capability*, that is when man is capable of being in uncertainties, Mysteries, doubts, without any irritable reaching after fact and reason."[1] Keats never precisely defines negative capability, but as it unfolds across letters, Li Ou points out, such capability requires abandoning "the comfortable enclosure of doctrinaire knowledge" in favor of "the actual vastness and complexity of experience."[2] Such receptive openness gives us two abilities important for my purposes here: the ability to contain contradictory ideas and to pass beyond the threshold of self-loss.

The ability to contain contradictory ideas entails the inability to make up one's mind, an inability that Keats regards not as weakness but as strength. Indeed "[t]he only means of strengthening one's intellect," Keats writes, "is to make up one's mind about nothing, to let the mind be a thoroughfare for all thoughts."[3] Only by relinquishing doctrinaire ideas, being "certain of nothing but of the holiness of the Heart's affections and the truth of Imagination," can we comprehend true beauty (54). Making the mind a passage for all thoughts evokes passivity yet strengthens the understanding, which in turn makes Shakespearean poetry possible. Epistemological weakness, for Keats, is a condition for poetic strength.

The second ability, an ultimately rewarding self-loss, follows from the first. When the mind becomes an open thoroughfare, the poet relinquishes stable selfhood, dissolving the cognitive boundaries, built over the course of a life, that include, exclude, and organize thought so as to characterize experience predictably. For Keats the poet "has no self—it is everything and nothing—It has no character . . . A Poet is the most unpoetical of anything in existence because he has no Identity; he is continually in for and filling some other Body" (194–5). Negative capability strengthens the intellect partly by granting the poet empathetic powers; the passivity of self-loss allows for the activity of entering other minds. Even more: the poet who for a time has "no Identity" finally—paradoxically—gains an identity far more impressive than the one initially lost (195). Negative capability dissolves the self so that it might be reforged, making the poet a "Soul"; "[t]here may be intelligences or sparks of the divinity in millions," Keats writes, "but they are not Souls till they acquire identities, till each one is personally itself" (290). Only the negatively capable accomplish this, with Shakespeare as the supreme example. Thus Lionel Trilling concludes that the Keatsian ideal is "anything but a 'negative' capability—it is the most *positive* capability imaginable," in part because it "is the sign of personal identity"; "[o]nly the self that is certain of its existence, of its identity, can do without the armor of systematic certainties."[4]

This is a book about skeptical practice, so I, like many readers, agree that Shakespearean texts suggest a mind "capable of being in uncertainties."[5] I agree, as well, that emulating Shakespearean cognition is worthwhile. But I disagree with Keatsian readings wherein weakness transforms into strength: wherein Shakespearean incertitude bolsters the mind, heightens its capacity for empathetic knowledge, and ends in self-refortification. As I read them, Shakespeare's works induce an epistemological weakness meant to be unremitting, a state in which readers are called to abide. Shakespeare does so by emphasizing how accepting weakness also means practicing weakness in response to fundamental problems, not so much of poetic as of everyday concern. Shakespeare addresses how a skeptic might: occupy an ethical field without normative coordinates (*The Winter's Tale*); be free while in doubt about metaphors of free movement by which liberty is conceived (*The Tempest*); love without knowing what it demands or what we can expect from it (*Othello*); and respond to violence amid incertitude about the separability of body and mind (*Lucrece*). Shakespeare, in other words, suggests practices for making skepticism livable yet for keeping negative capability negative. These practices, I show, are not the comforting ones often identified in studies of early modern skepticism in general and of Shakespeare in particular: of responding to uncertainty with conservative reliance on custom, liberal open-mindedness, or confident pragmatism. While Shakespeare keeps skepticism from lapsing into nihilism and from the consuming doubt later linked to Descartes, he takes the unsettling quality of uncertainty so seriously that the skeptical practices his works suggest are only just recognizable as practices.

Partly due to the classical provenance of practices of the self, we tend to think of them in firmly practical terms, as activities that aim to establish control in one or (usually) both of two domains. Practices aim inward, to promote inner order, calm, and self-cultivation; they also aim outward, at cosmic understanding and efficacy in the world. Despite serious differences, the two preeminent theorists of practices of the self, Michel Foucault and Pierre Hadot, show how these practices work toward meticulously calibrated control.[6] While Foucault I treat at some length in my chapter on *The Tempest*, this book's very title alludes to Hadot's conception of philosophy as a way of life, a conception that serves as a second jumping-off point for how I think about Shakespeare in this book.

Hadot conceives of classical philosophy first as a "choice of a way of life."[7] Far from being an "accessory or appendix" to an abstract system of philosophical discourse, this choice is at philosophy's origins (3). Philosophy aims to inform individuals, to transmit set knowledge to them, but it also—primarily—aims to form and even transform them (274). Hadot shows how, across philosophical schools, philosophy involves *askēsis*—exercises that range from the dietary and the dialogic to the mathematical and meditative—aimed at guiding the student toward wisdom, peace of mind, and a controlled, self-consistent life (102). If we emphasize aporia-free discourse, we often miss what ancient philosophy's goal was, and, Hadot suggests, ought to still be: not first to "communicate knowledge but to form and to train" (274). Hadot thus defines ancient philosophical discourse itself "as a spiritual exercise—in other words, as a practice intended to carry out a radical change in our being" (176).

Shakespeare's texts constitute and urge philosophical *askēsis* in many of Hadot's senses—in prompting a transformative, "existential choice," and in being concerned more with committing to a certain kind of life than with constructing or mastering elaborate philosophical systems (176). Indeed, the less-than-systematic nature of Shakespeare's skeptical practice helps explain why I read it alongside classical and early modern figures as disparate in their skeptical commitments as Cicero, Sextus Empiricus, Montaigne, and Descartes.[8] The thought of these figures overlaps only partially with that of Shakespeare, which seems less invested in a consistent relationship to skeptical lines of thought—themselves not overly precise—than in imagining skeptical practices for everyday existence.[9] I agree with William Hamlin and others that early modern "scepticism is less a school of thought than a temper of mind," a series of habits and tendencies rather than a system of dogma.[10] I also agree with Hamlin that many early moderns, Shakespeare included, either did not know or do not evince sustained interest in, say, the differences between Academic and Pyrrhonist skepticisms of antiquity, as Shakespeare lived in a time of "gradual fusion of common-sense skepticism with its philosophically grounded counterpart" (70). Shakespeare is as likely to exhibit common-sense doubts of the tavern—about miracles and about customary ways of thinking—as he is to dabble in more philosophically sophisticated skepticism.

Subsequent chapters detail Shakespeare's experiments with the staples of skepticism in its Academic, Pyrrhonist, more popular, and even Christian manifestations. In Hamlin's outline, these staples include: (1) a "sense of human weakness and mental frailty"; (2) "an awareness of the blatant fact of conflicting judgements and appearances"; (3) "an abiding fascination with the moment of *skepsis*, or judgemental suspension"; (4) a sense of "the untrustworthiness of sense-data"; (5) a distaste for "precipitous judgement, intellectual arrogance and credulity in various forms"; and, finally, (6) a doubt about "criteria for judgement" (120–36). All of these skeptical tendencies (not to mention others) help transform momentary epistemological weakness into a way of life, since for Shakespeare, being "skeptical" simply means finding ways to sustain this weakness.[11] Shakespeare is more concerned with how readers are formed than with how they are informed, and so it makes sense to speak not just of Shakespearean philosophy—as has been common since Hazlitt claimed that "Shakespeare was as good a philosopher as he was a poet"[12]—but also—as is less common—to speak of that philosophy as a way of life.

At the same time, Shakespeare as a way of life differs from philosophy as a way of life as Hadot understands it—and not just because Shakespeare is a poet and dramatist who may not have read widely in philosophy, or because I cannot find in the poems and plays a dietary-dialogic regime nor a course of training for aspiring philosopher-kings.[13] The difference becomes most clear when we compare Hadot's sense of skepticism's practical, controlled rigors with what I take to be Shakespeare's own sense of skepticism's methods and ends. Hadot, focusing on Pyrrhonist skepticism, reminds us that skepticism's end is *ataraxia* or unperturbedness, and that we can cultivate *ataraxia* by bearing in mind skeptical precepts that lend us subjective consistency and help us develop indifference: " 'This is no better than that,' 'Perhaps,' 'All is indeterminate,' 'Everything escapes comprehension,' 'Every argument is opposed by an equal argument,' 'I suspend my judgment.' "[14] Cultivating indifference through such precepts help us to cultivate control, no longer swayed by the false judgments that enslave us to false desires. In *Timon*, I will argue, Shakespeare puts Pyrrhonism, including some of the aforementioned precepts, to drastically different use, such that suspended judgment leads to just the opposite of classical Pyrrhonism's self-consistency and calm. In general, Shakespeare as a way of life does not offer the reassuring solutions of either the ancient or the Christian philosophies that interest Hadot.

Having said this, I will not deny that Shakespeare, eclectic in his skepticism, at times laments the foreclosure of skeptical practices that might grant control and convert epistemological weakness into strength. One of Shakespeare's central preoccupations, and my central preoccupation here, is with this: whether the serious doubt of skepticism can become a means for control, for negotiating our selves and our worlds with greater mastery and proficiency. To be sure, situations exist in Shakespeare where tragedy could be avoided only if characters could establish a pragmatic relationship to uncertain, competing conceptions. As we will see in Chapter 1, tragedy in *Lucrece* becomes inevitable when Lucrece cannot manipulate the uncertain, unstable relationship between body and mind to her advantage. Yet when Shakespeare turns from the early *Lucrece* to the mature tragedy of *Othello* and his late romances, he does not advocate the extensive self-control that interests Hadot. Instead, he acknowledges how illusory control so often is, and skepticism comes to mean practicing the impractical and un-pragmatic, the humble, the weak. Then, being free and behaving ethically come to seem more feasible. This is a way of saying that Shakespeare's skepticism, like all but the most unstinting skepticisms, ends in faith, but not in providence or tradition, nor in the best guesses of open-minded inquiry, nor even in the sweeping conviction that nothing can be known.[15] Shakespeare urges not faith that triumphs over or compensates for skepticism but faith in skepticism, faith not only that epistemological weakness can be a way of life, but that it should be.[16]

In a book about epistemological humility, it would be presumptuous to claim that the way of life that I find in Shakespeare is the only way to be found. There are, no doubt, other ways, other patterns; the one offered here, if characteristic of Shakespeare, is hardly exhaustive. Still, here is the pattern of Shakespearean skepticism as I see it.

In his texts there comes a moment when characters, readers, or both become aware that a frame by which they understand selfhood, ethics, or freedom is not the only or the natural one. Lucrece stops assuming that the body is an object, Othello that love is self-creation, readers of *The Tempest* that free action is self-directed action. There follows a moment when there arises the possibility—for characters, readers, or both—to control the framing of these concepts. There is then a decision: whether to adopt a frame that grants a greater or a lesser degree of control within the field of experience just called into doubt. This decision takes place as a response to the weakness we feel when deprived of our usual conceptual frames, to the skeptical sense that these frames do not afford access to objective truth.

Shakespeare entertains two kinds of response. According to the first kind, we seek to convert weakness into pragmatic strength. One can, for example, actively choose to think of freedom as self-direction, as a power available to any individual, a notion Shakespeare entertains but doubts in *The Tempest*. Or one can commit to frames only provisionally, choosing whichever frame seems empowering in a given instance, a choice that, I will argue, Shakespeare seems to wish were available to Lucrece in facing the mind-body problem.

According to the second kind of response, we accept epistemological weakness. Here, one can opt for a frame that deepens the initial sense of being weak—as, for instance, when *The Winter's Tale's* Leontes embraces a metaphor (of ethical behavior as the offer of a hand) that keeps him from knowing precisely where he stands. Or one can refrain from choosing between frames at all, as Shakespeare wishes Othello could do in facing frames by which love is, respectively, a discipline of being possessed or of possessing; or as readers themselves are asked to do when, reading *Timon*, they confront worlds that seem defined by scarcity on the one hand and abundance on the other.

Depending on the situation Shakespeare has imagined, any of these responses can seem legitimate. On occasion, if not often, Shakespeare wishes that skeptical practice could foster self-control, empowerment and confidence, that it could be a way of life as it is in Hadot's understanding. But only the second kind of response, the embrace of epistemological weakness, leads anywhere near redemption.

In my texts of focus, this response predominates and has the political consequences that most interest me. Still, there remains enough consistency across Shakespeare's thought about skepticism and self-control to include even the early *Lucrece*. Shakespeare habitually contorts commonplace metaphors that frame the notion of control, affecting how we conceive of a free or good life. George Lakoff and Mark Johnson show how commonplace metaphors emanate from early experience,[17] yielding relatively uncomplicated yet deeply ingrained conceptual frames for selfhood, ethics, and politics. For instance, our earliest experiences—when we learn to control things by manipulating them physically—dictate that self-control initially be metaphorized in terms of object-control, and selves understood as wholly responsible for themselves and their actions. Yet even in *Lucrece*, in which this metaphor has provisional appeal, Shakespeare counsels against any rigid assumption of a divided self so as to simplify control. And whereas ethical action tends to be pictured as movement by a self-directed agent along a clearly bounded path—and agents as fully accountable for keeping themselves within the boundaries—in a late play like *The Winter's Tale*, ethical behavior can be framed as the quite indeterminate offer of a hand and the infinitizing, even terrifying openness that the offer entails. Metaphors of freedom as self-directed movement, to cite a final example, grow out of our early experiences of excessive constraint, yet in *The Tempest*, Shakespeare can think of freedom not as control exercised from within but as transformative experience that arrives from the outside, not as a capacity we exercise but as an uncertain event for which we wait.[18] In his fidelity to epistemological weakness, Shakespeare elaborates an idiosyncratic pattern, one that scrambles categories that grow out of embodied existence, generating new experiences and relationships.

Often, early modern skepticism is not thought to have such unsettling consequences at all. Richard Popkin, in a classic study, displays how early moderns sought to put skepticism in service of systematic religion, to retain faith in established doctrine despite the advent of Reformation doubt.[19] More recently, Christian Thorne has argued that Renaissance skepticism can prop up authoritarian structures, inducing critical paralysis and passive acceptance of the status quo.[20] Shakespeare, by contrast, places faith not in doctrine or custom but only in the humility that comes with epistemological weakness. Unlike skeptics that Popkin describes, Shakespeare challenges readers to conceive of faith as something other than faith in a delimited set of articles, rights, or laws, as what can emerge from skepticism rather than what can serve as its antidote. While Popkin and Thorne show how skepticism's compatibility with faith can lead to stability—how each can balance the other out in coherent normative systems—Shakespeare shows how entwining the two can institute a subjectivity in which those systems lose some of their structuring power and even begin to recede. In this, Shakespeare's skepticism can help develop rather disorienting stances toward self, law, and liberty, stances that are radical not only in Shakespeare's time but even, I will argue, in our own. Shakespeare does not lead me where negative capability finally leads Keats, or philosophy as a way of life leads Hadot: to transcendent self-realization or to empowered self-confidence. Rather, Shakespeare induces exquisite cognitive disorientation and suggests how it might be extended without limit, how faith in epistemological humility might be sustained.

As implied earlier, I admit that Shakespeare does not, and should not, lead all readers where he leads me. The next section will take up other compelling accounts of Shakespeare's skepticism, but first I want to make a separate point and explain why I have chosen the works that I have and why *Shakespeare as a Way of Life* includes no sweeping assertions about Shakespeare's works. I have chosen the texts that I have simply because they are the ones that address my theme most intensely. Still, all but one of my principal texts come from the second half of Shakespeare's career; and all are either romances or tragic in nature. In *Lucrece*, I have suggested, Shakespeare thinks more practically about skeptical practice relative to other texts covered here; and I believe, but will not here argue, that many—not all, but many—other Shakespearean texts from the 1590s resemble *Lucrece* in this respect, particularly the early comedies. I focus on later tragedies and romances because they fixate on the impractical and keep negative capability negative.

Having said this, I do not wish to advance any unqualified assertions about Shakespeare's career. Such assertions need to be conscientiously hedged in order to have much humility and, in my experience, tend to fall into one of three categories. Some assertions are precise but finally indefensible, as in Peter Holbrook's recent argument that Shakespeare is a rugged individualist, an argument to which I turn later in this chapter.[21] Other such assertions are defensible but overly imprecise variations on Coleridge's claim that Shakespeare is myriad-minded.[22] Here there are numerous examples, but a few recent ones include Jonathan Bate's claim that Shakespearean "truth is not singular," that his plays are like duck/rabbit images, only more complex;[23] Marjorie Garber's claim that "Shakespeare always presents both his ideas and his character types contrapuntally";[24] and A. D. Nuttall's claim that "No sooner has one identified a philosophical 'position'" in Shakespeare "than one is forced, by the succeeding play, to modify or extend one's account."[25] A third, final kind of sweeping assertion about Shakespeare is at once indefensible and imprecise, for instance when Harold Bloom claims both that Shakespeare invented human nature as we now understand it and, vaguely, that the "ultimate use of Shakespeare is to let him teach you to think too well, to whatever truth you can sustain without perishing."[26]

I am unconvinced as to whether this search for the all-encompassing is worthwhile, and would fumble awkwardly in any attempt of my own. When I attribute an attitude to "Shakespeare," then, I do not mean Shakespeare the man or the full Shakespearean corpus; rather, I use "Shakespeare" as shorthand for the thought that informs my texts of focus. If at moments a line of thought sweeps me into a broader claim, I apologize. I have only found a habit in Shakespearean thinking, one that I try to keep.

Shakespeare, Skepticism, and the Politics of Cognition

Keats's account of Shakespeare's skepticism is far from the last, and while individual chapters engage in detail with contemporary readings of individual works, as part of this introduction I would like to review a few older, foundational accounts of Shakespearean skepticism and thereby clarify what my own adds.

In general, readers tend to situate Shakespeare historically, along a continuum with the roughly neo-Pyrrhonist, often therapeutic skepticism associated with Montaigne at one end and, at the other, the consuming skepticism expressed, then overcome (well after Shakespeare) in Descartes's *Meditations*. As one moves along the continuum, the skeptical outlook darkens. For Montaigne, that outlook offers a balanced viewpoint, protection from presumptuous, zealous belief, and, at least occasionally, the tranquility that comes as a result.[27] In the *Meditations*, by contrast, taking skepticism seriously makes the world and the self disappear, can make both seem the mystifications of an evil genius, arousing the overpowering state of doubt in which the meditator feels "suddenly thrown into deep water, being so disconcerted that I can neither plant my feet on the bottom nor swim on the surface."[28]

Stanley Cavell's *Disowning Knowledge,* the most prominent account of Shakespeare's skepticism, dwells on proto-Cartesian dimensions. Cavell begins the book by declaring that in Shakespeare "the advent of skepticism as manifested in Descartes's *Meditations* is already in full existence."[29] For Cavell, Shakespeare's "skeptical problematic" is Cartesian in degree, extending not just to the reliability of a given perception but to all that seems existent, raising the question of "whether I know with certainty of the existence of the external world and of myself and others in it" (3). This question consumes characters whose doubts produce ruination: Othello in his skeptical jealousy, and Coriolanus in his disgust at plebeian words; Lear with the world that steadily recedes from him, and Hamlet with the world that he refuses to join. As Lars Engle puts it, Cavell sees Shakespeare "as Descartes minus God."[30] Cavell dwells on how characters cannot live their skepticism except in and through catastrophe, going so far as to conclude that tragedy is "obedient to a skeptical structure," that skepticism itself bears tragic marks.[31] Skepticism destroys.[32]

Subsequent chapters—especially those on *Othello, The Winter's Tale,* and *Timon of Athens*—take up Cavell in more detail, so for now I will distinguish my view from his briefly. In *Disowning Knowledge* Cavell acknowledges that the presence of "Montaigne's skepticism is in various of Shakespeare's plays" and that there are Shakespearean skepticisms less grim than his own, but the book itself conceives of skepticism in resolutely Cartesian terms (3). Despite Cavell's initial concession, his book—perhaps by the sheer brilliance of its argument—leaves the impression that in order for Shakespeare really to be skeptical he needs to be proto-Cartesian, his characters on the verge of drowning themselves and their worlds, desperate for buoys not weighed down by doubt. I agree with Cavell that skepticism, at least in the texts I treat, rarely works as the straightforward therapy that it can be for Hadot. As I have already indicated, though, skepticism in these texts does not require recovery; the weakness and unease brought on by skepticism do not always make it a disease or a political dead end. Cavell maintains that the skeptics of Shakespeare's plays doubt the outside world's existence or seek to annihilate that world and thus refuse belonging in the political realm. I have argued that one of Cavell's own skeptics, Coriolanus, offers a political "world elsewhere"[33] and here I will argue that skeptical practice—in, for instance, *Othello* and *The Winter's Tale*—can serve as the precondition for sustaining new kinds of political community, where responsibility is at once unclear and infinite, where ties are amorphous yet entirely binding.

Readers who see Shakespearean skepticism as more livable than Cavell tend to regard Shakespeare as roughly neo-Pyrrhonist in his "double vision," a habit of seeing two opposed, yet equally compelling sides to philosophical questions. A. P. Rossiter, for example, writes that "Shakespeare's view is the double-eyed, the ambivalent: it faces both ways."[34] At the same time, Rossiter rejects the idea of a straightforwardly neo-Pyrrhonist Shakespeare in the sense that his skepticism brings satisfaction; the Shakespearean *epokhē* (suspension of judgment in the face of doubleness) fails to yield *ataraxia*. Rossiter remarks instead that "all this trading in incongruity" produces "a highly complex emotional effect, perhaps impossible to those who cannot face violently mixed feelings" (281).

Norman Rabkin offers another, more elaborate account of how Shakespeare's double vision burdens readers. In considering the juxtaposition of reason and passion as possible values in *Hamlet*, Rabkin writes that the play "puts us in a situation in which no matter how much we are tempted we are not permitted . . . to recognize a single good."[35] We do not know whether to praise or blame Hamlet when, first encountering the ghost, he claims that he will clear all but passionate vengeance from the book and table of his brain; or whether we are to believe or to doubt Hamlet when he speaks of man's godlike reason and praises Horatio for not being passion's slave. According to Rabkin, Shakespeare leaves us with a "set of questions to which there are no answers" (9). This sounds vexing, likely to arouse Rossiter's "violently mixed feelings," but Rabkin draws a different conclusion. Shakespeare brings us joy, helping us realize how important, if also how hard, it is to choose between opposed visions: "No matter how much the plays make us face up to the starkness of the world we live in, our response has always been in some mode of joy, of renewed pleasure in the world."[36]

Each chapter in this book centers on a text in which Shakespeare opposes competing conceptions. In some cases, Shakespeare resolves what would be double vision with a synthesis or with one possibility displacing another, but in certain chapters, especially the final one, the skepticism I describe is indeed mostly Pyrrhonist. Even then, though, the terms that I use differ importantly from Rabkin. In *Timon*, Shakespearean opposition prompts readers to see not the importance of choice but of refraining from choice, of abiding in uncertainty about the structure of self and world. Unlike Rabkin, I argue that this uncertainty is excruciating, akin to Rossiter's violently mixed emotions, and that our response to Shakespeare's double vision can be worthwhile without being joyous.

The political consequences of my argument, perhaps, best highlight the distance between what I find and what neo-Pyrrhonist readers do. Rossiter and Rabkin, of an earlier critical generation, do not articulate their arguments in overtly political terms as later critics would. According to Hamlin, for instance, the skepticism of drama in Shakespeare's age (including Shakespeare's own) emerges as a balancing of viewpoints that implies the importance of open political inquiry. The skepticism that interests Hamlin is "an irrepressible spirit of questioning," "an abidingly critical attitude towards all dogmatic or doctrinaire positions conjoined with an implicit and unceasing defence of open-minded enquiry. Scepticism," Hamlin writes, "provides an antidote for rash judgement and overconfident assertion."[37] Shakespeare's assault on presumption in a play such as *The Winter's Tale*, I will show, indeed opposes him to the "overconfident assertion" characteristic of political discourse. But skepticism that urges open-minded inquiry as an antidote to individual overconfidence suggests a degree of corporate confidence, a sense that an open society compensates for flaws inherent in individual perspectives. In my reading, Shakespeare's texts do not betray even this limited confidence, making his skepticism too radical to be pro-absolutist or proto-liberal.

As will become clear, I find Shakespearean skepticism more congenial to republicanism than to absolutism, but not because Shakespeare advocates republican institutions. As one might expect in a book whose concerns are partly political, republicanism will arise often: when we glimpse the beginnings of the Roman republic in *Lucrece*, when we see a withering critique of absolutist confidence in *The Winter's Tale*, and when we consider concepts of self-government in *The Tempest*. However, we never quite see Shakespeare put his faith in republican institutions. His political insight resides elsewhere. I thus may seem to suggest, with Northrop Frye, that Shakespeare has no theory of society, but I hope to suggest more than that.[38] Shakespeare has theories of the skeptical self and of a skeptical way of life, and we will see how these theories imply attitudes and approaches toward political practice, in terms of the politics of everyday life and in terms of what we can expect any polity to provide. Shakespeare is more concerned with reshaping the frames by which we view and negotiate politics than he is with forming specific political institutions, even if he also registers connections between the two.[39]

This means that the politics I find in Shakespeare differs not only from what Hamlin finds but also from the politics—akin to Hamlin's—found in negative capability by Roberto Unger, who has adapted Keats's concept most elaborately for political purposes and for reforming political institutions. Considered in purely cognitive terms, negative capability is the mind's "power to turn against itself, testing, denying, subverting, escaping, and transforming the presuppositions on which it has operated and the routines by which it operates."[40] But Unger's negative capability also promotes action in the world. For Keats, we have seen, taking nothing for granted, clearing the mind of comforting but finally constraining certitudes, enables Shakespeare to produce new poetry, to become a "Soul"; for Unger, turning the mind against its presuppositions and routines enables new agency: "the power to act nonformulaically, in defiance of what rules and routines would predict," the power to make "infinite combinations out of finite elements" (134–5).[41] It is up to states to cultivate negative capability with structural flexibility, to remain open to revision by closing the gap between context-preserving and context-transforming activity among citizens. Doing so promotes confidence in individual ability to effect change in the world.

In Unger's hands, negative capability becomes empowering, the source of a revitalized political pragmatism, much as in Lars Engle's hands, Shakespeare's texts become a nuanced resource for pragmatism's future.[42] My chapter on *Lucrece* shows that I do not wish to undermine pragmatic understandings of Shakespeare or of politics. I do, though, wish to outline a complementary way of thinking about how skeptical practice brings about the politically new. For Unger, as for Keats, the new arrives through a self-subversion that ends in confidence, ability, and agency, a finally strengthened sense of self. I, by contrast, explore how the new can arrive through humility and disorientation, through waiting and bearing-with, through serious and unremitting self-risk.

Hamlet *and the Politics of Friendship*

For a brief initial illustration of how skeptical practice suggests a politics of weakness in Shakespeare, we can look to *Hamlet*. We need not focus on Hamlet himself. In fact, it is best that we not, given his well-documented introspection and our tendency to praise his supposed subjective power,[43] though it is true that Hamlet confronts ambiguity and incertitude at every turn: with whether the ghost of his father is in fact a demon; with whether *The Mousetrap* can establish Claudius's guilt; with whether hell, purgatory, or nothingness awaits him after death. Bloom contends that by the play's end Hamlet accepts incertitude in a distinctly Keatsian way, that "Hamlet's final stance personifies Shakespeare's Negative Capability."[44] For reasons that I make clear in an essay on which I draw in the following pages, the prince's dying wishes contradict Bloom's characterization,[45] and as Janet Adelman shows in a psychoanalytic reading, Hamlet's career is very much shaped by a "pervasive boundary panic" that defines his desire for a certain, coherent identity: his lack, we might say, of negative capability.[46] Hamlet stands in for Shakespeare not so much because Hamlet himself "personifies" negative capability but because Horatio's friendship with him produces an epistemological weakness, and prompts an existential choice, suggestive of how politics can be modeled on friendship.

Elsewhere I discuss how a self-strengthening form of personal friendship is scaled into a form of political belonging.[47] Just as for Keats and Unger, a certain self-subversion opens the way for ultimate self-realization, so in this model of friendship, certain acts of self-sacrifice lead to final self-aggrandizement. As a politics of friendship, the initial sacrifice can range from personal resources to personal safety, given in exchange for certain entitlements and expanded possibilities for political action. This model requires epistemological confidence: about the friend, about what the friend can do for us, about friendship's positive outcome. Many early modern and more recent accounts employ this model, one that I believe is absent from *Hamlet*. Given Hamlet's antic disposition, his propensity for abstraction, and his edginess to a lethal degree—given that he plunges himself and others into ever-deeper levels of risk—we might justly ask how Horatio manages to be his friend at all, let alone how Horatio might benefit from friendship with such a puzzling, prickly figure. Hamlet praises his friend for being the paragon of self-mastery that he himself fails to be; Horatio, according to Hamlet, is a man "That is not passion's slave," "one, in suffering all, that suffers nothing, / A man that Fortune's buffets and rewards / Hast ta'en with equal thanks" (3.2.62–71). In testing this praise—in revealing how friendship with Hamlet diminishes Horatio's ability to live up to his friend's estimate—a practice of friendship and a skeptical politics emerge.[48]

We can perceive this emergence most readily in the exchange following Hamlet's poisoning. As Hamlet is dying, he asks Horatio to report recent events "aright," and Horatio tries to decline. "Never believe it," he explains. "I am more an antique Roman than a Dane. / Here's yet some liquor left" (5.2.332–4). Horatio conjures the Roman notion that self-killing can be a noble, rational act, one betokening laudable self-control in the face of evil. Were Horatio to drink, though, his death would hardly betoken self-mastery, since passion infuses his response. Not that we blame Horatio's wish to perish; being consumed by his friend's demise might well impress us. To be passionless, to separate the mind's judgments from the heart's affections, seems desirable elsewhere in the play—for example when Hamlet asks Horatio to observe Claudius during *The Mousetrap* in order to discern the latter's guilt. But not here, as Horatio's friend dies before him. We will see that this uncertainty about the separability of reason and passion, body and mind, appears as early as *Lucrece*, and can serve as the basis for skeptical practice. At *Hamlet*'s end, though, Shakespeare focuses most on Hamlet shaking Horatio to his core. He denies Horatio's wish to join him in death; with strength enough to wrest the poisoned cup from his friend's hand, the prince reiterates his earlier request:

> As th'art a man,
> Give me the cup. Let go. By heaven, I'll ha't.
> O God! Horatio, what a wounded name,

Things standing thus unknown, shall live behind me!
If thou didst ever hold me in thy heart,
Absent thee from felicity awhile,
And in this harsh world draw thy breath in pain,
To tell my story . . .
                    [*Hamlet dies*] (5.2.334–41)

Hamlet, a regicide, does not want to be remembered as a traitor and villain. He wants an unknown, Claudius's own treason, made known. Whether he wants Horatio to tell all that he knows is a separate question. On the basis of Hamlet's track record—the blithe unconcern with which he kills Polonius, the brutality with which he verbally assaults Ophelia, and the ease with which he dispatches Rosencrantz and Guildenstern—I struggle to see how Horatio could tell Hamlet's story with a commitment to honesty and without wounding his friend's name. Hamlet asks not that Horatio tell as unbiased a story as he is able but that he tell "my story"—his version of that story, in which he is not responsible for the demise of Polonius, Ophelia, or his old friends. "If Hamlet from himself be ta'en away," he earlier explains, "And when he's not himself that does wrong Laertes, / Then Hamlet does it not" (5.1.226–8). Hamlet asks Horatio to prove friendship, and preserve his friend's legacy, at least partly through deliberate dishonesty. Hamlet praises Horatio for being a man in whom "blood and judgment are so well commeddled," yet here asks that Horatio disregard honest judgment in favor of friendly affection (3.2.67). Committing to friendship and to an honest accounting seem very much at odds. In asking Horatio to ensure the integrity of his friend's identity, Hamlet also asks him to undergo a potentially disreputable self-sacrifice.

Horatio's penultimate speech best indicates where his commitments lie, and how being Hamlet's friend weakens his sense of everything. An English Ambassador enters and, having related that Rosencrantz and Guildenstern are dead, asks from whom they will have thanks. "Not from his mouth," Horatio replies,

Had it th-ability of life to thank you:
He never gave commandment for their death.
But since, so jump upon this bloody question,
You from the Polack wars, and you from England,
Are here arrived, give order that these bodies
High on a stage be placed to the view;

And let me speak to th' yet unknowing world
How these things came about. So shall you hear
Of carnal, bloody, and unnatural acts;
Of accidental judgments, casual slaughters;
Of deaths put on by cunning and forc'd cause;
And, in this upshot, purposes mistook
Fall'n on th' inventors' heads—all this can I
Truly deliver. (5.2.364–378)

Perhaps Horatio can truly deliver all of this, though it is unclear if this is truth (as he understands it, the play being notoriously divided both on truth and on our ability to perceive it). Horatio says nothing obviously misleading, but he does begin with some obfuscation; he remarks only that Claudius did not order the deaths of Rosencrantz and Guildenstern, concealing Hamlet's role in their execution. Yet as he continues Horatio appears to side less wholeheartedly with his friend.[49] While he emphasizes Claudius's unnatural murder, and while he uses twenty words to note the cunning by which Laertes and the king inadvertently did in almost everyone, Horatio also mentions "accidental judgments" and "casual slaughters," which conjures the death of Polonius.[50] Horatio may absolve Hamlet on several scores, but he does draw attention to Hamlet's culpability in at least one instance. Horatio implies he knows that Hamlet mistook Polonius for Claudius and deems the slaughtering casual. According to the *OED*, "casual" in the seventeenth century can mean "accidental" or "produced by chance" but also "unmethodical, haphazard, 'happy go lucky.'"[51] Horatio suggests that Hamlet's pass through the arras was both; presumably "casual" does not mean only "accidental," which Horatio has just used, and his words bring to mind Hamlet's unconcern about his error as well as suggest that this unconcern somehow changes the nature of a killing not initially intended as casual in any sense. Hamlet ascribes so little value to Polonius's life that Polonius effectively is dead in the prince's mind: the Lord Chamberlain's literal death merely manifests what Hamlet thinks of him to begin with. Killing Polonius by accident does not make the killing any less the expression of a flawed character. Horatio's speech registers this.

Given that Horatio lists Polonius's death as but one element in a heap of violent acts, none of which Horatio assigns to discrete agents, it is unclear with what degree of clarity—let alone in what condition—Hamlet's identity will emerge in his friend's telling. So I cannot resolve the issue of whether Horatio chooses friendship or honesty, blood or judgment, and can only imagine how vexed a full accounting of Hamlet's history would need to be. To the degree that Horatio conceals his friend's ill deeds, he chooses Hamlet, and to the degree that he brings these deeds to light, he chooses honesty. Horatio seeks to safeguard Hamlet's name yet also wounds that name. If honesty is paramount, it seems unconscionable that Horatio would absolve Hamlet for sending old friends to their deaths, and Hamlet might well turn in his grave, were he in one, to hear Horatio describe his casual slaughter. Instead of achieving a just balance between friendship and honesty, Horatio troubles his commitments to, and comprehension of, both.[52] In earlier acts he evinces perfect epistemological confidence on several issues: that Hamlet should not follow the Ghost; that Claudius reacted to *The Mousetrap* guiltily; that Hamlet should not duel Laertes. By the play's end Horatio is too shaken, too disoriented, too possessed now of humility—about himself and his powers, indeed about anyone's capacity to render the play's events other than confusedly—to embody a clear ideal.

Unlike friendships characterized by finally self-aggrandizing self-sacrifice, then, Horatio in the end unravels almost entirely.[53] To this point, simple commitments to friendship and honesty have held him together, such that we can ask whether his character has had another element of much significance. We know so little about Horatio that, figuratively speaking, he has seemed to exist for Hamlet, to exist in relation to him.[54] Now Horatio becomes incoherent, not filled with conflicting ideas or emotions, as complex Shakespearean characters are said to be, but instead broken by a psychic caesura, his subjectivity not so much rich as riven. He is epistemologically weak, unsure of who he is or who Hamlet was, unsure what is to be done. In the deepest sense, friendship gave him meaning, strength, purpose. As he struggles between honesty and affection, the mind that might strive for disinterestedness and the embodied fellow feeling that clings to attachments, brokenness becomes friendship's consequence.

Some commentators condemn Horatio's behavior as that of an equivocating politician, but I do not.[55] If politically responsible behavior means rule-bound behavior—here the rule might be against bearing false witness—Horatio behaves dubiously. If responsible behavior is best pictured differently, though, the issue is more complex. In having the poisoned cup wrested from him, Horatio loses the chance to perish with Hamlet. But in still offering Hamlet his hand—in still speaking for him—Horatio perishes in a deeper sense, sacrificing his sense of himself and of his ethical standing.

Horatio's unraveling has at least two political consequences. First, there is what seems a negative consequence: that attachments pull us apart and that any politics of friendship must account for the extreme difficulty involved in friendship itself and in making friendship scalable, indeed in combining personal and more broadly social commitments—here, to Hamlet and to justice—in any way whatsoever. Horatio's practice of friendship at the end certainly has perils: his skeptical commitment to Hamlet without a clear picture of him is coupled with, and further complicated by, his skeptical commitment to Danish politics without a clear solution to political difficulties.

But Horatio's skeptical practice also has possibility. I find undeniable sublimity in his abiding in weakness, in his still living, in his wish to appear amid devastation so soon after seeking to kill himself. In a lacerated state, he wishes to appear before an as yet unknowing world, to do so "[e]ven while men's minds are wild, lest more mischance / On plots and errors happen" (5.2.386–7). Shakespeare gives no reason to think that Horatio's speech will heal Denmark's wounds in any lasting sense—that it will, to use Unger's terms, restore any balance between preserving and transforming the Danish context writ large—but Shakespeare does give cause to admire Horatio's attempt to forestall needless violence, his commitment to politics despite disorientation and lack of answers. Friendship does not do for friends what negative capability ultimately does for Keats's poet or Unger's political actor, or even what *askēsis* does for Hadot. Friendship for Horatio becomes a practice of weakness: about how to account for what has happened or for oneself, for Denmark's future.[56] Horatio commits to Hamlet and to Denmark but also to uncertainty about both, to what is not well understood. Shakespeare, we will see, urges a similar commitment on readers in his treatments of freedom, ethics, and love. Horatio hardly models anything perfectly, but in a tragic world, his disoriented wish to forestall violence—the modest model he offers of a minimal, skeptical politics—may be the only kind imaginable. His embrace of epistemological weakness, his giving up of all mastery save what he needs to go on, brings me back to Shakespeare's play as a more confident story never could.

Looking to Horatio, rather than Hamlet, highlights the political stakes of Shakespeare's skepticism, and permits a last contrast of the politics that I find with that evident in recent studies. Consider, for instance,

Holbrook's provocatively titled *Shakespeare's Individualism*, which opens with the proclamation that "Shakespeare is an author for a liberal, individualistic culture."[57] Holbrook admires Hamlet for just the opposite reason that I admire Horatio: because Hamlet's selfhood "is remote, dignified and precious and, as a result, *worth fighting for*" (68). Holbrook opposes Hamlet's laudable, if incompletely realized dream of autonomy—his pursuit of values like individualism, self-realization, choice and authenticity—to a certain sort of ethical thinking, wherein "[t]he injunction of 'ethics' is that one listen to the 'Other' (defined in group terms) rather than oneself" (1, 63). If I have argued rightly about Horatio's vulnerability to Hamlet, Shakespeare's position cannot be Holbrook's, and would be closer to that offered by Julia Reinhard Lupton, who finds in Shakespeare not an advocate of self-sovereignty but a figure far more complex.[58] In Lupton's memorable formulation, one might "*live with* Shakespeare, as one might learn to live with AIDS, with cats, or with children."[59] Living with Shakespeare means honoring bonds and vulnerabilities, and so Lupton's chapter on *Hamlet* fastens not on Hamlet's infinite subjectivity but on how friendship tempers his loneliness, how he is "circled by a fellowship of friends who lighten and lessen [his] isolation" (86).

At the same time, if Lupton is as skeptical of Holbrook's version of self-sovereignty as Shakespeare in *Hamlet* seems to be, intersubjectivity for her nonetheless fosters subjective efficacy, expanded possibilities for action. Friendship in the play offers major safeguards for Hamlet and even progressive political potential: the play's language of classical friendship "courts deliberation, choice, and consent" (82).[60] Whereas Lupton focuses on how Hamlet's potential for action expands as he elects Fortinbras at the play's end—how the horizontal bond of friendship with Horatio enables his own agency—I am more interested in how those bonds wrench Horatio's agential capacities, how friendship yields not a dynamic increase in power, but an admirable, skeptical moment of near-powerlessness. For all that we share, then, I differ from Lupton in focusing on skepticism as a way to practice the impractical. In this I share with Daniel Juan Gil, who reads Shakespeare's plays as skeptical about practical politics and even about state structures.[61] While Holbrook's Shakespeare models possibilities for self-cultivation, and Lupton's models new vistas for action, Gil's dissolves the self in the political, even as Gil also sees aleatory possibilities in this dissolution.[62] Like Gil (albeit in in different terms), I find political possibility in intense, even extreme experience such as Horatio's. Unlike Gil, I see skepticism as a means by which these possibilities become livable in practices that, taken together, imply a way of life.

Shakespeare's Skeptical Practices

In Chapter 1, I read *Lucrece* in the contexts of Ciceronian skepticism and the mind-body problem, introducing the theme of self-control at the core of *Shakespeare as a Way of Life*. Critics have argued that Shakespeare's works in general, and *Lucrece* in particular, evince a resolutely monistic outlook whereby mind and body simply cannot be separated. My reading of the poem challenges the sweeping nature of this largely salutary critical trend. Often, mind-body dualism works in parallel to a patriarchal politics, where men are to rule women as minds are to rule bodies; but not in *Lucrece*, which throws parallels out of alignment even as it portrays the incident that precipitates the Roman republic. Cicero and *Lucrece* both are skeptical about selfhood's structure; both also suggest that, depending on context, one might establish control by acting as though the self may be either monistic or dualistic, regardless of the ontological "truth" at which we, as moderns, have supposedly arrived. If this rings of pragmatism, even in *Lucrece* Shakespeare is skeptical about using skepticism to cultivate self-control. Portraying Lucrece's inability to gain control even as she seems to verge on doing so—on finding a flexibility of self that would save her from devastation—Shakespeare suggests that control may be most desirable when least possible. *Lucrece* shows both the appeal and the limits of epistemological weakness as a basis for pragmatic action or therapeutic practice.

In my second chapter, on *Othello*, I consider skepticism and self-control as they pertain to love. In this play, Shakespeare asks what love is and whether self-control is possible in love. He suggests that only the most minimal self-control is in our grasp when it comes to love, and that that control is only possible when love itself—our sense of what it requires of us and what we reasonably can expect from it—is beyond our grasp. To make this argument, I consider the play alongside Cartesian texts, especially the *Meditations* and *The Passions of the Soul*, and I show that Shakespeare is a skeptic where Descartes is not, about how much self-control—in the terms of the chapter on *Lucrece*, how much dualism—is available and about whether love's structure can be comprehended. Whatever love is, love in the play has a certain, contradictory feeling: as being possessed by the beloved on the one hand and as wishing to possess the beloved on the other. Shakespeare indicates that tragedy in love is avoidable only so long as Othello acknowledges that the boundaries of this experience, the precise senses in which one is possessed and can possess, are unfixed. In making this suggestion Shakespeare helps us, along with theorists such as Michael Hardt and Lauren Berlant, to think through a politics of love without sovereignty at its core.

Chapter 3, on *The Winter's Tale*, explores the ethical consequences of epistemological weakness in Leontes, Shakespeare's reprisal of Othello. Through Leontes, Shakespeare shows in greater detail than *Othello* the dimensions of a politics of love founded on humility and non-sovereignty. I trace Shakespeare's inquiry into how Leontes can be king once he loses faith in himself and must instead rule with humility. When he does, Leontes must live not above law but under it, and Shakespeare explores two possible answers as to which kind of law, ones also explored in Paul's epistles, in Montaigne, and in radical theory's recent impressions of Paul. Leontes's first option is to submit to a law of works. His other option is submission to a non-juridical law of faith that demands neighborly love only. Shakespeare entertains both possibilities but sees greater virtue in the law of faith, a law emblematized by the offer of a hand—by Leontes's infinitizing, self-undermining gesture at the play's end. The play thus benefits when read in the present contexts of Agamben and Badiou, whose Paul is distinctly non-confessional, and when read in a Montaignean context rather than that of more systematic early modern thought.

My penultimate chapter, on *The Tempest*, also examines Shakespeare's skepticism alongside Montaigne's, this time in the domain of freedom. Here I ask what freedom is possible, given Shakespeare's doubt about straightforward conceptions of self-control and self-direction. Both Shakespeare and Montaigne are skeptical, I show, not in denying that freedom exists but in struggling to decide how it might be achieved. In this play, interestingly, freedom has no essential connection to the exercise of free will or even to ability; freedom sometimes seems to require the cultivation of rational self-control (for example, when Prospero is enslaved by passion) yet sometimes seems to require that such control be lost (for example, when Ferdinand might have found freedom in love and Caliban does find freedom in sublime poetic rapture). The *Essays*, likewise, entertain varying answers as to what freedom is, and when read together, *The Tempest* and the *Essays* seem almost Pyrrhonist in their skeptical treatment of competing viewpoints. Yet both Shakespeare and Montaigne's skepticism ends in faith when both, in different ways, repeatedly link freedom with uncertain transformation. In *The Tempest*, Shakespeare thus regards freedom as natality rather than sovereignty.

I conclude *Shakespeare as a Way of Life* by reflecting not on skeptical practices suggested by Shakespearean texts but on the cognitive value that reading can have as a practice in itself. In particular, I show how a late play, *Timon of Athens*, is informed by a skepticism that induces a wrenching but rewarding disorientation. The play drains readers of interpretive confidence, opening them to a reading experience that feels considerably twisted, an experience best captured by the idea of looking two ways at once. In one direction is a world of scarcity, the world of Athens, where personal boundaries must be preserved and a possessive relation to the world maintained; in the other is an abundant world, the wild where boundaries ought to dissolve. The attempt to look both ways, to see both worlds at once, leaves the reader incapacitated, in a cognitive world without fixed coordinates.

The value that I find in reading *Timon*, as a result, cannot be counted among the values often attributed to literature in general and Shakespeare in particular: that it clarifies our sense of ourselves, of others, and of the world; heartens us about human insight and invention; sharpens our ability to negotiate complex problems of ethics and politics; and supplies us with aesthetic satisfactions that offset the sundry disappointments of everyday existence. The experience of reading *Timon* offers only the most vexed pleasure. The play's skepticism scrambles my sense of myself, unsettles grounds for ethical action, and impairs my capacity for insight rather severely. As I point out in an epilogue to the book, Shakespeare's texts regularly yield cognitive discomforts of this order, yet it is these discomforts that make the texts worth reading.

CHAPTER I

Ciceronian Skepticism and the Mind-Body Problem in *Lucrece*

T hough this book dwells mostly on drama, this chapter focuses on the early narrative poem *Lucrece*. Considering the poem alongside Ciceronian thought, I show how *Lucrece* evinces skepticism about a problem important to other issues explored in this book: the problem of the relationship between body and mind. As we will see in later chapters, Shakespeare's approach to the mind-body problem colors his portrayals of love, ethics, and freedom.

Shakespeare responds to this problem—overlapping in the poem with the soul-body problem—with a pragmatic skeptical practice that has consequences for Shakespeare's thinking about gender and republicanism.[1] In a powerful and emblematic reading, Catherine Belsey reads *Lucrece* as a poem whose instructiveness resides partly in Shakespeare's awareness of the very inseparability of body and mind that much masculinist—as well as some republican—thought would deny, keeping the two apart in order to map masculinity onto a mind sovereign over bodies, and femininity onto a body in need of a sovereign. Rape, for Belsey, demonstrates that mind-body dualism depends upon a basic error about human ontology, an error that Lucrece herself avoids in deciding to end her life.[2] Belsey's essay is part of a much larger tendency in early modern studies aimed at displacing dualism as central to early modern thought. Here, I have in mind wide-ranging, influential collections such as *The Body in Parts*, *Politics and the Passions*, and *Reading the Early Modern Passions*, as well as important monographs by Michael Schoenfeldt and Gail Kern Paster.[3] Whether to show that reason cannot be separated from passion (or passion from reason), that thought is inherently embodied (and even distributed about the body),[4] or that selves are inseparable from the physical world, these works all attend to how productive early modern texts can be, often with reference to issues of gender, in refusing to separate body and mind. As I show in the chapter's final section, such work shares with, and occasionally also invokes, recent developments in cognitive theory, which assumes a thoroughly embodied mind and considers the implications.

This chapter challenges the sweeping nature of readings such as Belsey's and in doing so also challenges the idea that early modern conceptions of selfhood, not to mention models of cognition, are useful only—or even primarily—when they conceive of selfhood as fundamentally unified, embodied, and monistic. When *Lucrece* is read in the context of a specific, rarely discussed feature of Cicero's republicanism—his skeptical treatment of Stoic thinking about whether the self is unified or split, monistic or dualistic, in structure—we arrive at new answers about the poem's interest to us. Both Cicero and *Lucrece* present a difficult vision, infused with incertitude about selfhood's structure; both also suggest that the self can seem both monistic and dualistic, can seem to shade from one into the other and back again. Whereas we, as moderns, supposedly "know" that body and mind are inseparable, Shakespeare's poem suggests that viewing the two as somehow both separable and inseparable better conforms with experience, quite apart from questions of ontology, and also presents possibilities for the care of the self: in this case, for being republican before a republic has come into being, and for being so without falling into masculinist traps.

In my introduction I mentioned Shakespeare's partiality to republicanism but not necessarily to clear republican institutions, and I would like to add a brief word about this with regard to *Lucrece*. Until recently, debates about *Lucrece* and its potentially republican cast have tended to revolve around whether the poem celebrates or belittles Brutus's call for the overthrow of tyranny at the poem's end. If Brutus emerges as a hero—as in Annabel Patterson's account—the poem urges a republican polity; if not—as in the work of Heather Dubrow and Ian Donaldson—then *Lucrece* urges nothing of the sort.[5] More recently, Andrew Hadfield has redirected the terms of this debate, locating the poem's republicanism elsewhere than in the seven concluding stanzas, focusing instead on Tarquin's failure to embody or respect republican ideals.[6] Yet Hadfield, in keeping with earlier criticism, emphasizes ideals of negative freedom and positive liberty that fit within the frame of political structure. This chapter, by contrast, contends that the poem's republican elements extend beyond political structure to include a pair of practices of the self, distinctly Ciceronian as well as distinctly skeptical, which might allow for the preservation of republican forms of life in the absence of actual republics. I focus not on Shakespeare's interest in republican constitutions but on his engagement with how republicans are constituted: with the metaphors that inform their ethical outlooks. In the next three sections I consider the poem mostly alongside classical thought, with an eye to how the poem's skepticism urges a practice, leaving the poem's political implications for the final section. There, I show that whereas republicanism, masculinism, and mind-body dualism are often aligned, in *Lucrece* Shakespeare reconfigures all three, offering a skeptical way out of such unhappy alignment.

Battering Down the Consecrated Wall:
Body and Soul in Lucrece

After Tarquin rapes Lucrece, Shakespeare portrays the rapist's spiritual state:

> . . . his soul's fair temple is defaced,
>   To whose weak ruins muster troops of cares
>   To ask the spotted princess how she fares.
>
> She says her subjects with foul insurrection
> Have battered down her consecrated wall,
> And by their mortal fault brought in subjection
> Her immortality, and made her thrall
> To living death and pain perpetual;
>   Which in her prescience she controlled still,
>   But her foresight could not forestall their will. (719–28)[7]

Tarquin's soul, the text implies, could have been immortal, had her "subjects" (here figured as will and desire) not been in revolt. Yet there is no sense that the reasoning mind or soul has the capacity to quell revolt once it occurs. The soul is inert, if resistant, a consecrated wall unable to withstand fleshly desire: "My will," Tarquin remarks earlier, "is strong past reason's weak removing" (243). Tarquin assumes that selfhood is split into competing faculties, with reason struggling against the bodily desire that has overtaken will. What foresees cannot forestall what moves.

This split structure seems to present a philosophical problem commonly associated with dualism: that if the self really is split along the lines that oppose the reasoning soul and bodily desire, reason has no way of communicating with, let alone of controlling, desire. And yet desire can destroy the soul. Though a boundary separates Tarquin's soul and body, selfhood for him is only provisionally split; desire can violate the boundary irrespective of what the reasoning soul might wish, thus undermining the Stoic claim—a claim, we will see, which Cicero himself makes only inconsistently—that the self always can retreat into an inner citadel.[8] In Tarquin these confines collapse, making him monistic in structure. One part of the body / soul binary not only controls the other, as is possible in many dualistic frameworks, but overwhelms, suffuses, and pollutes the other.

The portrayal of Tarquin, then, implies a wish for dualistic or split selfhood, with either only enough connection between mind and bodily desire to allow the former to control the latter, or enough solidity in the boundary separating the two to bar the latter from ensnaring the former. Either Shakespeare wishes that Tarquin's reasoning soul were possessed of agency that could constrain and dominate desire,[9] or Shakespeare wishes for the boundary protecting the rational soul to be incapable of erosion. The structure of Tarquin's self disallows both possibilities, but we should bear in mind that that structure is, nonetheless, conditional. His body and soul could have remained separable; in the poem's presentation, no stable ontology forbids separation. A provisional soul-body split yields to a sinister unity.

Tarquin's structure, like Lucrece's, seems a function not of fixed ontology but of shifting context. After the rape, she also reflects upon the relationship between body and soul, in a way that implies a temporary unity:

> My body or my soul, which was the dearer,
> When the one pure the other made divine?
> Whose love of either to myself was nearer,
> When both were kept for heaven and Collatine?
> Ay me, the bark pilled from the lofty pine,
>   His leaves will wither and his sap decay;
>   So must my soul, her bark being pilled away. (1163–69)

In this stanza, Lucrece's eschewal of dualism parallels Tarquin's insofar as the body influences the soul but not vice versa, revealing the soul's dependence on the body. As the purity of Lucrece's body made her soul immortal, so its impurity makes her soul decay. Comparing her body to a protective covering for a soul that cannot survive when exposed, she verges on denying the soul any separate existence. Here her position resembles that of strong monism—in which body and mind are inseparable, and of one substance—but the end of the stanza indicates a change. Lucrece says of her soul that

> Her house is sacked, her quiet interrupted,
> Her mansion battered by the enemy,
> Her sacred temple spotted, spoiled, corrupted,
> Grossly engirt with daring infamy.
> Then let it not be called impiety
>   If in this blemished fort I make some hole
>   Through which I may convey this troubled soul. (1170–1176)

Lucrece now lays claim to a saving divisibility of body and soul, such that she might extract the soul from the blemished fleshly fort. So doing, Lucrece seems to have shifted from espousing strong monism to entertaining the possibility of either property dualism (in which body and mind are of one substance, but of differing properties) or substance dualism (in which the two are distinct substances).[10] Taken together, however, the stanzas suggest that Lucrece proceeds with a flexible self-conception, one that accommodates both monism and dualism; in her view, the body-soul relation is a matter of context and practice. She wishes for division yet does so on the basis that body and soul verge on being damnably indivisible.

I will focus on resemblances between classical philosophy and the flexibility that marks Shakespeare's portrayal of Tarquin and Lucrece, but Shakespeare's position also resembles ones inherited from Christian tradition. From Philo to Augustine to Aquinas, the body threatens to institute indistinction between itself and the soul, making the self monistic in making the soul as perishable as the body.[11] Yet unified selfhood, for Lucrece, if not always for early Christian figures, was unproblematic prior to Tarquin's crime. Lucrece believes in a world where selves, depending on situation, can be either monistic or dualistic without moral taint. To clarify Shakespeare's position, we thus do well to turn to classical ethics—and especially to Cicero. First, though, I want to examine how Lucrece's position both resembles and differs from that put forth by Epictetus, whose outlook on this point resembles that of early Christian traditions. Of the relationship between body and soul, Epictetus posits:

If a tyrant threatens me at court, I say, 'What is he threatening?' If he says, 'I will put you in chains,' I say, 'He is threatening my hands and feet.' If he says, 'I will behead you,' I say, 'He is threatening my neck.' If he says, 'I will throw you into prison,' I say, 'He is threatening my entire body'; if he threatens exile, I say the same. 'Well, then, aren't *you* threatened a little?' If I feel that these things are nothing to me, then no. But if I fear for any of them, then, yes, it is I who am threatened.[12]

Elsewhere in the *Discourses*, Epictetus assumes that selves are dualistic in structure—and that to think otherwise is to mistake selfhood's true nature. But in the previous passage, as in much early Christian thinking, whether the self is unified or split is a matter of practice. If one has cultivated the discipline necessary to make embodiment an inessential property of selfhood, then the tyrant's threats lack force. If that discipline proves insufficient, those threats induce terror.

Lucrece's thought shares with Epictetus's in that for her, selfhood has no inherent and unchangeable form. Lucrece differs from Epictetus, though, in suggesting the following: that dualistic self-conceptions are not always preferable (she was content to have her body preserve her soul's purity); that the self's monism or dualism is not entirely or even primarily within will's purview (Tarquin rendered her selfhood monistic); and that the self can, almost in the same moment, seem monistic and dualistic, shading from one into the other (as she considers the prospect of self-killing).

These differences justify a turn to Cicero's thought on the topic, which is less consistent than Epictetus's. Cicero at times seems a straightforward monist; in *De Oratore* he asserts that body cannot be separated from mind "without disaster,"[13] and in *De Finibus* he writes that "the mind is not some strange immaterial entity (a concept I find unintelligible) but is itself a species of body. It is not therefore satisfied with virtue alone but also desires freedom from pain."[14] In other texts, though, Cicero seems a straightforward dualist, for example in the first of his *Tusculan Disputations*, where he asserts both that body and mind are separate and that the project of philosophy is to minimize the latter's acquaintance with the former.[15] Matters become still more complicated if we consider the treatise on Academic skepticism, where confidence in either position seems absent: "[l]et me," he writes,

come back to the mind and the body. Do we have sufficient knowledge yet about the nature of the nerves or veins? Do we understand

what the mind is, where it is, or even whether it exists or, as
Dichaearchus thought, no such thing exists at all? If it does exist,
does it have three parts, as Plato thought (the rational, spirited, and
appetitive parts), or is it simple and unitary? If it's simple, do we
know whether it's fire or breath or blood, or, as Xenocrates held, an
incorporeal number? (Though one can scarcely imagine what that
would be like!) Whatever it is, do we know whether it's mortal or
eternal? There are many arguments on either side of these questions. One of these views seems certain to your wise person; but
the weight of the arguments on either side strikes ours as so equally
balanced in most cases that it's not even clear to him which is most
persuasive.[16]

In this treatise, Cicero counsels openness about the relationship between
mind and body, claiming that we cannot decide between these competing arguments. Lucrece offers no indication that we even should want
to decide: she feels compelled by opposed arguments to differing degrees in differing instances. So does Cicero, in his career as a whole.
From a perspective that expects to find systematicity, Cicero's shifts from
monism to dualism and back again might appear opportunistic or incoherent, signs of derivative, second-rate philosophy; Lucrece's position,
like Cicero's across his career, may seem naïve, un-rigorous, or stupidly
contradictory. But both positions offer a flexible, potentially pragmatic
skepticism: one that is open to being moved by powerful impressions
about the self but that also suspends ultimate judgment, never admitting one sense of selfhood as certain, stable, or even fully apprehensi-
ble.[17] Given the poetic world in which Lucrece moves, such a model
offers a means for dealing with the threat, and then the reality, of rape.
Much of the poem explores possibly therapeutic calibrations of body and
mind that might stop or at least slow tragedy. The following sections,
accordingly, describe two axes along which Shakespeare's exploration
of selfhood takes place: language and time.

Language

When it comes to verbal exchange, Shakespeare tends to favor a monistic self—who, rather than treat words as separate from things and
mind as separate from body, instead is open to being deeply, materially
affected by others' speech. The most obvious example, here, occurs when
Lucrece pleads with Tarquin, who fails properly to respond:

> His ear her prayers admits, but his heart granteth
>   No penetrable entrance to her plaining:
>   Tears harden lust, though marble wear with raining.
>
> Her pity-pleading eyes are sadly fixed
> In the remorseless wrinkles of his face;
> Her modest eloquence with sighs is mixed,
> Which to her oratory adds more grace. (558–64)

Tarquin falls short, here, when Lucrece's words have minimal physical effect on him. Since his will overrides all arguments that would oppose it—his "will is deaf," we read, "and hears no heedful friends" (495)—he, in this sense, if not in others, exemplifies a twisted, nightmarish form of split selfhood presumed in Epictetus:

> You've never heard sight speak up for itself, or hearing; both have been appointed to be slaves and subordinates to the faculty of using impressions . . . What opens or stops our ears, making us either receptive to a speech or unmoved by it? Not hearing; it is the will and the will alone . . . the determination whether to trust what someone says, and then, if we trust them, whether we should be angered by it—that also belongs to the will.[18]

Whereas earlier, Tarquin's evil stems from being insufficiently dualistic, unable to keep his mind separate from and sovereign over his body, here his evil stems from being too dualistic: from a concentration of power in the will that, though not identical with mind, allows him to remain unmoved by Lucrece's speech. She mixes her eloquence with sighs to blur the distinction between word and thing and intermingle willed judgment with bodily response, but in Tarquin, the two are kept separate. While her "behavior" feeds his heart's folly, her words are refused entrance.

Cicero regards a speaker's power to excite the entire individual as both personally and politically indispensable. In a series of works (including the three books of *De Oratore*, *De Inventione*, *Brutus*, and *Orator*), he ties persuasion and reason to passion by linking body and mind. When he explicitly parts with dualistic thinking in its Socratic form, Cicero writes that in "separat[ing] the science of wise thinking from that of elegant speaking" Socrates generated "the undoubtedly absurd and unprofitable and reprehensible" practice of "having one set of professors to teach us to think and another to teach us to speak."[19] As noted earlier, Cicero at times assumes that one cannot "without disaster" separate the passions that dualists associate with the body from the rational practice that he associates with the mind (21). Effective appeals must be addressed to the entire individual, and so persuasion requires not only "the winning over" and "the instructing" but also "the stirring" of one's audience.[20]

When Lucrece attempts this, the deficiency rests not with her—sighs add grace to her oratory—but with Tarquin.[21] It makes great sense that any republic would begin with Tarquin's everlasting banishment, so antisocial is his deficiency. Cicero attributes virtually no limit to how language can affect individuals, crediting a mythical orator's efforts for the genesis of civil society itself;[22] for Cicero, "bonding consists of reason and speech, which reconcile men to one another . . . and unite them in a kind of natural fellowship."[23] Tarquin, at the scene of mythical genesis, would be as stone. For Shakespeare as for Cicero, Tarquin must be expelled and the republic formed for many reasons, one of them being that words are, as Cicero puts it, "the governing force in every tranquil and free community."[24] For selves and states that function well, eloquence will shape the bearing of others, will "support the sinking and bend the upstanding" (331–333). Eloquence is the "soulbending sovereign of all things," enabling the orator "to transfigure a spiritless and misguided nation, to revive its sense of honour, to reclaim a whole people from its errors."[25] Eloquence serves this purpose in an ideal republic; in the midst of Tarquin, it is purposeless.

Tarquin's marble heart shatters Lucrece's own faith in linguistic force, her sense of what words might do drastically diminished:

> Out, idle words, servants to shallow fools,
> Unprofitable sounds, weak arbitrators!
> Busy yourselves in skill-contending schools;
> Debate where leisure serves with dull debaters;
> To trembling clients let you be mediators:
>   For me, I force not argument a straw,
>   Since that my case is past the help of law. (1016–22)

Lucrece had thought that words might alter Tarquin's heart. Now they work only in the legal domain or in solipsistic schools full of "Debate where leisure serves with dull debaters." Earlier her words sought to move, to gain entrance, to change; the above line, though, ends where it began, swallows its beginning. Words are futile:

> In vain I rail at opportunity,
> At time, at Tarquin, and uncheerful night;

> In vain I cavil with mine infamy,
> In vain I spurn at my confirmed despite;
> This helpless smoke of words doth me no right:
>   The remedy indeed to do me good
>   Is to let forth my defiled blood. (1023–29)

Smoky, insubstantial words cannot buoy her, the anaphora ("In vain . . . In vain . . . In vain") that might build rhetorical power instead vanishing into air. Earlier Shakespeare points to a moment of possibility in which the force of words could have forestalled violence,[26] but Tarquin's rejection of linguistic force, founded in his dualistic self-understanding, now becomes hers. The poem displays language's potential power as well as its potential futility—and once futility comes to be, Lucrece finds herself in a travestied intersubjectivity:

> So she deep drenched in a sea of care
> Holds disputation with each thing she views,
> And to herself all sorrow doth compare;
> No object but her passion's strength renews,
> And as one shifts, another straight ensues.
>   Sometime her grief is dumb and hath no words,
>   Sometime 'tis mad and too much talk affords. (1100–6)

Lucrece finds possibility for exchange with "each thing she views." Disputation, though, is a means not of reconciling but of comparison—and, finally, of multiplying sorrow. As Lucrece addresses the world and its creatures, we see only glimmers of conversational fellowship that would assuage pain, or at least relieve the self of suffering alone. "Should things go wrong," Cicero writes, "your misfortunes will indeed be hard to bear without someone who suffers as badly as yourself, or even worse."[27] The poem's speaker strikes a similar chord:

> Sad souls are slain in merry company;
> Grief best is pleased with grief's society.
> True sorrow then is feelingly sufficed
> When with like semblance it is sympathized. (1110–3)

Lucrece herself, imagining fellowship with a bird she calls Philomel, sounds the same:

> Come, Philomel, that sing'st of ravishment,
> Make thy sad grove in my disheveled hair.

> As the dank earth weeps at thy languishment,
> So I at each sad strain will strain a tear (1128–31)

Lucrece at least begins to imagine an embodied language that might have intersubjective potential, Philomel's sad strains and the tears distilled from her own eyes in perfect sympathy. But the potential is short-lived, as Lucrece observes that in singing she means to be reminded, not relieved, of pain:

> And whiles against a thorn thou bear'st thy part
> To keep thy sharp woes waking, wretched I,
> To imitate thee well, against my heart
> Will fix a sharp knife to affright mine eye,
> Who if it wink shall thereon fall and die:
>> These means as frets upon an instrument
>> Shall tune our heartstrings to true languishment. (1135–41)

Cicero emphasizes the binding force of language within a republic, but for him powerful words are as important without a republic. The exiled Cicero regrets what Lucrece's plight calls to mind: the difficulty of warding off "remembrance of our common misery, to forget which was one reason why I have spun out this discussion so long."[28] Some Ciceronian discussion is therapeutic not in preserving the past or ensuring a future, but in excluding past and future alike. When Brutus mentions that orators could have righted the wrongs of the crumbling republic, Cicero responds as follows: "Let us not speak of that, Brutus . . . It only adds to our sorrow; for while to recall the past is pain enough, dread of the future is a pain still sharper" (231). Cicero wants to dwell in an interactive present, one where he might follow conversation "to the exclusion of everything else."[29] For Lucrece, this is impossible, the rhyme of "instrument" with "languishment" suggesting that song's only remaining instrumentality is to clarify and sharpen a well-tuned sorrow. Language will be knife-like, the thorn with which Philomel reminded herself of pain. Even when Lucrece calls for her maid, a moment of deep sympathy avails little, the maid's cries giving Lucrece no solace:

> "My girl," quoth she, "on what occasion break
> Those tears from thee that down thy cheeks are raining?
> If thou dost weep for grief of my sustaining,
>> Know, gentle wench, it small avails my mood:
>> If tears could help, mine own would do me good." (1270–74)

The grief of Lucrece's "sustaining," we see, is not just the grief that she has felt but that now composes her. No words, no sympathy, can alter this. Dialogue can no longer be therapy.

Time

When Tarquin scrutinizes himself, forms of split selfhood could have stopped him from his crime. When this fails and he faces Lucrece's speech, a more unified self-conception might have halted him. Yet if we examine Tarquin's outlook on time, Shakespeare's sympathies seem to be once more with dualism.

Tarquin fails to dissuade himself from evil partly by failing to assume a broad temporal perspective that would diminish the embodied present's importance. "What win I if I gain the thing I seek?" he asks. "A dream, a breath, a froth of fleeting joy. / Who buys a minute's mirth to wail a week? / Or sells eternity to get a toy?" (211–14). Tarquin attempts to achieve a vantage in which body and mind are separable: in which he can, by imaginative self-projection, view himself and his bodily desire from an expansive spatiotemporal distance, one that would bar him from his ill deed and drive home his desire's insignificance. We have seen Cicero value a monistic outlook that severs the interactive present from the past and future. But he, in this respect akin to Stoics, also values a distant perspective. Reflecting on the time-bound nature of earthly reputation, Cicero enjoins us to

> Let others worry about what they say about you—and they will say things in any case. But everything they say is bounded by the narrow limits of the area, as you see, and it is never eternal about anyone, and it is overwhelmed by the deaths of men and extinguished by the forgetfulness of future generations.[30]

If one Ciceronian practice of the self, in the absence of a republic, is to generate a well-bounded, therapeutic present, another is to view the present from a broad, unbounded perspective. Doing so permits the republican self to cultivate virtue and ward off despair, driving home the reality, felt deeply by classical and early modern republicans alike, of *anacyclosis*: that not just subjects but states are fragile, mutable by nature, and apt to crumble.[31] Given such change, virtue, which the Ciceronian self can control, may become more crucial than the republican political structures whose glory is bound to fade.

In urging a perspective that transcends the spatiotemporal body, Cicero sounds similar to Marcus Aurelius, for whom a distant perspective reveals the smallness of the time-bound, embodied part of us: "[L]ittle the life each lives, little the corner of the earth he lives in, little even the longest fame hereafter."[32] Distance allows us not only to disregard present desire but to develop indifference about the length of life itself. "[S]ee the gulf of time behind and another infinite time in front," he counsels. "[I]n this what difference is there between a three-days-old infant and a Nestor of three generations?" (33).

Tarquin quickly gives up the attempt at such an Olympian perspective. Rather than adopting a distant, dualistic view where the present's importance drains into the huge gulf of time which surrounds it, Tarquin places an intensified present alongside a narrowly demarcated future and past, a present that begins with his encountering impediments while trespassing into Lucrece's chamber and that ends with his desire satisfied:

> The doors, the wind, the glove, that did delay him
> He takes for accidental things of trial;
> Or as those bars which stop the hourly dial,
>> Who with a lingering stay his course doth let
>> Till every minute pays the hour his debt.
>
> "So, so," quoth he, "these lets attend the time,
> Like little frosts that sometime threat the spring,
> To add a more rejoicing to the prime,
> And give the sneaped birds more cause to sing.
> Pain pays the income of each precious thing:
>> Huge rocks, high winds, strong pirates, shelves, and sands
>> The merchant fears, ere rich at home he lands." (325–336)

Desire frames Tarquin's understanding of past and future; he comprehends all in terms of his situated body.[33] Tarquin might have considered the doors, the wind, and the glove as barriers that reveal desire's futility, the present's trifling nature, and the larger world's indifference. Instead, he views these impediments in a foreshortened frame that infuses meaning into what might otherwise seem folly, turning a moment into the season of spring. Whereas Cicero and Marcus Aurelius view the present in the wide frame of the future in order to ward off desperate desires, Tarquin views the future in the narrow frame of the present. The scrupulously partitioned form of the lines that describe impediment ("The doors, the wind, the glove, . . . Huge rocks, high winds, strong pirates, shelves, and sand") dilate the present, walling out any future beyond landing "rich at home" in rape.

Lucrece's own conception of time shifts. Like Tarquin, she attempts to situate the rape in a broad context. But that context never broadens enough for the present to appear miniscule or empty of meaning. Instead, viewing the present in the frame of the future allows her to imagine, rightly, that she will be remembered through, not abolished by, time: "The nurse to still her child will tell my story, / And fright her crying babe with Tarquin's name; / The orator to deck his oratory / Will couple my reproach to Tarquin's shame" (813–6). More so than Tarquin, Lucrece assumes the broad temporal vantage that distances her from the embodied present, but doing so only makes the present stand out more sharply, an ever-fixed mark.

So Lucrece adopts another strategy. She addresses night, in a wish to thicken the present that displays a limit to the similar, Ciceronian practice discussed in the previous section:

> O hateful, vaporous, and foggy night,
> Since thou art guilty of my cureless crime,
> Muster thy mists to meet the eastern light,
> Make war against proportioned course of time;
> Or if thou wilt permit the sun to climb
>> His wonted height, yet ere he go to bed
>> Knit poisonous clouds about his golden head.
>
> With rotten damps ravish the morning air;
> Let their exhaled unwholesome breaths make sick
> The life of purity; the supreme fair,
> Ere he arrive his weary noontide prick;
> And let thy musty vapors march so thick
>> That in their smoky ranks his smothered light
>> May set at noon and make perpetual night.
>
> Were Tarquin night, as he is but night's child,
> The silver-shining queen he would distain;
> Her twinkling handmaids too, by him defiled,
> Through night's black bosom should not peep again.
> So should I have co-partners in my pain;
>> And fellowship in woe doth woe assuage,
>> As palmers' chat makes short their pilgrimage. (771–91)

Cicero, we have seen, imagines a therapeutic present that excludes past ills as well as potential suffering.[34] Lucrece, by contrast, constructs a present that expands, engulfing the future in a perpetual present that memorializes the past. However destructive the wish seems, Lucrece has a therapeutic purpose in mind. She fantasizes about a night prolonged so that she will have co-partners in pain: about extending this moment of embodied suffering such that, paradoxically, her suffering might slightly abate. The heavy internal rhyme of "war" with "por" and "cour" in "[m]ake war against proportioned course of time" enacts that war in slowing speech, as does the sodden chiastic structure of "fellowship in woe doth woe assuage." As we have seen, though, Lucrece enters an imagined intersubjectivity that is excruciating. She shows limits to Cicero's program for delimiting the present, shows how trauma makes past present.

Lucrece now seeks a third approach. This approach is dualistic, and so not that of a unified self forever rooted in the embodied present, but is also not exactly that of a split self able to view itself from a distance. Lucrece tests this third approach in an extended apostrophe to time:

> Misshappen time, copesmate of ugly night,
> Swift subtle post, carrier of grisly care,
> Eater of youth, false slave to false delight,
> Base watch of woes, sin's packhorse, virtue's snare;
> Thou nursest all, and murderest all that are.
>   O hear me then, injurious shifting Time;
>   Be guilty of my death, since of my crime. (925–31)

Lucrece so personifies time that it takes on virtually all capacity for action and, thus, for praise and blame. Rather than assume a perspective that makes praise and blame appear meaningless, Lucrece wishes to make time the guilty party and to empty the world of all other agents. If time nurses and murders all matter, Lucrece would be absolved of all guilt. In this sense like a Stoic, she wants to cultivate unconcern for things that are subject to time rather than to her free will; these things, which include her body, ought to be matters of indifference. Separating bodily trauma from her essential self, the part of her responsible for judgment, would offer her relief.[35] The next four lines, however, show that Lucrece cannot maintain a self-conception that upholds the division between body and mind: "Why hath thy servant opportunity / Betrayed the hours thou gav'st me to repose, / Canceled my fortunes and enchained me / To endless date of never-ending woes?" (932–35). The betrayal of time by opportunity enchains Lucrece to her anguish and threatens to make that anguish everlasting, inseparable from and corrosive of her spirit. While the desire for dualistic selfhood reappears, Lucrece becomes mired in a woeful monism.

Tarquin's rape of Lucrece binds her to whichever structure of selfhood is least useful at a given moment. In her reflections on time, Lucrece repeatedly attempts restructuring: first with a dualism that allows her to view herself from the outside perspective of a vast temporality, then a monism that would keep her forever rooted in the present, followed by a second dualism, one that would transfer agency to time. These efforts never meet with much success. Lucrece's difficulty stems not from misunderstanding her own ontology—from failing to grasp whether she is split or unified in structure. Rather, rape deprives her of the ability, moment to moment, to calibrate the apparently unfixed structure of selfhood for therapeutic purposes. Thus, the tragedy of *Lucrece* is not underwritten by the fact that the self is unified in its ontology: that Shakespeare rejects split selfhood, writing instead under the assumption that Lucrece cannot overcome bodily trauma by instituting some impossible division between body and mind. Rape drives the tragedy not because of selfhood's fixed ontology; rape drives the tragedy despite selfhood's apparently unfixed ontology, as rape forecloses the possibility for Lucrece to achieve any healing configuration of body and mind.

The foreclosure of these possibilities positions *Lucrece* curiously with regard to philosophy as a way of life in the sense put forth by Hadot (and covered in this book's introduction). The poem's affinities with Ciceronian flexibility—with the desire for a wide spectrum of practices—betoken Shakespeare's concern with philosophy as a way to achieve some measure of tranquility, self-control, and therapeutic perspective, rather than with philosophy as systematic discourse. Ciceronian possibilities for *askēsis* depend on not solving the mind-body problem, and the aporias opened by those possibilities far exceed those advocated by, say, Stoic philosophy. The *askēsis* suggested by *Lucrece* would, for instance, mean rejecting Stoic aspirations toward self-consistency. Zeno enjoins philosophers "[t]o live coherently—that is, according to a rule of life which is unique and harmonious. For those who live in incoherence are unhappy."[36] Lucrece's only chance at happiness, by contrast, requires incoherence in how she conceives of body and mind. The skeptical practice suggested in the poem also means rejecting the injunction to self-knowledge; whereas Marcus Aurelius believes we must always remind ourselves that we can retreat into an inner citadel—that we must know ourselves as dualistic beings—Shakespeare urges us not to presume to know something as basic as mind-body ontology. There is also a darker observation to be made, one which distances *Lucrece* not just from classical Stoicism but even from Ciceronian skepticism: that however desirable skeptical *askēsis* appears within the poem, its aims are thwarted at each turn. Shakespeare thus suggests that a practical *askēsis* may be most desirable when least possible.[37]

All the same, Shakespeare's early poem seems more invested in philosophy as a way of life in a classical sense, and thus in skepticism as a pragmatic pursuit, than any other work I treat. If Lucrece is denied such a skeptical practice, readers nonetheless are invited to reflect on the mind-body problem in ways that might make them more tranquil and give them some degree of self-command. *Lucrece*, in contrast to other texts, offers no other possibility for keeping tragedy at bay. So even as Shakespeare sees limits to philosophy as a way of life in a broadly classical sense, it is, in this early poem, the only way—the only skeptical practice—that he can imagine.

Lucrece *and the Politics of the Mind-Body Problem*

If I have argued correctly about *Lucrece*, Shakespeare's poem must seem retrograde, perhaps hopelessly so, from at least a pair of vantages: that of many early modernists, and of most cognitive scientists (if not all philosophers of mind).[38] I want to end this chapter by thinking about why this would be and about the political consequences of *Lucrece*'s skeptical practice.

The mind's embodied nature, cognitive scientists contend, has been well established for several decades. Yet they also note that the schema of a split self persists. It persists, according to Mark Johnson and George Lakoff, because of the widespread, unfortunate, and mostly unquestioned influence of folk theory, in this case theory that seems inevitable in that it grows out of sensorimotor experience. Since our first experiences of control involve manipulating objects, for example, it comes as no surprise when we metaphorize self-control as object control, with one of the self's faculties (reason, or mind, or soul) constraining and directing the others.[39] For Johnson and Lakoff, the conundrum is this: the theory of the split self stems from human experience yet is at odds with what we know about human ontology. Without being acknowledged, the theory has colored much of Western philosophy, beginning with the pre-Socratics but gathering most momentum from Descartes through Kant and beyond, to the point that, as Charles Taylor observes, the onus of proof still rests with those who oppose dualism.[40] Cognitive science aims to heighten and sharpen our awareness of the otherwise mostly unconscious metaphors by which we understand the ethical self as a split self, and self-control as object control; so doing, we open the possibility for new metaphorical understandings and, thus, new ethics.

Johnson and Lakoff acknowledge that the split self of folk theory occasionally has its uses. But they also—rightly—point out that this theory can generate an array of problematic assumptions: for instance, that ethical endeavors are essentially ones of a rational mind reining in a passionate body, with the former acting as a kind of strict father to the latter; that the body is inherently unruly; that reason is inherently ordered; that self-control conceived as object control is always possible and desirable; and that ethical problems, approached by right reason, will always yield single, clear solutions.[41] Mistaking our ontology, Johnson believes, not only dooms us to disappointment, but also impoverishes ethical discourse, suppressing reason's passionate, imaginative, and metaphorical underpinnings.[42]

From this perspective, it would come as no surprise that Lucrece and Tarquin fail to control their situations when they metaphorize selfhood in dualistic terms: that, say, Tarquin cannot maintain the consecrated wall that seems to separate body from soul or that Lucrece cannot attain distance from her embodied present and so diminish her rape's significance. Shakespeare, from this vantage, can refuse dualism so cannily because he precedes Cartesian thinking—explored in detail in Chapter 2—and the Enlightenment that, according to many, makes dualism hegemonic.[43] *Lucrece* was written before metaphors of a split self would have been likely to dominate neural pathways and literary texts.[44] Mary Thomas Crane draws explicit links between contemporary cognitive theory and "the pre-Cartesian, Galenic materialism that shaped early modern concepts of body and mind," arguing that we ought to abandon the frame of dualism if we are to understand Shakespeare.[45] Gail Kern Paster, likewise, observes that in order to comprehend early modern selfhood, "we must begin by understanding that the mind, the body, and the world are always connected,"[46] and Michael Schoen-feldt, though differing with Paster as to what this entails for self-control, also emphasizes how "bodily condition, subjective state, and psychological character are in this earlier regime fully imbricated."[47]

Writing of *Lucrece* in particular, Belsey argues that the poem helps us to understand this imbrication, registering keen awareness of how intensely visceral experiences shatter the brittle frame that would keep mind and body apart, a frame that Livy and Augustine require to suggest that the spoiling of Lucrece's body need not have spoiled her soul.[48] Belsey believes that many modern readers struggle to sympathize with Lucrece's reasoning because of "the dualism that would increasingly constitute the common-sense attitude from the moment when . . . Descartes was to identify the person with consciousness."[49] Pre-Cartesians could avail themselves of a more complex mind-body framework, and only the poem's men look forward to the Cartesian paradigm. "Lucrece herself," Belsey writes, "knows better":

> . . . if grief is registered physiologically, calling into question the distinction taken for granted by so many modern readers between mind and the organism of which it is a part, so, too, is rape, which violates flesh as well as self-respect, organic integrity at the same time as self-determination. Rape, in other words, deconstructs the opposition between mind and body which an exclusively dualist culture came to see as obvious. (331–2)

Belsey, like cognitive scientists, builds her argument on a foundation wherein dualism is ontologically untenable and thus unusable. Belsey's argument also reminds us of dualism's masculinist overtones, which raises a difficult question: of how one could find any utility in the dualistic framework employed to help underwrite early modern misogyny. From at least Plato forward, this framework links mind, soul, and reason more with men, and body and passion more with women, often so as to justify the domination of the latter by the former and to identify reason and self-control with masculinity.[50] Given that many republicans themselves often invoke this pernicious dualism, it may seem quite amiss to recuperate the poem by exploring its links to Cicero. In *The Commonwealth of England*, Thomas Smith, an avowed republican heavily reliant on Ciceronian discourse, masculinizes reason by applying a dualistic frame, the complexities of which I set aside in the interests of space and focus:

[I]n the house and family is the first and most natural (but private) appearance of one of the best kinds of a commonwealth, that is called *Aristocratia,* where a few, and the best, do govern . . . *God* hath given to the man great wit, bigger strength, and more courage to compel the woman to obey by reason, or force: and to the woman, beauty, fair countenance, and sweet words to make the man to obey her again for love. Thus each obeyeth and commandeth other, and they two rule together the house."[51]

Cicero himself urges that there "be a censor to teach men how to supervise their wives";[52] that women are those "whose wills and bodies are the weakest";[53] and that Marcus Antonius was unfit to rule partly because of his venal, womanish way of life.[54] For all that Cicero counsels incertitude about how selves are structured, then, he seems fairly certain about masculine supremacy, and his level of sensitivity toward Lucrece hardly equals that evident in Shakespeare's poem.[55]

Cicero's insensitivity seems especially worthy of scorn given how easy it is, in perusing his letters, to note an unhealthy alternation between cool, Stoic distance from the misfortunes of his embodied present and bottomless despair at those same misfortunes.[56] In detailing how rape affects the entire person, Belsey argues, *Lucrece* shows how selves are instead unified at their core and exposes dualism as a myth—both in the person of Lucrece and in showing how men, most obviously Tarquin, fail to make the myth at all plausible. *Lucrece* has, rightly, been read as exposing numerous features of masculinity as illusions, whether by revealing the pitfalls of possessiveness, shared by Collatine, Tarquin, and Lucretius alike;[57] by ridiculing the mimetic desire that sets Tarquin on his course to begin with; or by rejecting the notion, implicit in Livy, that Lucrece's rape is meaningful primarily in hastening the formation of a males-only republic.[58] Given all this, can *Lucrece* also be a poem that advances a form of life normally associated with masculinist enterprises? Is it either possible or desirable to read it as advancing, even if only contingently and provisionally, a separation between body and mind?

I think that it is both possible and desirable, mainly because Shakespeare in this poem does not seek to establish a stable ontology for selfhood. Crane, Paster, and Schoenfeldt have illuminated important monistic proclivities in early modernity, yet we need not be surprised by the presence in Shakespeare of both monistic and dualistic selfconceptions. David Hillman, himself also mostly focused on the "intimate connection between mind and matter," observes that although Shakespeare precedes Cartesian dualism, available conceptions of the mind-body relationship were not uniformly monistic. In early modernity, that relationship in fact is marked by "radical instability." "[W]hat is sometimes lost in [the] attempt to re-ground mental and emotional activity in the materiality of the body," Hillman writes, "is the instability of the relation, the fact that pre-Cartesian belief structures of earlier periods were already beginning to clash with radical new efforts." Hillman notes that "Shakespeare was writing at a crucial moment in this transition, at the juncture of two profoundly heterogeneous notions of embodiment . . . and the tension between these modes seems to have been profoundly creative for him."[59] The argument of this chapter does not rely on a marked paradigm-shift; though I focus on Cicero, currents of mind-body dualism run from Plato through Shakespeare's period. But Hillman's insight—that Shakespeare's creativity springs partly from the tension between monism and dualism—deserves further development. I have not been concerned here to establish uncertainty about selfhood's actual ontology, though I agree with David Chalmers's argument that it might not be possible to supply conclusive proof for a thoroughly physicalist account of the mind.[60] It is enough that Shakespeare's poem assumes an uncertain ontology, and shows how a flexible self-conception can serve therapeutic purposes, regardless of whether that conception matches selfhood's "true" nature.

So it is possible to imagine Shakespeare impressed by both dualistic and monistic structures of selfhood while suspending judgment about whether either matches actual human ontology. I also think it desirable for Shakespeare to do so. Since he, in *Lucrece*, does not conceive of the self in stable terms, the situational endorsement of dualism does not run afoul of the difficulties identified by either cognitive scientists or early modernists. The ethics of his poem, for instance, do not suffer from the problems of dualism enumerated by Johnson and Lakoff. The poem does not conceive of ethics as always founded in one part of the self reining in the others; Shakespeare, we have seen, has several metaphors for ethical behavior. Some, such as that of Tarquin's desire being so strong that it cannot be budged by reason, rely on images of force and constraint. Other metaphors in the poem urge openness, for instance when Lucrece's words fail to gain entrance to Tarquin's heart. And even when dualistic selfhood seems ethically superior—say, when Tarquin scrutinizes himself—Shakespeare nonetheless equivocates about whether those who think of themselves as split necessarily understand ethical situations with metaphors of force, constraint, and domination. The configuration of body and mind remains unfixed, kaleidoscopic. We will see this lack of fixity—if not a pragmatic orientation to it—time and again, for instance in Chapter 2, when we consider Othello's jealousy alongside but also outside the Cartesian practice of generosity, and when we consider Prospero's anger alongside but also outside Stoic practices of the self.

Because of this lack of fixity, *Lucrece*, like so much of Shakespeare, hardly encourages inattention to the metaphorical nature of ethics. The poem in fact displays how ethical lives are suffused with metaphor and how flexibility is necessary as we search for appropriate metaphors by which to frame a given situation. Katharine Eisaman Maus has drawn attention to the intensely metaphorical nature of Tarquin and Lucrece's thinking, and to how the poem's notorious rhetorical extravagance heightens our awareness of the imagination's role in understanding.[61] Maus also notes that Shakespeare insistently portrays "the metaphoric embodiment of mental events"—the rendering of thought in physical terms—thus showing how our metaphors may be constrained by sensorimotor experience. But Maus draws from this what seems to me an unwarranted conclusion: that mind and body, for Shakespeare, are inseparable.[62] Shakespeare's poem may well bolster the idea that we cannot metaphorize the relationship between mind and body except with recourse to embodied experience. This, however, only entails that mental life operates parallel to, and often may be influenced by, bodily life. It does not entail that we thus can or should always conceive of our minds and bodies as inextricable.

The instability of selfhood in *Lucrece* also keeps the text from being tinged by the masculinism that so often colors dualistic thought. The poem's affirmations of a separation between mind and body are hard to map onto a masculinist framework, as those affirmations do not privilege reason, masculine or otherwise. *Lucrece* engages with Ciceronian thought by showing how its chauvinism can and should be abandoned, but also by preserving the best part of that thought: not that it is free of split selfhood but that, in its skepticism, it refuses to choose between monism and dualism. In *Lucrece*, Shakespeare declines any final decision about whether minds and bodies are divided or unified, taking it not as matter to be solved once and for all, with recourse to established ontology, but as a question to be addressed again and again, context by context.

If kept in mind when we reach the poem's end, Shakespeare's in-decision also highlights the complexity of *Lucrece*'s engagement with republican thought. Near its final stanzas, Brutus upbraids Lucretius and Collatine, father and husband to the slain Lucrece, for their lack of self-possession. Instead of establishing control over themselves and their grief, Lucretius and Collatine can only imagine control over Lucrece. Without question, Shakespeare portrays this complete lack of self-possession, coupled with intense possessiveness, in unappealing terms, much as he will in *Othello*. Brutus himself, by contrast, seems to have found a way to bring mind and body, reason and passion, into a harmonious relationship—into a workable sort of dualism, in which he gains enough distance from the present horror of Lucrece's death to transform Rome's future. When Brutus castigates Lucretius and Colla-tine, he does so not to extirpate passion but to replace the "dew of lam-entations" in which their hearts are steeped with adoration for the Capitol, to change paralytic passion into a controlled, orchestrated affect, the sort that can issue in virtuous action (1828–9, 1835).

Brutus's words work; the republic comes to be. Yet just as we can-not view Shakespeare as unequivocally monistic, so also must we not mistake the dualism that Brutus advocates here as of absolute value. To privilege Brutus with respect to *Lucrece* is to over-value the ending and reduce the poem's complexity. As we have seen, self-control—an oft-cited hallmark of early modern masculinity—is hardly of absolute value, in republican tradition and *Lucrece* alike.[63] Lucretius and Collatine must cultivate self-control as a kind of object control, must develop the tem-perance requisite for the republic's genesis. Still, we must bear in mind that in Shakespeare's early poem, the republic's birth becomes exigent only in the aftermath of Lucrece's death; and it is that death, not the republic's birth, that matters most to Shakespeare. As Coppélia Kahn has observed, the poem's end—most especially, the status of Lucrece's bleeding body as an icon for a new republic—is more than a little disturbing.[64]

To privilege Brutus and the republican dualism he champions is to misconstrue *Lucrece*, in terms of its *askēsis* and its politics alike. We have seen how Tarquin, like Collatine and Lucretius, himself fails in part by the sort of intemperance that earns Brutus's contempt. Yet Tarquin fails equally when he refuses to relinquish control in the face of Lucrece's plea. Shakespeare presents this, too, as a failure of virtue, of what could have been the courage of being open to rebuke and to how weak his position is. Had Lucrece's words affected Tarquin viscerally, he might have welcomed it; and this would be no less, but also no more, republican than the temperance that splits the self in two.

Never again, I think, does Shakespeare so readily—if, even here, reluctantly—suggest practical solutions for problems of life and living. To be sure, he continues to explore both monism and dualism—dualism when he queries, with terrible precision, whether Othello, Prospero, or Timon can cultivate control to separate volitions from passions, and monism when he portrays Othello's quayside ecstasies, Leontes enraptured by the statue-event, or Caliban's sublime dream. Shakespeare never offers an ultimate answer to the mind-body problem. What does change, what does diminish as his career unfolds, is the concept that skeptical practice is a practical endeavor, a way to establish calm and control, a way available to readers if not to Lucrece. As Shakespeare elaborates skeptical practices, more and more he detaches them from pragmatics, as though Lucrece's tragedy stayed with him, gradually overshadowing his early neoclassical optimism. Shakespeare as a way of life becomes far more modest, becomes about learning how to be skeptical not to gain control but to accept its loss.

CHAPTER 2

"It stops me here": Love and Self-Control
in *Othello*

In this chapter, I consider Shakespeare's skeptical practice through the workings of love and self-control in *Othello*. Shakespeare, I argue, casts a skeptical, withering eye on what love is and on whether self-control is one thing that love involves. In the end, Shakespeare allows only for self-control that is attenuated and love that is unknown, and even suggests that Othello can only have such control when his sense of love is elusive. When Othello thinks he knows love's precise demands and entitlements, by contrast, he renounces all control; when Othello thinks he has a grasp of love, he loses his grip. The minimal self-mastery available in love demands humility, especially epistemological humility.

To make this argument I read the play—consistently if not, I hope, to a fault—alongside Descartes. I do so not because Shakespeare thinks along proto-Cartesian lines more in *Othello* than in other plays (which may well be the case), but because a Cartesian background provides the sharpest contrast for Shakespeare's skeptical thinking about love and self-control. In *The Passions of the Soul*, Descartes argues for an acute degree of such control even as he represents—and celebrates—love as that which evacuates control, praising self-possession even as he praises being possessed by desire for the beloved. Shakespeare takes a more modest position in *Othello*, not because love does not undermine self-sovereignty—it does, to the point that, as Stanley Cavell notes, Othello places "a finite woman in the place made and left by Descartes for God"[1]—but because self-control, oddly enough, actually depends on a certain weakness, on giving up control over the beloved as well as our ideas about the event of love. Shakespeare, I will argue, is a skeptic where

Descartes is not: with regard to whether much self-mastery is within our reach and to whether we can master love even in a conceptual sense.

While Shakespeare doubts whether we can know what love is, it does have a consistent structure of feeling. Love in *Othello* involves a pair of seemingly contradictory yet mutually reinforcing movements, ones that correspond to Cartesian thinking about God and about love: a feeling of being possessed by the beloved on the one hand, and, on the other, a desire to possess the beloved. Love so conceived allows Othello to at once deify Desdemona as a being of infinite good, akin to the Cartesian God, and regard her as a finite piece of property, akin to the Cartesian beloved. While Shakespeare offers no outside to the general form in which love is felt as being possessed and wishing to possess, he does, I argue, distinguish between the form's livable and fatal manifestations. Love is livable when the thing thought to be possessed is not literally the beloved, but is instead either an affective infinitude (in the scene near the Cyprian harbor, when Othello beholds Desdemona) or a shred of self-possession (as when Othello asks to be left a little to himself even as he vows to deny Desdemona nothing). In these moments, love is livable not only because Othello is less possessive of Desdemona but also because he assumes himself to be less possessed of a precise sense of what she owes to him and he to her. Love becomes fatal when Othello assumes sovereignty not only over Desdemona but also over an experience that ought to have overmatched him. Othello thus is not a victim of proto-Cartesian skepticism, as Cavell has claimed, but of a twisted proto-Cartesian faith in sovereignty's feasibility and appeal. In this, I conclude, *Othello* helps advance a project undertaken by theorists such as Michael Hardt and Lauren Berlant: that of building a politics of love on a non-sovereign foundation.

Before beginning in earnest, I want to make a brief remark about Cavell, who uses similar terms to read the play for different ends. While Cavell believes, as I do, that Desdemona is to Othello like what God is to Descartes, Cavell also believes that Othello has certainty about just the opposite of Desdemona's supposed deity—that she is another human—and that Othello's refusal to accept this certainty drives the play's tragedy. Cavell's precise words, worth quoting in full, are these:

> Nothing could be more certain to Othello than that Desdemona exists; is flesh and blood; is separate from him; other. This is precisely the possibility that tortures him. The content of his torture *is* the premonition of the existence of another, hence of his own, his own as

dependent, as partial. According to me further, his professions of skepticism over her faithfulness are a cover story for a deeper conviction; a terrible doubt covering a yet more terrible certainty, an unstatable certainty. But then this is . . . the cause of skepticism—the attempt to convert the human condition, the condition of humanity, into an intellectual difficulty, a riddle. (To interpret "a metaphysical finitude as an intellectual lack.") (138)

Cavell's Othello cannot bear finitude, imperfection, and separation. Instead he turns these features of his existence, intrinsic to being human, into an "intellectual difficulty," a cause for skepticism. "What this man lacked was not certainty," Cavell writes. "He knew everything, but he could not yield to what he knew, be commanded by it" (141).

Cavell's fascinating reading enables my own in basic respects yet—in my view—misconstrues the experience of love in *Othello*. Cavell argues that Othello cannot come to terms with the fact that humans are finite, separate and, thus, unknowable to each other. I agree that Othello cannot love Desdemona as another human; at the same time, I think that love in the play induces deep uncertainty about human separation. Cavell focuses on skepticism's tragic dimensions, and offers as antidote fidelity to what we know: that the beloved is separate. While fidelity to this knowledge requires acknowledging our incomplete understanding of the beloved, it also requires confidence about the extent of our separateness—confidence that, I point out in the chapter's conclusion, underwrites some theories of love. In *Othello*, Shakespeare asks for epistemological humility deeper than this, asks readers to have sufficient discipline to cling to love despite its incoherence, despite being unable to know truths as basic as the domains in which and the degrees to which lovers are together and apart.

Love and Self-Control: Descartes, Iago, Othello

Does love require discipline, and if so, of what sort? In commonplace conceptions of love, Zoltán Kövecses rightly notes, the answer is "no," largely because we treat love and self-control as mutually exclusive. Kövecses writes that "If we really are in love, we are unable to function normally," as we can see in expressions like 'He was blinded by love' and 'She swept me off my feet.'[2] This perceived, even clichéd tension between love and self-control pervades many of Shakespeare's plays, including *Othello*, where the tension assumes complexity best illuminated against a Cartesian background. In the previous chapter, I showed that when critics bring Descartes into discussion with Shakespeare, they usually distinguish Cartesian dualism and faculty psychology from the more integrated selfhood evident in Shakespeare's pre-Cartesian texts, but in *Othello* matters are more muddled. While some characters (for instance, Iago) speak of love with a clear vocabulary of faculty psychology, others (for instance, Othello) tend not to do so. To show how Shakespeare adjudicates between them, I want to explore three models of self-control: Descartes's, Iago's, and Othello's.

Toward the end of *The Passions of the Soul*, Descartes justifies an ambitious claim made earlier in his treatise: that "[e]ven those who have the weakest souls could acquire absolute mastery over all their passions."[3] Descartes argues that the surest way to establish mastery is to cultivate "generosity," by which he means the continual recognition of limits to self-control and, within those limits, control's virtuous, scrupulous exercise. At once modest and exacting, Cartesian generosity consists in two things: first, in "knowing that nothing truly belongs to him but this freedom to dispose his volitions," and, second, in "feeling within himself a firm and constant resolution to use it [this freedom] well" (384). Generosity means knowing how little belongs to us; it means putting to good use what little we have.

Generosity might seem merely to separate volitions from passions. In fact, generosity not only keeps volitions uncontaminated but also allows us to control passions such as jealousy, fear, and anger. For instance, since Descartes believes that we should only esteem what is within our control, and since generosity stipulates that only volitions are within that sphere, we should never have the esteem needed to be jealous of another's position or possessions. If we feel jealous, we must tell ourselves this. Generosity keeps anger at bay similarly, diminishing our esteem for things that depend on others and, thus, our disappointment when others fall short of our expectations (385). When we "feel our blood agitated" with what could be excessive anger, we should seek "to separate within ourselves the movements of the blood and spirits" that cause angry feelings "from the thoughts to which they are usually joined"—from, say, thoughts of vengeance (403). We can help make this separation by reminding ourselves of excessive passion's distortions. We

> should take heed, and recollect that everything presented to the imagination tends to mislead the soul and make the reasons for

pursuing the object of its passion appear much stronger than they are, and the reasons for not pursuing this object much weaker . . . we must refrain from making any immediate judgement about them, and distract ourselves by other thoughts until time and repose have completely calmed the disturbance in our blood. (403)

Rather than bridle passions directly, then, generosity gives us self-control by striking at the foundation that supports passion and serves as the platform for rash decisions. We employ volition with caution and care, adopting a skeptical attitude toward the distorted thoughts that passions produce. The stakes here are truly monumental; the final section of *The Passions*—entitled "*It is on the passions alone that all the good and evil of this life depends*"—ends with this pronouncement: that "the chief use of wisdom lies in its teaching us to be masters of our passions and to control them with such skill that the evils which they cause are quite bearable, and even become a source of joy" (404).

Cartesian generosity, though, does not extirpate passion and induce Stoic apathy. Far from it: Descartes writes of passions "that they are all by nature good"; "we have nothing to avoid," he explains, "but their misuse or their excess" (403). Concluding his treatise, Descartes even asserts that "persons whom the passions can move most deeply are capable of enjoying the sweetest pleasures of this life," those that arise from well grounded love and joy (404). But what really complicates *The Passions* is that love, which Descartes also praises, seems not to admit of Cartesian self-control. At first, Cartesian love seems straightforward enough; it "is an emotion of the soul caused by a movement of the spirits, which impels the soul to join itself willingly to objects that appear to be agreeable to it" (356). We love on a commonplace basis: that of "perfections we imagine in a person who we think capable of becoming a second self" (360). Love so conceived sounds more compatible with generosity, and even with the self-sufficiency of classical friendship, than it actually is. "Nature," Descartes writes, has

implanted certain impressions in the brain which bring it about that at a certain age and time we regard ourselves as deficient—as forming only one half of a whole, whose other half must be a person of the opposite sex . . . when we observe something in one of them which is more attractive than anything we observe at that moment in the others, this determines our soul to feel towards that one alone all the inclination which nature gives it to pursue the good which it represents as the greatest we could possibly possess. (360)

Cartesian language shifts from sufficiency and self-possession to deficiency and possessiveness. Drawing on a traditional view at least as old as that voiced by Aristophanes in Plato's *Symposium*, Descartes claims that nature implants in us a sense of our deficiency, and a drive toward an external good. And for all that he lauds self-control, Descartes does not rue the deficiency and the dependence implied by love; rather, he remarks that when love joins with knowledge—when we know what merits love—it is "extremely good because by joining real goods to us it makes us to that extent more perfect. I say also that it cannot be too great" (377). In justified love, only the limit imposed by embodiment—by the fact of our finitude—mandates moderation at all. "[I]f we had no body," Descartes claims, "I venture to say we could not go too far in abandoning ourselves to love and joy" (378). Descartes draws no closer to acknowledging this tension in *The Passions*—between his praise of self-possession on the one hand and, on the other, his approval of love wherein selves are incomplete and self-possession ceases to be an option. Descartes offers no sense of whether or how we could exercise self-control in a matter that exceeds control's limits.

A kindred tension can be found in Iago's own praise of self-control. Iago exhorts the love-struck Roderigo, who has just said that he cannot temper his love for Desdemona, in language full of the faculty psychology that frames much Cartesian thinking. "Virtue?" Iago asks,

> a fig! 'Tis in ourselves that we are thus or thus. Our bodies are our gardens, to the which our wills are gardeners; so that if we will plant nettles or sow lettuce, set hyssop and weed up thyme, supply it with one gender of herbs or distract it with many—either to have it sterile with idleness or manured with industry—why, the power and corrigible authority of this lies in our wills. If the beam of our lives had not one scale of reason to poise another of sensuality, the blood and baseness of our natures would conduct us to most prepost'rous conclusions. But we have reason to cool our raging motions, our carnal stings or unbitted lusts; whereof I take this that you call love to be a sect or scion. (1.3.317–332)[4]

While Iago employs metaphors—of gardening and counterbalanced scales, of raging passion and cool reason—too flagrantly metaphorical for Descartes, Iago's conception of self-control resembles Descartes's in that bodily passions exert force that reason and volition seek to oppose and control. Initially, Iago attributes greater scope to, and a simpler mechanism for, self-control than Descartes later would. He begins by figuring the body as passive, as a garden that the gardener, "will," can cultivate as he pleases.[5] Iago posits limitless control over passion. Midexhortation, however, his metaphors shift, such that reason and sensuality become counterweights. We have reason, he claims, to slow and assuage passion's already existing motions, stings, and lusts. Replacing an image of total control with one of balanced opposition, Iago's conception of self-control grows more modest. Reason limits passion not by bridling it—by seizing control—but by balancing it out on the scales of the self.

Iago may or may not believe what he says. But the shift between metaphors registers that Roderigo's affection for Desdemona must persist for Iago, in turn, to use Roderigo in his own plot against Othello; were the gull's affection extinguished, he would become inert, no longer of use to Iago or anyone else. Iago seems to realize that life without passion—whether love or hate—is life without action. A problem, a motorlessness, arises when we value only our volitions. Iago inadvertently runs into a quandary at the heart of the concept of self-control: that if control were to become total and the self to become truly selfsufficient, desire might cease to exist. It makes sense that Iago would try to escape the quandary by striking a compromise whereby reason moderates, restrains, and directs passion instead of extirpating it. In general outline, this is also Descartes's later solution in *The Passions*, though, as we have seen, not a solution that Descartes applies to love. Iago's solution, utterly vague, itself cannot apply to Roderigo, whose love is never less than desperate. Iago's lame exhortation fails to solve the problem of whether self-control could have a place in love.

If Iago vaguely affirms the place of self-control in love, Othello denies that place in complicated ways. Early in the play, Othello accepts that love imposes limitations on self-possession and that he is not quite the "all in all sufficient" Moor later described by Lodovico (4.1.259). In love his "unhoused free condition" has been "[p]ut into circumscription and confine" (1.2.26–7); he thrives not on his own but in Desdemona, "in this fair lady's love" (1.3.124–5).[6] He acknowledges his lack of selfsufficiency from the outset: in the Venetian Senate chamber he stakes his life on a fair report from her, and, after her report, stakes his life upon her faith (1.3.114–120, 294). As the play unfolds and he begins to suspect Desdemona of infidelity, his sense of dependence and of compromised control escalates. In act 4, he expresses to her what betrayal means for him, beginning in a register of patient perseverance that gradually gives way: "Had it pleased heaven," he speculates,

To try me with affliction, had they rained
All kinds of sores and shames on my bare head,
Steeped me in poverty to the very lips,
Given to captivity me and my utmost hopes,
I should have found in some place of my soul
A drop of patience. (4.2.47–53)

Othello claims the ability to endure all manner of physical constraint and affliction—"sores and shames," captivity without hope—implying that soul and body, however intimate their connection, can be separated. Whatever happens to his flesh, some part of his soul would remain untouched. Potential for self-control still exists; Othello imagines a "drop" of his soul over which the body has no dominion. While lacking the optimism evident in Iago's speech or in Descartes's treatise—let alone the Stoic optimism that we encountered in the previous chapter—Othello believes that a modicum of self-control might survive amid severe trials.

Othello next contrasts physical trials with cuckoldry: "But, alas, to make me / The fixed figure for the time of scorn / To point his slow and moving finger at!" (4.2.53–5). Being "fixed" socially is more difficult to endure, yet even this, Othello claims, he can bear ("Yet I could bear that too; well, very well" [line 56]). Othello cannot bear infidelity and maintain self-control in its midst—cannot, in Cartesian terms, enforce any separation between his volitions and his passions—for another, stranger reason: because Desdemona not only determines his existence in making him a cuckold but actually sustains his existence as such. In her, not in him, is he thus or thus. To be betrayed, as his next utterance suggests, is to be nearly annihilated:

But there where I have garnered up my heart,
Where either I must live or bear no life,
The fountain from which my current runs
Or else dries up—to be discarded thence,
Or keep it as a cistern for foul toads
To know and gender in—turn thy complexion there,
Patience, thou young and rose-lipped cherubin! (4.2.57–63)

Lines 57–60 are complex. In claiming that Desdemona is the site at which he lives or "bears no life," Othello suggests that he lives by her and, thus, that he remains an effect contained within, and thus wholly dependent on, the cause that his beloved is.[7] Othello figures Desdemona as encompassing him completely; when he exclaims "My life upon her faith!" (1.3.294), he is not being hyperbolic. It is not in her that he lives or dies, precisely, but in her that he lives or *bears no life*, as though, were she not to love him, he could exist deprived of life, a being who bears a lack. As for what it would mean to exist but not to live, we can infer that to so exist is to be without a drop of patience—and, thus, that patience is one facet of truly living. Existing without living means being in impatience's grips, in desperate need for change, for one's situation to be otherwise than it is. If total self-control means being without desire, to depend on Desdemona so completely means being nothing but desire, moved and shaped by the beloved as water is by a fountain. To have no self-control is to exist without living.

As the speech unfolds, Othello's dependence deepens. He figures Desdemona as that from which his current either runs or dries up, as what gives form and motion to his otherwise unbounded existence. Without the form that is her fidelity, he would evaporate. When he is nothing but desire, he may soon be nothing at all. And yet—as his speech registers—Othello does still exist. He himself seems aware that he has not evaporated, that he thinks and speaks despite being certain of Desdemona's adultery. In this he resembles Descartes, not in *The Passions* but in the second meditation, when, prior to arriving at proof of a benevolent God's existence, he nonetheless knows that he himself exists. Othello might be deceived in all that he once believed about Desdemona but, still, it is he who believes, he who is deceived. Othello can exist and bear no life because Desdemona, in his mind, is like the Cartesian evil genius.[8] So Othello revises his figure a bit, imagining not his own evaporation but existence as water in a toad-filled cistern, as the passive element in which infidelity occurs. Once a benevolent, faithful guarantor of life, now Desdemona is a deceiver; what he took for a fountain is a hideous cistern.[9]

How can Othello deify Desdemona and thereby make self-control seem so unthinkable? So far I have connected the play with Descartes's *Passions*, but a more detailed comparison with the *Meditations*—and particularly, with the meditator's thinking about God—can clarify what Othello has to suppose to conceive of love and self-control as he does. Two Cartesian thoughts, both serving to prove a benevolent God's existence and both having to do with causation, are of special relevance.

First is the Cartesian meditator's solution to a seemingly paradoxical idea: that he, a manifestly finite, imperfect person, has the idea of an infinite, perfect divinity. Descartes remarks that the light of nature tells him that there must be as much reality in a cause (here, whatever generates his idea of an infinite being) as in the effect (the idea itself).[10] According to this causal axiom, finite humans cannot have created the idea of an infinite God on their own, nor have derived it from any source in the finite world. The idea's source, indeed, must be an infinite, perfect God. An axiom, then, allows Descartes to conclude that a perfect, benevolent God must exist.[11]

Othello thinks of causation similarly. Early in the play, he conceives of Desdemona as a being on whom he can stake his life, not questioning whether she, as the cause of this conception, might differ from his idea of her. "Look to her, Moor, if thou hast eyes to see," Brabantio warns. "She has deceived her father, and may thee" (1.3.292–3). Brabantio suggests that Desdemona is not what she seems—that, in Cartesian terms, there might be less reality in the cause (Desdemona) than in the effect (Othello's idea of her). Othello responds by declaring his conviction about the absoluteness of her faith, so trusting in the relation of ideas to their causes as to be oblivious of love's tendency to idealize. When Iago arouses Othello's doubt, this causal principle turns pernicious. Othello assumes that Iago "sees and knows more, much more, than he unfolds" (3.3.242–3), and soon enough there appears the play's unforgettable effect, the handkerchief, aptly described by Karen Newman as a "snowballing signifier."[12] When he sees the handkerchief in Cassio's hands, Othello assumes the cause must be infidelity, Desdemona somehow having slept with Cassio a thousand times, never considering whether she might have lost the handkerchief in, not in opposition to, her concern for him.[13] The handkerchief can be part of Iago's designs—"[t]rifles light as air" can be "proofs of holy writ"—not just because of Othello's jealousy but also because of how he reasons from effects to causes more generally: by assuming at least as much reality in the cause as in the effect (3.3.322–3).[14] The axiom that saves Descartes from an evil genius allows Othello to turn Desdemona into one.

The second relevant Cartesian thought follows from the first: that the idea of God cannot be self-generated reveals but a corner of the meditator's dependence on God. Whenever, for instance, the meditator considers himself properly, dependence comes to mind, and whenever dependence comes to mind so does another idea, "of a complete and independent being, that is, of God."[15] Proper self-conception itself cannot occur without an accompanying conception of God—on whom, it turns out, the meditator depends not just for self-conception but for every moment of his existence. Since a human's life "can be divided into an infinite number of parts, no one of which is in any way dependent upon the others," he himself can at no point be the cause of his own life; rather that life, "to be conserved at every moment that it endures, needs the same power and the same action which would be necessary to produce it and create it anew if it did not exist" (47). Only God can accomplish this. So, from his inability to have generated the idea of God on his own—his dependence on Him for this—Descartes arrives at the conclusion that he depends on God for his conservation, moment-to-moment.

Othello, too, cannot think of himself without also thinking of Desdemona; virtually every thought he has of himself in the play is accompanied—and not just accompanied, but conditioned—by thoughts of her. As he seems unable to conceive of himself without conceiving of her, it makes sense that Othello would speak as if he depends on her for his own conservation, that she would not only be the source of desire but also make of him a creature who is nothing but desire. As his evil genius, she is also his source of doubt. Othello lacks self-control because of his total dependence on Desdemona, and the idolatrous aspect of his love surely is a problem.[16]

It is not, however, the problem in its entirety. Othello lacks self-control not only because he feels mastered by Desdemona but also because he—in keeping, as critics have pointed out, with patriarchal ideology—feels desperate to master her.[17] Othello's sense of being possessed by Desdemona increases in proportion to his possessiveness, the sense, most vividly evident in 3.3, that she is not his possession but should be:

> O curse of marriage,
> That we can call these delicate creatures ours,
> And not their appetites! I had rather be a toad
> And live upon the vapor of a dungeon
> Than keep a corner in the thing I love
> For others' uses. (268–73)

Othello's lament over husbands' less than absolute possession of their wives precedes the claim about Desdemona's absolute possession of him. I see no simple causal relationship wherein the feeling of imperfect possession produces the sense of being possessed, the latter a byproduct of patriarchy's impossible dreams of absolute ownership; after all, Othello stakes his life on Desdemona in the first act, when he seems least possessive. I do, however, see mutual reinforcement at work, such that Othello's excruciating sense of non-possession and his intense sense of being possessed catalyze each other. The more he imagines a part of his wife over which he has no dominion, the more he thinks she has utter dominion.[18] The more he would rather be a toad than lack control over a corner of Desdemona, the more he sees himself immured in that corner, a toad-engendering element.

Descartes, we have seen, believes that love springs from a sense of deficiency, and that thinking of God redoubles our awareness of this deficiency. When we love, the beloved becomes for us the greatest good we could ever possess, while God is the greatest good we could ever imagine. Othello's thought is proto-Cartesian not just in putting Desdemona in God's place, but in melding thoughts of love and divinity, in figuring Desdemona as at once woman and deity, a being that he might possess but that also conserves him and gives him life. This is his love's greatest vexation: that it induces the desire to control the creator, to be an effect in control of his own cause, the master of that by which he is mastered.[19]

Such vexatious doubleness exacerbates Othello's jealousy, whose form itself seems twistedly proto-Cartesian. "Jealousy," Descartes writes,

> is a kind of anxiety which is related to our desire to preserve for ourselves the possession of some good. It does not result so much from the strength of the reasons which make us believe we may lose the good, as from the high esteem in which we hold it. This causes us to examine the slightest grounds for doubt, and to regard them as very considerable reasons.[20]

Othello esteems Desdemona highly even after he is jealous and she becomes his evil genius. Even after she is a "lewd minx" she remains to him an alabaster idol (3.3.476). The esteem he has for his beloved, the desire he has to control she who seems so beyond him, makes shaky grounds firm, makes relatively weak reasons—Iago's recounting of a dream, the handkerchief in Cassio's hand, an inconclusive conversation between Cassio and Bianca—strong grounds for doubt.

Descartes's condemnation of jealousy helps highlight the tragic potential, in *Othello*, of trying to master what masters us. "[W]e have contempt for a man who is jealous of his wife," Descartes remarks, because this indicates that he does not love her in the right way and that he has a bad opinion of himself or of her. I say that he does not love her in the right way, for if he truly loved her he would not have any inclination to distrust her. But what he loves is not strictly her: it is only the good he imagines to consist in his having sole possession of her. And he would have no anxiety about the loss of this good if he did not think himself to be unworthy of it, or his wife to be unfaithful. (390)

Descartes believes that the jealous man must have a low opinion of himself, of his beloved, or both, and that he loves not so much the beloved as he does the pure sense of possession. Othello develops a poor opinion of himself, partly because of his status as a Moor in Venice and partly because Desdemona is not the deity he wants her to be.[21] Not only can he never feel worthy of a woman who is his God; he also, as many critics remark, can never love her as a fellow, flawed human—as she is, for example, in lying about having lost the handkerchief and in obstinately advancing Cassio's suit despite her husband's obvious agitation.[22] Othello does not love Desdemona as a finite, imperfect being; if anything, he loves the idea of her as a benevolent deity who possesses him, and the idea of having sole possession of her, of the delicate creature and her appetite.[23]

Caught in these impossibilities, Othello renounces so much self-control as to renounce agency altogether. His soliloquy just before he murders Desdemona shows how he believes in agentless action, and how his love, involving unshakeable faith both in being possessed and in the rightness of possessing, issues in tragedy. In this soliloquy, Othello convinces himself of the necessity of killing his god:

> It is the cause, it is the cause, my soul.
> Let me not name it to you, you chaste stars!
> It is the cause. Yet I'll not shed her blood,
> Nor scar that whiter skin of hers than snow,
> And smooth as monumental alabaster.
> Yet she must die, else she'll betray more men.
> Put out the light, and then put out the light. (5.2.1–6)

"It is the cause," while ambiguous, can mean something like: "In her unfaithfulness, Desdemona has caused the killing about to occur." Her adultery is the antecedent to "it" because the infidelity is so heinous as to be unspeakable before the stars. Othello assures himself that her infidelity—rather than, say, his own refusal of her mortal love[24]—is behind her impending death, displacing agency and responsibility onto Desdemona and designating himself as but an instrument of justice. Just as Desdemona in her faith was responsible for his life lasting, so she in her faithlessness is responsible for her life's end. It is the cause. He is not. Not the standard excuse—*you made me do it*—but one more extreme—*you did it*. Given his viewpoint, Othello at most could form part of the occasion on which Desdemona, his world's omnipotent god, destroys herself. Othello adopts so thoroughly occasionalist a view of causation that as soon as he invokes his own will ("Yet I'll not shed her blood"), he also says that the perfection of her appearance, her being more alabaster idol than living flesh, prompts his unwillingness. He will not even claim unwillingness as his.

Othello says that Desdemona "must" die, not that he would like her to die, and he realizes that he cannot take Desdemona's life so long as his senses are in command. He cannot kill her except in the darkness where justice can be done. In the *Meditations*, Descartes himself repeatedly ascribes value to ignoring his senses as a means for avoiding error. "I shall close my eyes," opens the third, saving meditation. "I shall stop my ears, I shall disregard my senses, I shall even efface from my mind all the images of corporeal things; or at least, since that can hardly be done, I shall consider them vain and false."[25] Descartes turns inward to learn about his own mind and, in doing so, to prove God's existence. Othello turns inward to banish the image of Desdemona from his mind and, in doing so, to end his god's existence. Whereas Descartes ignores his senses so as to heighten self-control, Othello does so to forswear self-control altogether. Caught in absolute but contradictory framings of love, Othello can only reconcile the frames for an instant, can only possess Desdemona absolutely by claiming that he is absolutely possessed, that he is not death's agent; complete denial of self-control allows complete control over Desdemona. His faith about what love is—his being absolutely possessed by the beloved—has increased in equal measure with his faith about what love ought to be—his absolute possession of the beloved. Only now, smothering her, does his love's 'ought' become its 'is.'

Othello's life ends soon after Desdemona's. The play, as Michael Neill observes, finishes unusually abruptly, with relatively little space used for resolution.[26] One wonders, staggering away from the play, if Shakespeare undermines love entirely, whether by bringing to light its tragic structure—the crazy, contradictory faith that love brings about, a point made long ago by John Middleton Murry[27]; or by illuminating desire as "a too-muchness that cannot be explained, and that proves utterly disastrous to all who encounter it," a point made recently by Madhavi Menon.[28] One wonders if Shakespeare is not a skeptic but a cynic. I see two possibilities for avoiding such a conclusion, both of which involve skepticism, not about whether love is but about what it is.

'Tis in ourselves after all?

Given the rigidity of Othello's thinking—what Kenneth Gross describes as Othello's "naïvely oppositional, inflexible, but wholly undialectical manner of framing reality"[29]—one escape from tragedy might be found simply by conceiving of the relation between love, self-control, and causation more nimbly, with greater awareness that the seemingly fixed framings of these concepts are, in fact, contingent.[30] Othello thinking of Desdemona as a fountain and himself as water, or even of marriage as a husband possessing a wife, may not be inevitable. Admitting this might not grant Othello the freedom that Iago promises Roderigo, but it could grant a saving degree of cognitive mastery, enough pragmatism to make his love livable.[31]

To consider how this could work in Othello's case, let us begin with causation, a concept framed by a wide range of metaphors, many of which are well beyond Othello's ken. George Lakoff and Mark Johnson, for instance, describe a range that includes metaphors by which causes are: forms; necessary conditions; laws of nature; uniformities of nature; correlations; and applications of force or "power."[32] On the basis of this range, Lakoff and Johnson conclude that "the skeletal structure of causation is so minimal and impoverished that hardly any significant inferences can be drawn from it" (177).[33] Mark Turner, likewise, observes that even in early childhood we have multiple ways to think about causation, and in light of this variety Turner finds most value in one especially complex metaphorical structure: that of causation as progeneration, of metaphors such as "death is the mother of beauty."[34] Within this structure, cause is neither isolated ("a mother," Turner points out, is "not the exact sum total of the causal conditions" for a child, just as death is not the sum total of the conditions of beauty) nor deterministic (which means that "the same cause can have different effects," just as death does not always end in beauty) (146–7). Praising open-endedness, Turner goes so far as to say "that in representations of causation, there can be great utility in indistinct concepts, and either utility or no harm in indeterminate concepts" (177).

Othello himself cannot form indistinct concepts. We have seen him constrained by thinking of causes as forces (in the "it is the cause" speech) as well as related metaphors such as "causing is making" and "effects are objects made" (in the "Had it pleased heaven" speech).[35] We have also seen Othello assume that causes contain at least as much reality as effects. What if he developed more conceptual flexibility—if, for instance, he were to think that Desdemona were not "the exact sum total of the causal conditions" of his jealousy, or that Desdemona's devotion could issue in losing the handkerchief as well as in treasuring it—that the same cause might have different effects? Then the play may have ended as the romantic comedy that, as Susan Snyder points out, it appears to be until the second act.[36]

Similar observations might be made about love, itself as various as causation in its metaphors, ones that—like those for causation—allow for activity and passivity, self-control and lack of control. Kövecses, despite emphasizing the conflict between love and self-control, reviews metaphors by which love is: a journey; a unity; a commodity; a game; a war; a fluid; a moving object; a hidden object; an opponent; a captive animal; magic; a magnetic, chemical, or gravitational force; insanity; a rapture; a nutrient; a flood; a storm; wind; and fire.[37] Our varied framings of love, Kövecses maintains, derive from our experience of love as power and as powerlessness—from, for instance, the fact that it involves physical proximity and increased bodily heat and strength, as well as the disruption of everyday perception. In what Kövecses calls the "typical" case of love, metaphors suggest a definite measure of control, with love as a hidden object for which the lover actively searches, or as an opponent against which the lover struggles. In what Kövecses calls the "ideal" case, though, love—as an overpowering physical force or as insanity—immediately strips the lover of control.

In the depth of his dependence, Othello's own love seems an extreme, completely constraining version of Kövecses's ideal case. The dominant metaphor for that case frames love as a unity, which entails that love fulfills a need (for completion), that the beloved is irreplaceable, and that love creates a harmony (62). In Othello's case, these entailments obtain but are intensified. Love creates a harmony that keeps chaos at bay but, more than complete Othello, lets him bear life. Moreover, Desdemona the beloved, though unique, is replaced by Desdemona the evil genius. The metaphor most germane to Othello's case, "the object of love is a deity," also pertains to Kövecses's ideal case and also is twisted in Othello (72). While Kövecses shows a conceptual link between love and devotion in "that the lovers see themselves as being devoted to each other in much the same way as a priest sees himself as being dedicated to the service of God," Othello's deification of Desdemona entails both much more and much less than this (73).[38] He assumes Desdemona's omnipotence to the point that his own service seems irrelevant; all that matters is that she defines and conserves him. Action is not even within his own domain, let alone among love's requirements. Othello fails to adopt a complex view of love, fails even to accomplish the simple task of adopting closely related metaphors such as "the object of love is a deity" and "love is devotion," such that Desdemona would sustain him yet merit responsibility, admiration, and sacrifice.

Drawing on Kövecses's enumeration of the several dozen metaphorical frames we have for thinking about love, Raymond W. Gibbs, Jr., makes a point about love quite like the points that Lakoff, Johnson, and Turner make about causation: that the mere existence of such multiplicity suggests "that we do not have a single cognitive model for love" and that "[e]ach of these metaphorical models offers different entailments appropriate for thinking and talking about different aspects of our love experiences."[39] When love is particularly unpredictable, for example, "love is a natural force" might make most sense, whereas when we experience love most securely, "love is a unity" might obtain. Were Othello to consider his concepts for love as Gibbs counsels, "not as fixed, static structures, but as temporary representations that are dynamic and context-dependent," he might conceive of love more deftly.[40] Instead he insists on contradictory yet fixed structures of possessing and being possessed, on a pathological, mutually reinforcing pair of deadly metaphors.

"It stops me here"

This therapeutic, practical solution to Othello's problem would be compelling were the ostensibly practical option not so hopelessly impractical within the play's world.[41] The impracticality derives partly from racial and patriarchal ideology's structuring power; while Othello may be able to resist the conflicting ideologies that would place Desdemona beyond him (as white) and below him (as a woman), he cannot simply cast off ideological pressures to freely, radically restructure his cognitive architecture. But the impracticality of such restructuring also derives from love's general form in *Othello*, which cuts across categories of race and sex. Not only does the hero believe himself to be absolutely possessed by someone else; several other characters do, too, as if the belief were inevitable so long as one loves (Emilia, who loves no one, being the one principal character free of the belief). If Othello depends on Desdemona, she, Iago, and Cassio all depend on him.

For Iago, Harold Bloom observes, "Othello was everything, because war was everything; passed over, Iago is nothing, and in warring against Othello, his war is against ontology."[42] He seems to exist only in relation to his general, possessed by him while wanting desperately to possess him: to be Othello's own forever (3.3.480).[43] Cassio, once fallen out of Othello's favor, considers his own existence a function of the general's love; he implores Desdemona to help him so that he "may again / Exist, and be a member of his love / Whom I with all the office of my heart / Entirely honor" (3.4.110–12). Desdemona, finally, vows to control Othello ("I'll watch him tame" [3.3.23]), but ends up relying so heavily on him for her self-conception that she, when asked who smothered her, answers "Nobody—I myself," as though unable to distinguish between her agency and his (5.2.125). Given the uniformity of this structuring of love—given that, whatever love is, love is felt as being possessed and wanting to possess—a more sensible solution to Othello's problem might be less in learning to choose appropriate frames for given experiences of love, and more in learning to make livable the excruciating frames of possession that love thrusts upon us. As a tragedy, *Othello* is not replete with examples of how this might work; I see two that merit attention.

The first takes place near the Cyprian harbor. Othello, having survived "[t]he great contention of sea and skies" on the voyage to Cyprus (2.1.92), beholds Desdemona and is overcome by an almost intolerable joy that reveals how much—and how little—Shakespeare believes that lovers can possess as they are possessed. His first words conjure an intricate picture of the passions overpowering him: "It gives me wonder great as my content," he says, "To see you here before me. O my soul's joy!" (2.1.182–3). The conjunction of wonder and contentment startles; wonder implies that one does not possess the wondrous object—wonder pierces, so that, as T. G. Bishop puts it, "[a] delicate, vital economy between outside and inside has been disrupted"—while content implies possession, possibly even self-possession.[44] Othello's love, though, consists both in being possessed by wonder and in possessing content.

With respect to wonder, at least, Descartes's later formulations again help. Descartes describes wonder as

> a sudden surprise of the soul which brings it to consider with attention the objects that seem to it unusual and extraordinary. It has two causes: first, an impression in the brain, which represents the object as something unusual and consequently worthy of special consideration; and secondly, a movement of the spirits, which the impression disposes . . . to flow with great force to the place in the brain where it is located so as to strengthen and preserve it there[45]

Cartesian wonder's power "depends on two things: the novelty and the fact that the movement it causes is at full strength right from the start" (353–4). Wonder makes a powerful impression of novelty that the brain and body do all they can to retain. Even as the self tries to establish cognitive mastery, though, wonder undermines self-possession in generating dependence on the impression's object.[46] Descartes counsels freeing ourselves from wonder on these grounds yet he also admits that it, like other passions, has utility in being able to "strengthen and prolong thoughts in the soul which it is good for the soul to preserve and which otherwise might easily be erased from it . . . things of which we were previously ignorant" (354). That Othello's wonder is of a proto-Cartesian order becomes clear further in his quayside exchange:

> I cannot speak enough of this content;
> It stops me here; it is too much of joy.
> And this, and this, the greatest discords be
> [*They kiss.*]
> That e'er our hearts shall make! (2.1.195–8)

Othello's wondrously arresting contentment—it "stops" him—is practically the opposite of the freedom and control that comes from Cartesian self-direction. Desdemona's form possesses Othello, strikes him with the force of something never before seen. Shakespeare may be more skeptical than Descartes about self-control but also may have more faith than Descartes in its loss—even as he also admits the perils of that loss.[47] Othello does not try to possess his wife here, does not even try to capture love in a verbal frame. Othello kisses his wife to prolong this moment and, perhaps, preserve within himself the wonder which he feels upon seeing her and of which he, in a life of broils and battle, once was ignorant.

Much less possessive here than later in the play, Othello feels his "soul's joy," which gives him two things: the idea of love as an infinite good, and the feeling of being possessed by that good. In this livable version of the play's tragic paradox, Othello possesses only that which exceeds limits, possesses only in his imagination and without mastery. Othello neither deifies nor objectifies Desdemona; wonder and content come not from owning or controlling his wife but merely from seeing her before him and from being overcome by love. It stops him here.

In a further paradox, Othello's openness to risk, even his welcoming of death, makes love livable. Though he has just survived a "desperate tempest," he would embrace another (2.1.21). "If after every tempest come such calms," he says,

> May the winds blow till they have wakened death!
> And let the laboring bark climb hills of seas
> Olympus-high, and duck again as low
> As hell's from heaven! (2.1.184–88)

It may seem hackneyed for Othello to describe death in describing love, but the import of his reference has less to do with orgasm than with the fact that love, at this moment, entails his death as an entity with any mastery over what puts him beside himself. For love, Othello welcomes the world's reordering, the horizontal made vertical, hills of seas joining hell with heaven. As ecstatic about descending into fiery depths as about ascending Olympus, Othello feels internally the external state that he invites. The storm he has passed and the calm that has come cannot be distinguished.

To appreciate how totally Othello embraces this extremity, we might compare his thinking to that of Georges Bataille, discussed at greater length in this book's final chapter. Bataille contends that *eros* signals the end of the individual as a discontinuous—a bounded, discrete, and clearly delineated—being. For Bataille "[t]he whole business of eroticism is to strike to the inmost core of the living being . . . to destroy the self-contained character of the participators as they are in their normal lives."[48] The violent agitations of *eros* break established patterns, jar selfhood's stability. Yet even the avowedly radical Bataille limits the desirability of *eros'* undoings. "Continuity is what we are after," Bataille writes, "but generally only if that continuity which the death of discontinuous beings can alone establish is not the victor in the long run. What we desire is to bring into a world founded on discontinuity all the continuity such a world can sustain" (18–19). Our everyday worlds are populated by discontinuous beings, and though we desire the continuity of personal boundaries being undone, we do so only with the expectation of the everyday world's eventual return. Otherwise, we literalize the symbolic death that continuity brings. Othello, on the other hand, wants a new world, founded on boundaries eroded once and for all, wants this to be distinct from death even as he suspects that it cannot be. Stephen Greenblatt rightly notes that "the death [Othello] invokes may figure not the release from desire but its fulfillment," yet also sees in Othello "an anxious sense of self-dissolution."[49] Bataille registers this anxiety, and so does Desdemona; in remarking that bodily limits keep us from abandoning ourselves to love, so does Descartes. Othello, for now, does not:

> If it were now to die,
> 'Twere now to be most happy, for I fear
> My soul hath her content so absolute
> That not another comfort like to this
> Succeeds in unknown fate. (2.1.188–92)

Othello fears not self-dissolution but self-reconstitution, the quotidian disappointments that may succeed this ecstasy. Desdemona, not only anxious but actually taken aback by the volatility of Othello's vision, heightens her husband's awareness of what he has said, of how his wishes threaten love's duration: "The heavens forbid," she says, "But that our loves and comforts should increase / Even as our days do grow" (2.1.192–4). She wants their love to last, a prospect to which Othello says "amen," remarking that kisses, rather than an upended world, may be their only discord after all. Desdemona recalls her husband to the world of discrete beings, turns his gaze from oblivion and toward what little he can possess. When he says amen he does not offer any extended reformulation of love, as though he now comprehends its essence. He instead says that he cannot speak enough of his content, that it halts him. Likening love to death might not mean claiming to understand love, but it does, as Greenblatt points out, suggest a wish "for decisive closure" (48). Now Othello fully acknowledges that he cannot grasp love, that it exceeds his words and his wish. Though Desdemona works to preserve him and their love, to restore stability in that sense—and though Othello accepts this—he also accepts another instability in admitting, overcome, that love eludes cognitive capture.

This moment is not comic. Snyder notes that here we see tragedy's beginnings: "at the same time that Othello celebrates his peak of joy so markedly," she writes, "his invocations of death, fear, and unknown fate make us apprehensive about the postcomic future."[50] I also think that tragedy tinges the scene, not only in making us apprehensive but also in suggesting, as Rollo May suggests, that all love—even enduring love—must involve a tragic element if it is to avoid being saccharine, if love instead is to mean being "taken over by an event" that opens us "to an intensity of consciousness we did not know was possible before."[51] Such intensity requires a skeptical admission about love, one that further distinguishes Shakespeare's vision from Descartes's own. While Descartes defines love as desiring to possess the beloved as a great good, near the Cyprian harbor we find love largely undefined; love is only fidelity to being taken over, to an experience not fully known.

Othello clings to love with ease in such a joyous moment. Most of love's moments are unlike the one near the harbor at Cyprus, though, and we can also find possibility in a moment of deep perturbation, one in closer proximity to tragedy. Near the start of 3.3—by the end of which tragedy is all but inevitable—Othello and Desdemona have their first fraught conversation. Desdemona has just assured Cassio that Othello "shall never rest" until he recalls his lieutenant. "I'll watch him tame and talk him out of patience," she promises. "His bed shall seem a school, his board a shrift" (3.3.22–24). When Othello and Iago enter, we scarcely expect the ecstasies of 2.1, and expect still less after Iago raises some initial suspicions by suggesting that Cassio, unless he conceals something awful, ought not to "steal away so guiltylike, / Seeing your coming" (3.3.39–40). Desdemona presses Cassio's suit and, when Othello avoids a precise answer, implores him to recall his lieutenant within three days. Her plea prompts an irritated Othello to interrupt: "Prithee no more," he says. "Let him come when he will! / I will deny thee nothing" (75–6). The caesura in line 75 leads to the unexpected: agreement that follows immediately upon agitation. Cassio can come when he will. Othello will deny his wife nothing. Desdemona, herself now irritated by this peremptory reply, finishes line 76 by asserting that Othello has, in point of fact, granted precious little, helping no one so much as himself:

Why, this is not a boon;
'Tis as I should entreat you wear your gloves,

Or feed on nourishing dishes, or keep you warm,
Or sue to you to do a peculiar profit
To your own person. Nay, when I have a suit
Wherein I mean to touch your love indeed,
It shall be full of poise and difficult weight,
And fearful to be granted. (76–83)

Recalling Cassio promotes Othello's own well-being. Restoring his lieutenant would nourish him, and is akin to protection from the elements
that Othello earlier wished would overwhelm him. In acceding to her
wish, Othello merely guards against his own oblivion. The plea leaves
his love untouched, untested. Desdemona has not yet made him feel
love's burden, or so she believes, not knowing that Iago's insinuations
have already started.

Now Othello ends a line begun by Desdemona. "I will deny thee
nothing!" he repeats. "Whereon I do beseech thee grant me this, / To
leave me but a little to myself" (83–85). Othello and Desdemona finish lines started by the other in ways that betoken a complex, trou-
bled acceptance of union and separation in love. In his initial exclamation
Othello pledges to disregard his interests for hers even as his irritation indicates the gulf that yawns between the two, while Desdemona,
completing the line, denies any difference between their interests only
to then remind him that a time may come when they differ so radically, the distance between their positions so vast, that granting her
suit shall be "fearful." Othello insists that nothing will be withheld,
yet also asks that Desdemona give him space: "leave me but a little to
myself." We sometimes imagine that by love we might set aside or
even erase differences in pure, perfect union.[52] Othello and Desdemona here realize that this is but a dream. In asking to be left a little
to himself, Othello registers that the difference does and will remain. He asks for this little, this modest self-possession, even as he accepts that she possesses him and vows to deny her nothing. He will
be open to her without merging with her, totally vulnerable to desires of hers that war with his. Othello vows to embrace this vexing
intensity.

The play's tragedy, partly, is that Desdemona holds to a similar vow
to the end—"Shall I deny you?" she asks at this conversation's end,
"No . . . Whate'er you be, I am obedient" (3.3.86, 88)—whereas Othello
lapses into patriarchal tyranny, refusing her every request in the pathetic
cascade that ends with him smothering her:

DESDEMONA
O banish me, my lord, but kill me not!
OTHELLO
Down, strumpet!
DESDEMONA
Kill me tomorrow; let me live tonight!
OTHELLO
Nay, if you strive—
DESDEMONA
But half an hour!
OTHELLO   Being done, there is no pause.
DESDEMONA
But while I say one prayer!
OTHELLO   It is too late. (5.2.78–83)

Othello again finishes Desdemona's lines, now so that he might deny her everything, unable to grant anything at odds with what he sees fit. In his promise to deny Desdemona "nothing," Othello admits that he cannot limit or define what love will demand of him, yet pledges to meet those demands, having accepted not only what runs counter to what he would wish but what in love exceeds his comprehension, the features of its horizon that remain in haze. When that horizon clears for him, his humility about what he can know and possess evaporates, replaced by tragic presumption.[53]

I have written of love and self-control in *Othello* as though they are irreconcilable, but this is not quite the case. Othello's brief acceptance of humility in 3.3 demands a modicum of self-control, so small as to be almost indiscernible. His vow to deny Desdemona nothing is admirable partly because the vow, and the volition that grounds it, runs so counter to his ire.[54] There must be some separation between passions and volitions. And while I have largely contrasted Shakespeare and Descartes's views on self-control, Shakespeare's position might be called proto-Cartesian in according with some of Descartes's less ambitious (if also less common) moments, those more cautious about self-control's scope. A few passages of *The Passions* register the impossibility of full control over passions of special power. These, Descartes writes, so impress us because

> they are nearly all accompanied by some disturbance which takes
> place in the heart and consequently also throughout the blood and

the animal spirits. Until this disturbance ceases they remain present to our mind in the same way as the objects of the senses are present to it while they are acting upon our sense organs. The soul can prevent itself from hearing a slight noise or feeling a slight pain by attending very closely to some other thing, but it cannot in the same way prevent itself from hearing thunder or feeling a fire that burns the hand. Likewise it can easily overcome the lesser passions, but not the stronger and more violent ones, except after the disturbance of the blood and spirits has died down.[55]

One cannot do much in such situations, but one can do something: "The most the will can do while this disturbance is at its full strength," Descartes writes, "is not to yield to its effects and to inhibit many of the movements to which it disposes the body. For example, if anger causes the hand to rise to strike a blow, the will can usually restrain it" (345). Early in 3.3, Othello has not yet felt, and failed to resist, the impulse to strike his wife, though he has at least felt, and resisted, the spirit of denial, the wish to simply say "no" and send his wife away. The struggle evident in Othello's "it is the cause" speech may even suggest a last lingering potential for the self-control that consists merely in restraining a blow. Were he able to restrain his anger merely to this degree—were he to gain a grasp of himself by admitting, with a shred of humility, that he might not grasp his situation—Othello's strong passion could have abated a bit. Time might have been all that Othello required to grant Desdemona's pleas and so restore fidelity to love.

When Desdemona exits early in 3.3, Othello, still filled with intense affect, utters one of the most famous exclamations in the play: "Excellent wretch! Perdition catch my soul / But I do love thee! and when I love thee not, / Chaos is come again" (3.3.90–92). Othello here seems to misconceive of love in terms of volatile, mutable feeling rather than in terms of works, but in a sense Othello has already performed one of love's most important works: declaring fidelity to the event of love, vowing to deny his beloved nothing without knowing what love is or may ask of him. Othello fails in his vows not by basing love in feeling but by becoming presumptuous about love: about what he can and should expect from his beloved, the precise domains in which and degrees to which he is possessed and ought to possess. In *The Passions*, Descartes attempts his own precision, and it is only in Descartes's more skeptical moments that we can see Shakespeare in accord with him.

Conclusion

The discipline of love that Shakespeare intimates would not bring extensive self-control or much knowledge of love. Rather, it would be a discipline of learning to cling to what we cannot master or even fully grasp, of learning to stop here. To clarify some consequences, I want to finish by comparing Shakespeare to other philosophers of love, with a final aim of discussing love not only in personal terms but also in more overtly political ones.

I have said that for Bataille, love is a discipline of incorporating as much continuity as possible in a world of discontinuity, of the state of being separate. *Eros* helps us to discover how much of the self we can erode, and how much control we can relinquish, given our constitution as separate individuals. Bataille values the erosion of boundaries in *eros*; as we will see in the chapter on *Timon*, this erosion spells self-possession's end, a point to which I return in a moment. Yet for some philosophers love should not end self-possession but establish it.[56] Indeed, according to some—for instance, Erich Fromm—love should do so even though it overcomes our default experience as bounded, discrete beings. Fromm writes that our sense of being separate arouses anxiety, that "it is, indeed, the source of all anxiety." Love allays this anxiety in delivering us to "interpersonal fusion," yet if it ended aloneness with a self-dissolving union, love would be an unhealthy symbiosis.[57] Luckily, love does not do this. No one would dispute that love also involves concern for a beloved conceived of as separate, so the union love produces must be less complete and more complex. Fromm thus writes that "*love is union under the condition of preserving one's integrity* . . . In love the paradox occurs that two beings become one and yet remain two" (19). In this paradox, we are separate enough that love can be "*active concern for the life and the growth*" of the beloved, a concern that involves dimensions of care and respect for the other, responsibility to the other, and knowledge of the other (24). Affection is an art, a discipline of "'standing' in love" that demands an acute degree of self-control (3). Knowledge of the other is the most crucial dimension of this discipline, as we cannot know how to properly care for, respect, or be responsible to the beloved without a keen sense of the beloved. In love we strive to move from narcissism toward objectivity, to develop "the faculty to see people as *they are*, objectively, and to be able to separate this *objective* picture from a picture which is formed by one's desires and fears" (109).

It seems obvious how Othello might have learned from Fromm. With rare exceptions, Othello fails to tolerate the paradox of being one but two; abandons care, respect, and responsibility; and never approaches anything resembling objectivity in his view of Desdemona, instead swinging wildly from symbiosis to total loathing. On the other hand, it is not as though the play would not be a tragedy if Fromm were to slip its protagonist a copy of *The Art of Loving*, and not only because of standard issues having to do with the drama—for instance, that the degree to which the beloved cannot be known is greater than Fromm allows.[58] Shakespeare also is skeptical that the self can retain its integrity in love, not because the self is lost in total union—a notion about which he is equally skeptical—but because to love is to experience the incoherence of feeling possessed and desiring to possess, an incoherence far more unsettling than is Fromm's paradox of love. Love, for Shakespeare, cannot be stabilized by developing active concerns of responsibility and respect. Love's incoherence can only be made livable, its indeterminate, unstable demands accepted. *Othello* cannot offer any system for loving not just because it is a play but because love in the play demands a single thing: that lovers cling to love, that they keep going.

In a recent set of interviews, Alain Badiou gives depth and dimension to Fromm's paradox of love in a fashion that does not fully answer this Shakespearean demand but that does demonstrate how radical the demand really is. For Badiou, lovers require discipline not in order to become objective but to adopt a complexity of perspective. Love begins with an overwhelming event, an encounter in which the beloved has "erupted, fully armed with its being, into my life thus disrupted and re-fashioned."[59] Love offers neither an easy communion, in which differences dissolve, nor a simple separation, in which differences are respected and sustained, but creates a "unique Subject, the Subject of love that views the panorama of the world through the prism of our difference" (26). This means both that love is an outward, not an inward-looking construction and that that construction is made not "from the perspective of One but from the perspective of Two" (29). Whereas Fromm's paradox of love demands that one develop as objective a view of the beloved as possible, love in Badiou's view requires incorporating the beloved's perspective into one's own. Love is not love without fidelity to this new perspective, to constructing a life-world through the prism of difference. Love is a disciplined search for truth in which two questions are posed time and again: "what kind of world does one see when one experiences it from the point of view of two and not one?" and "What is the world like when it is experienced, developed and lived from the point of view of difference and not identity?" (22).

Shakespeare's thinking in *Othello* resembles Badiou's in that both yearn for love that yields neither simple unity nor simply sustained difference. Yet Shakespeare does not seem to think that love could institute the "unique Subject" that Badiou describes inasmuch as this Subject's new perspective offers stability and knowledge of a truth—in this case, of the sort of world we build when we assume the point of view of difference. Badiou doubts love's power to unite, but this doubt gives lovers a considerable degree of control, enabling them "to handle difference and make it creative" and to persevere in "the onerous development of a truth that is constructed point by point" (54). In *Othello*, the skepticism of Shakespeare runs deeper than that of Badiou—at least the Badiou of *In Praise of Love*.[60] Love would lead to the onerous development not of a truth but of a relation whose truth eludes us, to disorienting intensities of extraordinary and quotidian kinds.

At the close of *A Lover's Discourse*, Roland Barthes offers an aphorism about the "non-will-to-possess" that nearly captures the discipline of acceptance urged on readers of *Othello*: "to let come (from the other) what comes, to let pass (from the other) what goes; to possess nothing, to repel nothing; to receive, not to keep."[61] In *Othello,* Shakespeare allows for minimal possessions (of a memory of wonder, of being left a little to oneself) but aside from this requires a non-will-to-possess, one with obvious and less-than-obvious cognitive politics. There is the obvious point that love offers a way around one of possessive individualism's major pitfalls: namely, that once one conceives of the self in terms of strict self-possession, as Leo Bersani points out, one becomes more likely to think of all relations as property relations.[62] For other points we can look to Lauren Berlant, who (at times in concert with Michael Hardt) also has been thinking through a political concept of love[63] wherein love "always means non-sovereignty."[64] Love, Berlant writes, not only is "one of the few places where people actually admit they want to become different"—where they might lose interest in the mastery of remaining selfsame, as Othello does near the Cyprian harbor—but also a place where they accept that love brings changes beyond their control, as Othello does, however briefly, at the start of 3.3. Love is "change without guarantees, without knowing what the other side of it is" (8).

Love forces us to consider ourselves as non self-identical, as wanting to be so, and as not expecting polities to guarantee self-identity or supply political fora as sites at which coherent identity emerges. When summoned to the Venetian Senate chamber, by contrast, Othello expects just this. "I must be found," he explains to Iago. "My parts, my title, and my perfect soul/Shall manifest me rightly" (1.2.30–2). His accounting of love's genesis makes him seem what he is not, changeless, perfect, "all in all sufficient" (4.1.259). Love itself, when he holds to it, is an experience of change and imperfection, of livable insufficiency.

Politics must accommodate these things, Berlant believes, because political actors are filled with "[i]ncompatible needs and fantasies," as Othello is quayside, desperate to die but also to give love duration, and at the start of 3.3, denying Desdemona but vowing to deny her nothing.[65] Love offers "[t]raining in one's own incoherence," and by doing so it offers us "training in the ways in which one's complexity and contradiction can never be resolved by the political," which Berlant views as crucial to any theory of non-sovereignty.[66] Such training drives home that the political could never resolve our own contradictions or render us whole, protected, and empowered.

So love adjusts what we expect of politics. As Berlant puts it, love "is one of the few situations where we desire to have patience for what isn't working."[67] *Othello* shows how we can have patience—if perhaps not desire patience—for what isn't working when we stop pretending to know precisely how it should work: we can be faithful to love, can bear its incoherent senses of possessing and being possessed, only when we admit that we do not know exactly what love is or how it should unfold. Love in the *polis* thus might diminish expectations while increasing patience, which is not the same as quietism, since love also might affect political practice. Berlant offers a list of elements that a political concept of love would provide, two of which are relevant to *Othello*. First, it would "provide the courage to take the leap into a project of better relationality that would give us patience with the 'without guarantees'" part of love. Second, it "would open spaces for really dealing with the discomfort of the radical contingency that a genuine democracy—like any attachment—would demand" (690). Berlant thus argues that we need "space for enigmatic, chaotic, incoherent, and structurally contradictory attachments" and that we need to provide this space "without promising to deliver a 'life' that feels cushioned" (685).

Changing political expectations, love issues in a call for spaces that accommodate incoherence without also promising the false assurance of a cushioned life. We have seen how Shakespeare structures the cognitive space needed for patience with love's lack of guarantees, its discomforts and deep contingencies. Reading *Othello* alongside Berlant, though, allows us to also imagine how political spaces might change. What if we were to reimagine act 1, scene 3, when Othello appears before the Duke, the scene of interrogation now made like the space for which Berlant calls? We would not have a liberal space in which Othello is not derided for being a Moor and Desdemona is granted unfettered freedom of choice, Venetians having lost their prejudice and Brabantio now a loving father concerned for his daughter's personal flourishing. This is what the Senate chamber would become were it shaped by the pressures of promoting individual sovereignty.[68] Brabantio, in a distinctly nonmodern way, already thinks of the chamber as a stronghold for his own sovereignty, a place to be reassured that Desdemona belonged to him and that her match with Othello infringes on his individual right to dispose of daughterly property. Love disrupts Brabantio's model of sovereignty, but not in order to restore Othello and Desdemona to self-sovereignty. Were love fully to erupt into the chamber, it would release those within from the imperative to appear sovereign and from the pressure of narrative self-fashioning: of having to present a controlled, impressive, all in all sufficient self.

This pressure released, discussion's dynamics would change. There would, to begin, be no question of whether Othello has won Desdemona with powerful, incapacitating charms, or of whether Desdemona was "not herself" when she fell for him. To legitimize and sanitize their love, Othello shifts charm's terms from literal spell-casting to autobiographical magic, an enhanced version of a humdrum courtship; but if love were assumed to be enigmatic, chaotic, and structurally contradictory, its causes unknown, there could be no onus to explain their love coherently, let alone to satisfy Brabantio's demands.[69] Brabantio accuses Othello of infringing on his sovereignty by compromising Desdemona's, but if love is a phenomenon of non-sovereignty and discussion in the Senate chamber were shaped by non-sovereign aims, Brabantio's accusation would lose force. Othello would feel no burden to claim that Desdemona loved him for the dangers that he had passed and that he loved her because she pitied them. Few readers believe this story to begin with. Othello would not need to pretend, nor would Desdemona. In asking to accompany Othello to Cyprus, she would not need to insist that she "saw Othello's visage in his mind" and that she, in rarefied love, has consecrated her soul to him. She would not have to claim that their love is a spiritual union when their attachment is far more complex and more contradictory than that.

Were the Venetian Senate chamber to become a space that accommodates an unknowable love, it would not be a sphere for open debate among sovereign individuals, one where Brabantio could accuse Othello of coercion and Othello and Desdemona could assure everyone present that her freedom of choice was unconstrained. The chamber would instead become a space of diminished presumption and pretense, a skeptical space that accommodates and even encourages incoherence, a space where chaos—this time without tragedy—is bid welcome. Expecting to know "the whole course of love" would be deemed ludicrous (1.3.91). If, as Shakespeare often suggests, falling in love is reasonless—if we do not know why we fall in love, and if the explanations we offer seem hopeless, painful in their inadequacy—perhaps this is partly because we do not and cannot know what love is.[70] *Othello* suggests that the best way to stand in love is to admit that you do not know exactly where you stand, to acknowledge that the ground seems always to shift, and to hold onto love despite its disorientations and its disruptions of sovereign thinking. If *Othello* allows us to glimpse the politics of this humility, *The Winter's Tale*, we will now see, gives us a more extended look.[71]

CHAPTER 3

The Winter's Tale: Faith in Law
and the Law of Faith

I n Othello, Shakespeare asks for faith in a love whose demands cannot be defined in advance. The Winter's Tale, a late romance that reprises Othello's themes of jealousy and possession, also investigates skepticism and faith as they extend not just to love but to a range of things—to sovereigns, to the rule of law, even to statues—and in doing so imagines a more robust political humility than is possible within Othello's world. In The Winter's Tale we see skepticism yield to faith when it comes to law, to the sort of law that merits faithful submission. Shakespeare, we will see, looks into how Leontes can be a husband and king once he loses faith in himself and realizes he is not the king James I so often claimed to be. Shakespeare asks how Leontes can go on when the nature of his office fails to "[agree] very wel with the office of the head towards the body, and all members thereof"—when Leontes must rule and love with epistemological humility and, thus, must live not above the law but under it.[1]

The question is which kind of law. Shakespeare explores two possible answers in The Winter's Tale, answers also explored in Paul's epistles, in Montaigne, and in radical theory's recent readings of Paul. One option for Leontes would be to submit to a law of works, to a system of injunctions and prohibitions—a system founded, and dependent for its ground, on faith in a series of beliefs (at minimum, about the rightness of certain actions, but also about the clarity of evidence, the transparency of intention, and the extent of human discernment), parallel to beliefs about love that Othello seeks to form. Leontes's other, quite different option is submission to a law of faith neither normative nor juridical; without much underpinning in propositional belief, this law demands only that subjects love their neighbors. Shakespeare entertains both possibilities but ends with emphasis on the law of faith: law that both assumes and induces intense epistemological weakness. This means that if Shakespeare critiques absolutism, he does not do so, as much criticism argues, in order to adopt a clear confessional or political vocabulary. Rather, Shakespeare does so in order to explore faith without firm belief in any particular code, be it republican or religious. *The Winter's Tale* thus benefits when read in the present contexts of Giorgio Agamben and Alain Badiou, whose Paul is distinctly non-confessional, and when approached from (if not fully captured by) a Montaignean perspective rather than the perspective of a more systematic early modern thinker. Read so, we can see how Shakespeare presents a Pauline, yet skeptical—and strikingly unsystematic—practice for the cultivation of virtue.

Law based in epistemological strength, as James I imagines it, enables "right interpretation and good execution" from above and, if "made as plaine as can be to the people" below, eliminates "the excuse of ignorance" about their standing as loyal or rebellious[2]; when law fails to contain unruly elements, the wise king has license to "cut them off for feare of infecting the rest."[3] Such law institutes divisions—between people and categories of people, between acts lawful and transgressive—while also elaborating a framework that locates selves as undivided subjects. This chapter shows how the Pauline law instituted at *The Winter's Tale*'s end divides the above divisions, such that subjects no longer coincide with themselves, no longer know where they stand with regard to an imprecise, infinitizing law of neighbor-love, one that gives depth and dimension to Othello's swiftly broken promise to deny Desdemona nothing. In the play's world, this law, though unsettling, disorienting, and to some extent unsatisfying, is also the most fundamental, just, and peaceable law that Shakespeare can imagine.

Saint Paul, Skepticism, and The Winter's Tale

This chapter brings Pauline concepts of law to bear on skeptical readings of the play and skepticism to bear on Pauline readings of the play. Numerous critics have described the play's skepticism.[4] Particularly influential among these critics is Stanley Cavell, for whom skepticism is a markedly destructive way for Leontes to negotiate separation from, and connection to, the subjects and objects of the world.[5] More recently, David Hillman and Anita Gilman Sherman have offered book-length treatments of Shakespeare's skepticism that include chapters on *The Winter's Tale,* both developing and parting ways with Cavellian lines of thought.[6] Hillman and Sherman's accounts are brilliant in their own right, yet there is more to be said about the play's contributions to our thinking about law in general and Pauline law in particular. While Cavell, Hillman, and Sherman all link skepticism with separation and detachment, I will trace another skeptical practice that inflects the play, one that enjoins being absorbed and transported by a distinctively Pauline law of faith.

Paul interests critics of *The Winter's Tale* as well as the radical theorists germane to this chapter. Critics often claim that the play bears traces of Pauline influence; the play invites such claims, given that one of its principal characters is called Paulina. But criticism that claims this—reaching back to G. Wilson Knight and continuing through to Roy Battenhouse and, more recently, to Huston Diehl—either does not treat that influence as involving skepticism at all or, at most, links the play with a targeted, Reformation skepticism (about transubstantiation, miracles, and so on) and with fairly clearly delimited religious belief.[7] Like much thinking on religious influence in Shakespeare, such criticism regards the play as engaged with confessional questions.[8] Diehl, for example, reads the play as Protestant, arguing that it offers a confident set of prescriptions about the gentleness (and the severity) with which Paulina ought to lead the wayward Leontes; Diehl shows how Paulina can employ both sharp rebuke and seeming idolatry and still remain within a Protestant framework.[9]

Radical theorists such as Agamben and Badiou, by contrast, have an interest in Paul, if not in Shakespeare, as a figure whose "teachings" resist systematization. Since their interests have important affinities with Shakespeare's, I will review them in some detail. Both theorists, as Julia Reinhard Lupton puts it, "aim to think the implications of Paul beyond any confessional framework."[10] For Badiou, for example, "Paul is not an apostle or a saint"; Badiou has "never really connected Paul with religion," and simply sees him as "a subjective figure of primary importance."[11] Specifically, Paul holds interest for Badiou as a theorist of the "truth-event," in this case Christ's Resurrection, and of how events produce subjects who in turn cannot fully comprehend what brought them into being (4). Badiou's Paul assumes that the Christian subject, in some strong sense, cannot exist as a subject until exposed to the truth-event of Christ's Resurrection (14). Indeed, for Badiou, the subject's subordination to the event is axiomatic: "I call 'subject' the bearer [*le support*] of a fidelity," he writes, "the one who bears a process of truth. The subject, therefore, in no way pre-exists the process . . . the process of truth *induces* a subject."[12]

Committed to the event and its truth, Badiou's framework might seem resistant to all skepticism; but this is not so. The Pauline subject is subordinated to the event not only because his existence depends on it, but also because he cannot capture its truth by rendering its consequences in normative, systematic language.[13] In his treatment of Pauline epistles, Badiou draws attention to 1 Corinthians 2:1–5, where the apostle claims to offer not words of wisdom but rather a demonstration of spirit. Such a claim amounts to what Badiou calls a "radical antiphilosophy."[14] Submitting to the event means being skeptical about one's own conceptual powers, about others' wisdom, and about systems of thought. The event exceeds all, and is a rupture in, these things. Agamben describes Pauline faith similarly in that he also de-links faith from propositional belief. Focusing partly on Paul's use of the conjunction "Jesus Messiah" rather than the copulative "Jesus is Messiah," Agamben writes:

> what then is the world of faith? Not a world of substance and qualities, not a world in which the grass is green, the sun is warm, and the snow is white. No, it is not a world of predicates, of existences and essences, but a world of indivisible events, in which I do not judge, nor do I believe that snow is white and the sun is warm, but I am transported and displaced in the snow's-being-white and in the sun's-being-warm. In the end, it is a world in which I do not believe that Jesus, such-and-such a man, is the Messiah, only-begotten son of God, begotten and not created, consubstantial in the Father. I only believe in Jesus Messiah; I am carried away and enraptured in him.[15]

Like the Pauline event for Badiou, Pauline faith for Agamben does not and cannot involve elaborating a series of assertions; faith is not faith in a belief system. It is, instead, the experience of being so carried away that we cannot translate messianic faith into propositional form.

Giving faith this sense, Agamben and Badiou describe a very different Paul than the one described by Diehl in her account of *The Winter's Tale*. If her interest resides in how Shakespeare, through Paulina, offers a body of Pauline laws regarding rebuke—a practical guide for calling wrongdoers to account—Agamben and Badiou are interested in how

Paul's thinking might not amount to a system. Diehl's argument has merit, as there is a prescriptive quality to Paulina's handling of Leontes (and to many moments in Paul's epistles!). As various commentators have pointed out, Agamben's and Badiou's models are nothing if not partial, a point to which I return in my conclusion.[16] Yet their models have much to add to our thinking about *The Winter's Tale*. Whereas Diehl regards the play's Pauline element as a Protestant antidote to thoroughgoing skepticism, Badiou and Agamben describe a faith far more consonant with such skepticism and, thus, with Shakespeare's late romance.

This epistemological point carries legal consequences—ones that will carry the following reading of *The Winter's Tale* well beyond the issue of whether the play offers a set of prescriptions about rebuke. The most famous consequence derives from the Pauline distinction between (a derogated) law of works and (a privileged) law of faith, drawn in Romans 3:27–8. The distinction interests Agamben keenly. While the law of works, obviously, assumes propositional form enjoining performance of certain acts and abstention from others, the law of faith eschews this kind of prescription in favor of imprecision. According to Agamben, Paul opposes the law of faith and the law of works in order to set "a non-normative figure of the law [which never moves beyond the non-specific injunction, delivered in Romans 13:8, to love one's neighbor] against the normative figure of the law."[17]

For Paul, the displacement of a law of works by one of faith has much to recommend it. To begin, it allows an escape from the ironic effects that normal, prescriptive law has on human desire. Positive law, according to the framework set out in Romans 5:20 and 6:14, not only makes transgression possible but also in some sense actually produces the desire to transgress.[18] Second, since the law of faith suspends normative law, a world under such a law would qualify as a "state of exception," and a salutary one at that. The Pauline state, in Agamben's description, is not nearly so terrifying as the states of exception that he discusses elsewhere, in the context of concentration camps and Guantanamo Bay. The modern state of exception captures subjects within inclusive exclusions, where they are "legally" reduced to bare life even though the reduction does not occur through recognizably legal channels; one (extrajuridical) form of "legal" practice replaces another (juridical) one. The Pauline state resembles the state of exception in that an extrajuridical law of faith replaces the juridical law of works. But since

Paul "radicalizes the condition of the state of exception," he not only emancipates the faithful subject "from any obligatory conduct and from positive law" but also makes faith "a manifestation of 'justice without law.'"[19] While the modern state of exception reduces the subject to bare life—as life that can be killed without recourse to normal legal channels—in the Pauline state of exception, individuals can never be so reduced. To fulfill the law you must love your neighbor, but since this love's dictates cannot be specified, punishments both legal and extralegal lose their warrant. Whereas the suspension of normative law permits all sorts of "legal" violence in the modern state, then, suspension in the Pauline state makes such violence almost unthinkable.

In this fashion, Agamben turns epistemological weakness—not knowing precisely what the law enjoins—into virtue. Agamben dwells on a point observed in this chapter's first pages: that law, when articulated from an epistemologically strong position, institutes divisions, boundaries that permit the capture of subjects found on the wrong side of those boundaries.[20] The generality of Pauline law, on the other hand, "divides the divisions of the law themselves and renders them inoperative, without ever reaching any final ground" (52). By this cryptic formulation, Agamben means that Paul never intends to move beyond divisions—between Jew and Greek, man and woman, and so on—"to pinpoint a sameness or a universal lurking beyond" (52); even as Paul famously claims, in Colossians 3:11, that Christ breaks down distinctions that lend subjects identities, Pauline law does not unite subjects by eliminating what divides them.[21] Rather than undo the division between Jew and non-Jew, for instance, this law plunges the Jewish subject into incertitude as to whether he has fulfilled the injunction to love his neighbor, making that subject always also potentially non-Jewish.

For Agamben, then, the law of faith divides divisions themselves and so is unlike normative law, which more straightforwardly identifies and defines subjects as obedient or rebellious. Introducing the impossibility of coinciding with oneself, Agamben's account also differs from Badiou's, at least insofar as Badiou's Pauline law of faith creates a subject possessed of a kind of consistency, defined by his fidelity to the event. If, for Badiou, fidelity to the event opens the possibility for a "Sameness and an Equality,"[22] Agamben claims that the Pauline project is to drive an epistemological wedge "between every identity and itself."[23] Badiou himself would never go so far, which is not to say that Agamben and Badiou are diametrically opposed as to the law of faith and its relationship to the subject. If, for Badiou, the Pauline event produces a subject consistent in its fidelity, that fidelity itself is pledged to an ungraspable object, pursuit of which introduces division. This event "regulates subjective consistency" only insofar as it requires the individual to "persevere in that which exceeds your perseverance," to "[s]eize in your being that which has seized and broken you."[24] According to both Agamben and Badiou, the law of faith divides subjects. For Agamben, this division comes from how that law divides the divisions that define subjects: from not knowing whether one has been faithful. For Badiou, the division comes from fidelity itself: from the pursuit of that which exceeds the self, a perseverance that ends stasis.

In what follows, I show how *The Winter's Tale* anticipates Agamben's and Badiou's ideas about skepticism, law, and the Pauline subject. Like both theorists, Shakespeare in *The Winter's Tale* advocates faith without belief, evincing a skeptical attitude toward positive law that locates subjects and, indeed, toward positive law in all its forms (in this play, distinctions between bodies of common, civil, and canon law go mostly unobserved). I will show how we can turn to Shakespeare's play in order to expand and add nuance to the discussion between Badiou and Agamben about faith that is drained of belief and the sort of subjects possessed of such faith. By carefully delineating outlooks that thwart and enable an embrace of epistemological weakness, and by giving texture to our sense of how law in the Pauline state of exception differs from its modern counterpart, the play helps us to think Agamben and Badiou together, to see both possible combinations of their thought as well as limitations to that thought. In *The Winter's Tale*, we encounter something like Badiou's event—overwhelming those who are party to it. We also see that the law of the event, far from producing defined subjects, instead has the salutary and even saving effect of unsettling subjects irreparably, both in Agamben's sense (in inducing incertitude about one's standing with respect to the law) as well as in Badiou's (in inducing fidelity that assumes the form of moving outside the self toward an always ungraspable object).[25] But if *The Winter's Tale* resembles Agamben and Badiou's thinking in attributing a salutary quality to such an unsettling law it also, unlike either theorist, operates with deep awareness that this law, however salutary, could never be fully satisfactory.

Whatever its differences from contemporary radical thought, *The Winter's Tale*'s connection to such thought means that Shakespeare's play need not be viewed as fitting within religious and political systems of early modernity. Though it is valuable to pose confessional questions about the play, we need not focus on how it may be Catholic or Protestant in outlook, or on how it seems to straddle, waffle, or metaphorize when it comes to confessional divides. Rather, the play's Pauline quality consists also in its being open to a thoroughly non-confessional reading; I will show how one early modern context of *The Winter's Tale*'s Paulinism is not that of Calvin or Luther (whom I discuss in this chapter's conclusion), but that of another figure altogether: Montaigne, often discussed alongside Shakespeare but never yet for the ends introduced here.[26] Montaigne—a skeptical, experimental Christian, and a moderating voice in the French Wars of Religion—offers a Pauline concept of epistemological weakness that helps further the exchange between Shakespeare's Paul and that of contemporary radicals.[27] In this, we will see, the play proves similarly resistant to systematic political thinking of early modernity. While clearly anti-absolutist in its portrayal of Leontes, the play, like the early *Lucrece*, does not quite advocate republican institutions. To be sure, *The Winter's Tale* wants nothing to do with Jacobean absolutism; yet in supplying an antidote to that absolutism, we will see, Shakespeare also looks outside republican frameworks for a Pauline solution.

Tyranny and Belief in The Winter's Tale

> Presumption is our natural and original malady. The most vulnerable and frail of all creatures is man, and at the same time the most arrogant.
>
> Michel de Montaigne, "Apology for Raymond Sebond"[28]

Badiou and Agamben argue that Paul undergirds his anti-philosopher's outlook—one opposed to propositional beliefs and to coherent normative systems—partly with remarks about wisdom in 1 Corinthians. (To cite just a few examples: "Hath not God made the wisedome of this worlde foolyshenesse?" [1:20]; "God hath chosen the foolyshe thynges of the worlde, to counfounde the wise" [1:27]; "If any man among you seeme to be wise in this worlde, let hym be a foole" [3:18]; and "If any man thynke that he knoweth any thing, he knoweth nothing yet as he ought to know" [8:2].[29]) Agamben and Badiou underscore the presumption that Paul ascribes to those who would offer wisdom and claim to reveal truth in words. For their Paul, man cannot capture the truth-event of

Christ in all its implications, cannot derive from it a codified way of life; indeed, for their Paul man cannot even properly grasp the world at its most mundane.

The Winter's Tale's Leontes springs to mind as a character of stupendous presumption. His failings emerge with particular clarity when considered alongside Montaigne's "Apology," which elaborates on the Pauline position just outlined, often invokes Paul directly, and describes the presumptuous mind in terms that capture Leontes nicely. Montaigne writes, for instance, that notions of wisdom and intellectual capability are foolish because "[o]ur mind is an erratic, dangerous, and heedless tool,"[30] and Leontes's mind is just the same. Whereas Paul claims that no one "knoweth the thynges of a man, saue ye spirite of man which is in hym" (1 Cor. 2:11), Leontes claims access to others' interiors and infers infidelity on a bizarre, almost wholly imaginary basis—on even less basis than Othello has and far less than is offered in Shakespeare's source, Greene's *Pandosto*.[31] Leontes's scattered, confused utterances are nothing if not erratic, and he, once convinced of Hermione's infidelity, attempts to execute all who are dear to him. Montaigne observes that "[t]he mind is a dangerous blade, even to its possessor" (510), and Leontes's mind is precisely this. He is, as Camillo puts it, "in rebellion with himself" (1.2.354).[32]

The Sicilian king surely ranks among Shakespeare's most presumptuous characters. The way his mind operates merits pausing over, as his thoughts follow paths that help clarify both how his beliefs come to be, and why those beliefs have bad aftermath. The intricacies of both arise when Leontes calls his son, Mamillius, to him in order to verify his parentage:

> Thou want'st a rough pash and the shoots that I have,
> To be full like me; yet they say we are
> Almost as like as eggs. Women say so,
> That will say anything. But were they false
> As o'erdyed blacks, as wind, as waters, false
> As dice are to be wished by one that fixes
> No bourn 'twixt his and mine, yet were it true
> To say this boy were like me. Come, sir page,
> Look on me with your welkin eye. Sweet villain!
> Most dear'st! my collop! Can thy dam?—may't be—
> Affection, thy intention stabs the center!
> Thou dost make possible things not so held,

Communicat'st with dreams—how can this be?
With what's unreal thou coactive art,
And fellow'st nothing. (1.2.129–143)

Leontes's analysis here opens with a perception: that Mamillius lacks only signs of cuckoldry to be "full like" Leontes, implying that only the effects of age and infidelity separate him from the boy. Yet the initial 'perception' involves no reference to Mamillius looking like Leontes; rather, it refers to the boy being like Leontes, as though likeness were to be perceived by intuition rather than tuition. This initial assay is followed—spoiled and interfered with—by the springing to mind of others' judgments. With striking misogyny, Leontes distrusts these judgments as made by women who hold truth in low regard and will utter anything at all. Still, others' untrustworthy opinions cannot spoil his own simply because the two accord. Leontes notes that even if women simply tell him what he wants to hear and are thus not worthy of trust, he nonetheless cannot deny that he and Mamillius are alike. His intuition trumps the consensus that he deems dubious.

Then, just as Leontes insists that he will see through his own eyes, he refuses to, and ends up denying what Cavell calls "the all but undeniable."[33] Leontes asks Mamillius to approach, presumably to conduct empirical observation, as though the matter remains unsettled and he has judged intuition inadequate. Oddly, it is now that his speech becomes excited: "Sweet villain! / Most dear'st! my collop! . . . . / Affection, thy intention stabs the center!" This moment of accurate observation and acute self-awareness—a moment in which both he and his son appear clearly and distinctly—could correct the ocular impression that instigated Leontes's suspicion. If we assume that what Leontes reports in his first aside, as he looks at his wife Hermione and his friend Polixenes, is what is there to see—the two of them "paddling palms and pinching fingers, / . . . and making practiced smiles / As in a looking glass"— nothing in his visual field necessarily suggests infidelity (1.2.116–8). What he reports seeing could be interpreted as a pair of narcissists pretending to look in the mirror, so oblivious of each other that they inadvertently pinch each other. What he sees is open to, but hardly demands, sexual interpretation. Montaigne argues that "external objects surrender to our mercy," in part depending on our bodily states, and one would be hard pressed to find better proof of this assertion than Leontes's *tremor cordis* and the incredibly willful interpretation that follows.[34]

"*A strong imagination creates the event,*" Montaigne writes. "Everyone feels its impact, but some are overthrown by it."[35] If, in his first aside, Leontes's imagination overthrows him, with Mamillius before him he gains some distance on himself and, with it, the chance to stand his ground. Self-awareness before his son might place a partition between passion and final judgment. Registering affection's role in altering perception, Leontes seems no longer symptomatic of what Montaigne describes, but actually voices Montaigne's own position, in which our senses are "often completely stupefied by the passions of the soul."[36] Leontes recognizes that affection, for him, is coactive with the unreal. Yet even as Leontes attains a self-reflexivity, none of its familiars— self-control, diminished willfulness, and tempered affection—follow in its train. Distance allows him to see that he lacks the power to properly judge Hermione or their unborn child, but the distance that should be humbling, bizarrely, fails to impede him from judging.[37] The "infection" of his brains spreads and the ex-stasis of critical distance becomes inseparable from the dangerous ecstasy it was to allay. The movement toward objectivity does nothing to alter his subjectivity. Helpless before passion, his sense of vision so compromised by envisioned infidelity, Leontes's observation generates more feeling than even his initial feeling did.

Leontes is slave to a *tremor cordis* that disables discernment of any sort. Lorna Hutson has demonstrated a rise, during Shakespeare's period, of forensic rhetoric and evidential concepts;[38] Leontes, too, invokes evidential notions, but only to abandon them. What stirs Leontes seems impossible to pinpoint and, according to Leontes himself, insubstantial. He is, despite himself, "a feather for every wind that blows" (2.3.153). Leontes is man as portrayed by Montaigne, for whom "[a] contrary breath of wind" is "enough to overthrow him and bring him to the ground."[39]

Moved by a false belief in Hermione's infidelity, Leontes declares Sicilia a state of exception, a place of pure prerogative. For him, her infidelity has made Sicilia a nest of traitors, and so he seeks to make legal what the play suggests is extralegal—in, for example, the discussion between Leontes, Antigonus, and a Lord, during which they urge Leontes to allow the oracle's judgment to prevail, "lest [his] justice / Prove violence" (2.1.127-8).[40] To not defer to the oracle, as Hermione puts it, would be "rigor and not law" (3.2.113). Links between false belief, passion, and tyranny—and the implied case against absolute power—seem ironclad. This being so, Shakespeare's portrayal of Leontes registers as a critique both of Henry VIII turning adultery into a form of treason[41] and of James I's many attempts, outlined by Rebecca Lemon, to extend emergency power in the wake of the Gunpowder Plot.[42]

But the Leontine state of emergency, unlike its Jacobean counterpart, is laughably inept. Leontes's proclamations are as ineffective as his beliefs are inaccurate. He commands Camillo to poison the king's own former best friend, Polixenes, upon threat of death, and instead Camillo flees Sicilia with the person he was supposed to poison (1.2.348). When he does, Leontes takes their flight as proof that "[t]here is a plot against my life, my crown," then repeatedly tries and fails to banish Paulina, his most insistent critic, from his presence (2.1.47). Leontes complains to Paulina's husband Antigonus that he "canst not rule her," issuing numerous commands—"Force her hence," "Out!"—always to no avail (2.3.46, 61, 66). When this fails, Leontes tells Paulina that he will "ha' thee burnt," only to have her assure him that doing so would make him, not her, a heretic (2.3.113). His commands lack force; his words neither reveal nor produce truth. Nevertheless, Leontes continues to accuse, labeling Antigonus a traitor for having allowed Paulina to talk to him, instructing the noble to make up for it by exposing the daughter that the king will not acknowledge as his, also—as with all things—upon threat of death.

Leontes declares a state of exception, but no one seems to be listening. He believes, with James I, that "Rex est lex loquens" ("the King is the law speaking").[43] But if the king, for James, is as the head toward the body, in a position of epistemological superiority and fit to command, the body of Sicilian subjects rightly revolts against its Leontine head.[44] His commands do not work as law does for legal theorists as disparate in their understanding of royal prerogative as John Fortescue, Thomas Smith, and James himself; his commands fail to solicit obedience, whether by provoking fear of God, as for Fortescue,[45] by bringing subjects "neerest to the straightnesse," as for Smith,[46] or by rendering rebellion unthinkable, as for James.[47] Rather, the king's commands work as they normally do for Paul: by soliciting subjects to transgress.

In fact, his commands make transgression the only option. When Leontes orders Camillo to poison Polixenes, Camillo cannot but disobey. "[M]y ground to do't," he remarks, "Is the obedience to a master, one / Who in rebellion with himself will have / All that are his so too" (1.2.352–355). Leontes would have others perform actions that imperil the king and in this issues edicts that turn subjects into rebels—either from his perspective or that of normality—regardless of whether they obey.[48] Hermione, herself observing how obedience and its other have come to seem one and the same, remarks that her supposedly treasonous involvement with Polixenes consists only in "a love even such, / So and no other, as yourself commanded" (3.2.64–65). Insane, Leontine law makes everything, including obedience, into treason. Those who obey are as fit for death as those who transgress, and so it seems only fitting that Antigonus does more or less as he is told only, famously, to be torn apart by a bear.

But Leontine tyranny is ultimately not so ursine; it has dull teeth. Delineating the flaws of *dominium regale* versus more limited monarchy, Fortescue argues that for a king to act outside existing law and according only to will is not power but powerlessness; and if James sought to overturn this idea, Leontes, accidentally, ratifies it.[49] If he deals death to anyone, he does so inadvertently. Unlike in *Coriolanus,* where Brutus and Sicinius declare a state of emergency in order to successfully banish the play's eponymous hero, Leontes's impotence as a tyrant is darkly comic.[50] Eventually, perhaps dimly aware of the absolute malfunction of his absolutism—and despite also saying, in Jacobean fashion, that his royal prerogative requires no counsel—Leontes agrees to subordinate his will to that of "sacred Delphos," the oracle whose spiritual counsel will spur or stop him in a way that others deem legal (2.1.183–187).[51] Since Hermione has been publicly accused, he notes, "so shall she have / A just and open trial" (3.1.203–4). Through his repeated failures, Leontes seems to have realized that what others think actually matters; he hopes not to be accused "[o]f being tyrannous," "since we so openly / Proceed in justice, which shall have due course, / Even to the guilt or the purgation" (3.2.5–7). Of course, when the oracle's verdict contradicts Leontes's expectation, he restores the state of exception: "[t]he sessions shall proceed" (3.2.139). Only the sessions do not proceed, because as soon as Leontes says that they will, word of Mamillius's strange, sudden death arrives. Leontes changes just as suddenly, abandoning his beliefs and his state of emergency alike.

Leontes's miserable failure might seem to imply a politics increasingly familiar to recent thought about England in the early seventeenth century. A majority of characters hold the right beliefs—about Hermione's innocence, about whether the baby should be set aflame, and so on—and undermine tyranny relatively readily. Shakespeare's portrayal of Leontes thus might appear to link false beliefs with a pathetic absolutism and true beliefs with a triumphant republicanism, one that upholds negative freedoms and positive liberties of citizens and that places strict limits on emergency power. In accord with a long tradition of republican thinking in the British Isles in the sixteenth and seventeenth centuries—from Thomas Smith and George Buchanan before Shakespeare to Marchamont Nedham and James Harrington after him—the play might be seen as connecting true beliefs about selves with true beliefs about ideal political structures. Once we see individuals for the fallible beings that they are, we realize the folly of absolutism, of allowing one, unfettered, to choose for all.[52] Though not avowedly republican, Montaigne also has this folly in mind when he writes that it seems "very iniquitous to want to subject public and immutable institutions and observances to the instability of a private fancy."[53] If Leontes's inept campaign of terror implies as much, *The Winter's Tale* might be said to advance an epistemological humility more limited—and a politics a bit more programmatic—than that of Agamben's Paul.

To be sure, Shakespeare critiques the epistemological confidence behind Jacobean absolutism, a critique also evident in Shakespeare's portrayal of Bohemia and especially in the contrast between Polixenes and his son Florizel. Unlike Leontes, Florizel sounds Pauline from the outset. He seems free, for instance, from the two main aspects of Montaignean presumption: thinking too highly of himself and not highly enough of others.[54] Florizel instead fêtes Perdita and affects a sheephook, humbling himself. The first two verses of 1 Corinthians 13, juxtaposed with an early speech of Florizel's, bear out the point:

> Though I speake with the tongues of men and of Angels, and have not loue, I am [as] a soundyng brasse, or [as] a tinckling Cimball: And though I coulde prophesie, and understoode all secretes, and all knowledge: Yea, if I had all fayth, so that I coulde move mountaynes out of their places, and have not love, I were nothyng. (1 Cor. 13:1–2)

>   were I crowned the most imperial monarch,
> Thereof most worthy, were I the fairest youth
> That ever made eye swerve, had force and knowledge
> More than was ever man's, I would not prize them
> Without her love; for her, employ them all;
> Commend them and condemn them to her service
> Or to their own perdition. (4.4.371–77)

Paul and Florizel both suggest that life's goods lose their value without love. Such recognition of dependence distinguishes Florizel from Leontes; he rejects the atomism to which Leontes aspires early on.[55] Florizel says that he "cannot be / Mine own, nor anything to any" if he does not belong first to Perdita (4.4.43–45). In a love that defuses *Othello's* tragic paradox—of wanting to possess even as one feels possessed—Florizel can only have anything resembling a possessive conception of himself by being possessed by someone else.[56]

And yet Bohemia is not quite a world elsewhere. Florizel and Perdita's courtship is overlaid by his father Polixenes's despotic edicts and death threats, issued when he sees that his son will marry without seeking his consent; ruthlessly, wildly overconfident, Polixenes declares an old shepherd (who does not even know Florizel's identity) an "old traitor" for joining him with Perdita, and laments "that by hanging thee I can / But shorten thy life one week" (4.4.419–21). Florizel's self-effacing Paulinism is endangered by Polixenes and his false convictions. Heading into the final act, the play has portrayed two rulers, neither of whom would rule through usual legal channels and both of whom try to declare states of exception. A question that remains is where an outlook such as Florizel's can find a home, and how that outlook could become more general. While a temptation, at this point in the play, is to offer as solution the structures of a republic, *The Winter's Tale* does not quite do so, much as *Lucrece's* primary concern is not with the republic whose birth it represents. Instead, it turns from concern with positive, customary law to another, more subjective law. The play's concern, we will see, becomes less about the epistemological humility and the sort of laws that might help constitute republics, and more about the level of humility and the sort of law that might help constitute virtuous subjects.

I will argue that Shakespeare offers a solution at the play's end that is more radical than republican. But first we must consider a more conservative solution, one that Shakespeare could be said to offer through his portrayal of Leontes's reformation. Realizing how inadequate he is on his own, Leontes seeks a new guide for action. His search involves a sustained period of utter humbling—of submission, humiliation, and abjection at Paulina's hands. Here, again, Montaigne's Pauline position is germane. Near the opening of the "Apology," Montaigne writes that he aims

> to crush and trample underfoot human arrogance and pride . . . to wrest from their hands the puny weapons of their reason; to make

them bow their heads and bite the ground beneath the authority and reverence of divine majesty. It is to this alone that knowledge and wisdom belong.[57]

Invoking the Pauline idea that those who think themselves wise do not yet know as they ought to know, Montaigne seeks to reform "the man who is presumptuous of his knowledge" for being the man who "does not yet know what knowledge is"; man "is nothing if he thinks he is something, seduces and deceives himself" (398).[58] Paulina's project, when Leontes submits to her, seems almost precisely the same as Montaigne's. She excoriates Leontes time and again, trampling him underfoot just as Montaigne counsels.

Leontes proves a quick study in humility. He immediately realizes how deserved Paulina's excoriations are: "Go on, go on," he remarks, "Thou canst not speak too much. I have deserved / All tongues to talk their bitt'rest" (3.2.213–215). Leontes imagines total transformation, effected through daily shame, vowing to list himself, on his wife and son's graves, as the cause of death, "unto / Our shame perpetual. Once a day I'll visit / The chapel where they lie, and tears shed there / Shall be my recreation" (lines 235–38). He believes that he will exist, will be re-created, as the tears he sheds, that he will become nothing more than repentance's product. The shift from a closed, unaccountable form of sovereignty to a radically exposed and open one could hardly be more marked. Cavell points out Leontes's earlier reluctance to acknowledge connection;[59] of Hermione, he has said that "While she lives / My heart will be a burden to me" (3.1.204–5), unaware that in Sicilia, to sever connection pains everyone, that existence there is as it is for Paul in 1 Corinthians 12:26: "yf one member suffer, all suffer with it." Leontes realizes that as Hermione fares, so does he.

Open to this suffering, Leontes also opens himself to Paulina's sole authority. And he seems to acquire the right beliefs. She makes him well aware of his tyranny; she underscores that that tyranny proved him weaker than a child; even after sixteen years pass, she reminds him that he "killed" Hermione, who, Paulina reiterates, was a perfect, unparalleled woman, thus curing Leontes of his inordinately elevated self-estimate and an unfairly low estimate of others (3.2.173, 5.1.15).

Leontes's epistemological abjection and willing submission go hand in hand. As this happens, Shakespeare entertains a possible, more retrograde reaction to epistemological weakness, one also entertained, and

at least temporarily endorsed, by Montaigne in the "Apology." Citing
1 Corinthians, Montaigne claims that "participation in the knowledge
of the truth" might be possible so long as we choose the right person—
by divine intervention exempted from complete ignorance—"to in-
struct us in his admirable secrets." Montaigne writes that "[i]t is not
by reasoning or by our understanding that we have received our religion; it is by external authority." Thus, "[t]he weakness of our judgment
helps us more in this than its strength."[60] Leontes, similarly, accepts
authority because he is weak. Paulina replaces his former sovereignty
with what Montaigne calls "the sovereign good in the recognition
of the weakness of our judgment" (440). As Leontes's misogyny and
malice drain away he, arguably, comes to exemplify a Montaignean
maxim: that "humility and submissiveness alone can make a good
man" (436).

What we see here differs from forms of epistemological humility so
far introduced and the law that each entails. First, Paulina's use of this
Pauline method differs markedly from the method outlined by Agamben and Badiou. For them, the Pauline embrace of weakness means
abandoning systematic philosophy, but Paulina, as I implied earlier, is
nothing if not systematic and philosophical, instructing Leontes to live
according to precepts. Her Pauline quality derives, in part, from the
epistles' many prescriptions, which Agamben and Badiou disregard so
as to see Paul as an anti-philosopher. In Paulina's renovation of Leontes,
faith is determinately faith *in*; Leontes can inhabit a redeemable form
of life by believing in certain propositions, and by acting in accordance with laws that Paulina derives from those propositions. (For
example, believing Hermione peerless entails not remarrying without
Paulina's leave.) This, as implied earlier, is Diehl's Protestant Paul,
and in this respect the play adds to current discussion of Pauline political theology by refocusing attention on the epistles' prescriptive
investments.

Second, Paulina's program is not only systematic; it is also anti-
republican. Paulina may not be a Leontine tyrant, but she is absolutist.
Her word is law, and her rehabilitation of Leontes places no emphasis
on liberty, republican, or otherwise; a king's submission to a subject need
not lead to freedom. But the implication—that the play does not undermine absolute power and epistemological confidence so much as it
details who deserves that power and that confidence—does not quite

hold. As above quotations suggest and as T. G. Bishop points out, for much of the play Paulina treats Leontes with an unmistakable, perhaps unredeemable cruelty.[61] As Anita Gilman Sherman puts it, Paulina may keep "male forgetfulness" helpfully at bay, but her role as a "dogmatic memorialist" has a coercive, sadistic quality.[62] It is only at the end, during the statue scene—when all characters, including Paulina, are humbled—that the play's world ceases to be cruel.

The Winter's Tale *and the Law of Faith*

Given how the play has unfolded, it is not surprising that Shakespeare would end *The Winter's Tale* by imagining a world in which Florizel's lack of presumption becomes everyone's, and in which law might reflect such humility. The final scene's demolition of confidence, especially of the epistemological variety, has been explained time and again. Though Paulina urges Leontes to "awake" his faith when she presents him with what may be a statue of his long-dead wife, and what later is his wife alive, most critics do not see much faith at play. Walter S. H. Lim, for example, writes that the end "refuses to grant to faith a privileged position" since it suggests both that "faith cannot be extricated from superstition" and that "the foundation of our sure knowledge is perhaps nothing more than ignorant or fond credulity."[63] Lim builds on Julia Reinhard Lupton's now seminal work, wherein the statue scene "stages the visual conditions of Catholic image worship, but only as canceled"; "[n]o heretical transubstantiation or pagan magic, we are assured, has in fact taken place."[64] For Lupton as for Lim, the play addresses the confessional question mentioned above in order to eschew Catholic faith in favor of the theatricality and transparent artifice of the purported "miracle" of a statue brought to life.[65] Some critics do not read the play's end as quite so demystifying, but these, too, do not see an embrace of faith. Kenneth Gross, for example, argues that the play leaves its audience in a zone of undecidability, that it "allows us neither self-evident faith in magic nor the quiet comforts of disenchanted irony."[66] Bishop, who also sees indeterminacy at the end, suggests that there "[o]ur skepticism and our pleasure at the pretenses of the theatrical meet," that our disbelief both is and is not suspended.[67] For Gross and Bishop, Shakespeare does not let us know what Hermione is or is not, instead plunging us into a state of perplexity about what she is and means.[68]

Such criticism accounts elegantly for the final scene's complexity, for how difficult it is to believe anything determinate about that scene—how, for once, characters and audience alike are plunged into epistemologically weak states. Understandably, this criticism also assumes that the final scene blocks faith because faith, here, would be faith that Hermione is a statue come to life: faith in a propositional statement. I agree, with Lim and Lupton, that we lack warrant to believe that Hermione is a statue brought to life; I agree, with Gross and Bishop, that we lack warrant to believe that Hermione is pretending to be a statue until Paulina calls her down. I want to propose, though, that the final scene does not only ask its audience to suspend belief, though it surely does so. The scene also asks for adherence to a certain Pauline faith—a faith without belief—as a path to virtue.

After Paulina reveals the figure of Hermione, she likes Leontes's silence; "it the more shows off / Your wonder" (5.3.21–22). His silence suggests an inability to generate beliefs that, earlier, he had generated effortlessly. But his silence does not last. Leontes wants to verify that the thing before him somehow is his wife—"I may say indeed / Thou art Hermione"—and not merely a statue resembling her (5.3.24–5). To do so he asks her to chide him, and then, since he believes he has a good grasp of her, to not chide him, "for she was as tender / As infancy and grace" (5.3.26–7). Leontes reconciles beliefs, in himself as a weak, loathsome figure deserving of rebuke, and in Hermione's tenderness: reconciles what he deserves and what he is given. Leontes, as Roy Battenhouse observes, begins to believe in a Protestant grace, knowing the inadequacy of works.[69]

Soon enough, though, he stops enunciating beliefs altogether. Now, the figure of Hermione overwhelms him. He surmises that she may be somehow alive ("Would you not deem it breathed? and that those veins / Did verily bear blood?") without assuming that he sees Hermione herself, in the flesh; rather, he wonders if perhaps he sees a sculpture that can somehow "cut breath" (5.3.64–65, 79).[70] Paulina deems him "almost so far transported that / He'll think anon it lives," the emphasis for both on the "it," on Hermione's uncertain, unclassifiable status. If, earlier, Leontes's madness consisted in generating wildly inappropriate beliefs about the world, his present madness simply transports him; he does not hold beliefs about what "it" is, does not even yet think that it lives. This event transports him to a point beyond belief, beyond thinking in terms of predicates.

Leontes's loss of belief ushers in a new fidelity, a now salutary ecstasy to which he pledges faith. When he urges Paulina not to draw the curtain, he asks her to prolong his mental state, to "Make me to think so twenty years together!" as "No settled senses of the world can match / The pleasure of that madness" (5.3.71–73). Given this plea, we do well to consider anew some lines from Agamben, cited earlier in this chapter. "What then," Agamben asks, "is the world of faith?":

> Not a world of substance and qualities, not a world in which the grass is green, the sun is warm, and the snow is white. No, it is not a world of predicates . . . but a world of indivisible events, in which I do not judge, nor do I believe that snow is white and the sun is warm, but I am transported and displaced in the snow's-being-white and in the sun's-being-warm. In the end, it is a world in which I do not believe that Jesus, such-and-such a man, is the Messiah . . . I only believe in Jesus Messiah; I am carried away and enraptured in him.[71]

During the final scene, Leontes comes to inhabit a world like Agamben's and Badiou's worlds of Pauline faith. Drained of predicates, Leontes's world becomes indivisible, the world of the event. He no longer believes the figure before him to be alive as humans are; the figure's being-warm transports him, unsettles his senses. He is given over to the Hermione-statue event, carried away and enraptured by that event, one that he cannot evaluate properly but to which he means to remain faithful. In this, the play suggests that it is better to be below the level of discourse—better for Leontes to have *tremor cordis* upon him and be faithful to it—than to formulate a propositional belief ("Hermione is unfaithful") that would justify the *tremor cordis;* better, too, in his experience at the end, not to try to assign Hermione a copulative as to whether she is resurrected. It is better that he embrace being overwhelmed by her stirring, that he allow his fidelity to consist in being so overwhelmed.

This new faith institutes new law. I have shown how Shakespeare portrays a world in which beliefs lead to tyrannical threats from those in position to tyrannize. Law has no tyrannical aspect at the play's end, though what is left of law is hard to specify—this, despite the fact that Paulina and Leontes opine about law's function pretty explicitly. Just before Paulina instructs Hermione to descend, she asks those who think she is about "unlawful business" to depart; then, just after Hermione descends, Paulina remarks that "her actions shall be holy as / You hear my spell is lawful" (5.3.96–97,104–5). Leontes agrees. "If this be magic," he says, "let it be an art / Lawful as eating" (5.3.110–11). It would be wrong to say that for Shakespeare, a world without belief—this world of epistemological weakness—is a world without law. But the form that law assumes requires close attention.

In early-seventeenth-century England, according to the *OED*, "lawful" has several meanings: for example, "permitted or sanctioned by" law; "not contrary to" law; and simply "pertaining to, or concerned with" law. Paulina's usages of the word seem to carry all three meanings. She wants to clear herself of sacrilege and idolatry—to place her action on the right side of the law—but the spell itself, she seems to hope, will institute a new law, one that binds Leontes and Hermione, though not in any easy unity. In this way, she implies a commentary on law, a point on which I will build in a moment.

In his own usage, Leontes, similarly, gives royal sanction to Paulina's act in declaring it lawful, yet the spell undermines characters' sense of themselves even as it might seem to sharpen that sense. For example, just after Paulina orchestrates this scene, and just after Leontes positions her on the right side of the law, her authority evaporates and she quickly diminishes, calling herself an "old turtle" fit for a "withered bough" (5.3.132–33). The scene's most powerful character is suddenly also the weakest. Other characters also come to embody contradiction. Both Perdita and Leontes begin to approach the condition of stone, and believe they can do so by looking upon Hermione faithfully, for a score of years (5.3.83–84). When Hermione steps down, it is she who embraces Leontes, she who hangs about his neck; if she is unclassifiable, somewhere between flesh and stone, so, evidently, are Leontes and Perdita. Characters repeatedly ask for the context that would bring others into focus—Polixenes wants the last sixteen years of Hermione's past filled in, and Hermione wants the same for Perdita—but the play ends with characters under the law of a spell that renders them strange to each other and to themselves.[72]

Law in both Sicilia and Bohemia had been the matrix within which subjects located themselves and were located as obedient or rebellious. But Paulina's Pauline law here does just the opposite: instead of fixing characters into position, the law instituted by her magic—the fidelity to each other that it demands—makes existence such that characters cannot coincide with themselves. This magical law does not bring subjects together by eliminating difference. It does not cement bonds with what Daniel Boyarin, in a critique of Paul, would call a coercive universality;[73] rather, this law brings subjects together by dividing them, unites them by separating them from themselves.

So we find in this scene what Agamben finds in Paul: a radicalized state of exception. Characters are certainly not reduced, as Leontes had earlier tried to reduce them, to bare life; the scene does not draw the extralegal within the domain of the legal in this way. But nor are characters reinserted into a normative juridical framework; none are bound to the obligatory conduct enjoined by any positive law. The most stringent command is delivered from Paulina to Leontes: "Do not shun her," she tells him, "Until you see her die again, for then / You kill her double. Nay, present your hand" (5.3.105–7). Paulina, giving up more detailed prescription, prohibits only turning away, commands only the presentation of a hand and faith in the openness of doing so. The destruction of tyranny in *The Winter's Tale* ends not in the negative freedoms and positive liberties that we associate with republican frameworks. Leontes's state of emergency does not give way to a state of just law or institute a clear law of works. Rather, what emerges is a Pauline state, one whose subjects are under a law of faith and no other. To love is the only injunction.

To be under this law is to embrace epistemological weakness, to exist in a state where the most important "freedom from" is freedom from presumption. As mentioned earlier, such an embrace helps reconcile Badiou's thought about the Pauline legacy with Agamben's. The ending of the play resembles Badiou's event in destroying the play's philosophical systems and in subordinating what individuals are to the event that overwhelms them. The end is unlike Badiou's event, though, in that its law does not bring subjects into being. If in the wake of the event, as Paul suggests in Ephesians 4:22, we ought to lay aside the old self, we ought not to expect a "new self" who is single-minded, heroic, or whole. *The Winter's Tale* implies that events just do not—and should not—work like this. The law of the Hermione-event, like Pauline law for Agamben, explodes the notion of individual integrity and suggests that only then does peace become possible. We are thus better off when we do not expect law to foster self-assurance. Recent criticism—such as that of Victoria Kahn and Lorna Hutson—has shown how in early modern England, skepticism exists about how law can be separated from rhetoric and thus about how to establish the rightness of laws: about how they define actors as occupying a given juridical position.[74] *The Winter's Tale* takes its skepticism still further, questioning whether law should help define subjects to begin with, assume positive form, or serve normative purposes, be they Catholic, Protestant, or republican. Instead, the play asks that we embrace a law of faith that leaves us divided and undefined.

The play ends on this note, satisfying in some ways though not in all. *The Winter's Tale* suggests that if we were all to accept this Pauline lesson about epistemological humility, there would be a reward: the tyranny of those who exercise power, and claim to have knowledge, becomes unthinkable. We also escape the cycle of law and its transgression that drives much of the play. Further, while *The Winter's Tale* is not republican in any programmatic sense, it might be said to offer a Pauline solution to a crucial republican problem: that of cultivating virtue. Shakespeare, obviously, writes four decades prior to the headstrong republican answer furnished by James Harrington: that good orders would make good men. But Shakespeare might well have known the classical, Polybian theory of *anacyclosis* discussed in Chapter 1, whereby governments are, inevitably, subject to change. As Cicero and, after him, Thomas Smith, put it, "[n]o form of government is maintained for very long";[75] government is bound "never to stand still in one maner of estate."[76] Thus virtue, while fostered by republican political structures, must also, often, be fostered without reference to those structures if virtue is to survive in their absence. *The Winter's Tale*'s end presents one skeptical strategy for such survival: one way to cultivate, say, wisdom, courage, and temperance, is to embrace the law of faith and the neighborly love that it requires. Such an embrace could give Leontes the wisdom not to presume, the temperance to forestall hasty judgment, and the courage to love, even when doing so proves remarkably hard.

If we, like Leontes, accept this Pauline lesson—if we embrace a law of faith and make of it a skeptical practice—we also have to accept that this law will not give us the certainty of self-consistency or of rightness, of knowing precisely who we are and where we stand.[77] Unlike Agamben and Badiou, the end of the play evinces a tentative, even ambivalent attitude about the supersession of a law of works by one of faith. As Lars Engle has noted of another play, the end "embodies scepticism in social practice partly in order to show how awkwardly it performs there."[78] Leontes can never know whether or not he is law-abiding, whether he has embraced Hermione once and for all—whether he is human, no longer stone. The law of this embrace, like the Pauline injunction to neighborly love, is open-ended, infinite. In a recent account of early modern conversion, Jeffrey S. Shoulson argues that the fact that "conversion was not a finite, discrete process" raises a series of anxious questions; "[w]hen conversion is said to have transpired," Shoulson writes, "how can one be certain that the transformation is complete, reliable, or stable? Has the transformation genuinely captured and changed the essence" of the one converted?[79] The event of Leontes's "conversion" keeps such questions about his transformation alive.[80] Consenting to a marriage without statutes, Leontes gives up the law of works for one of faith, for a law that will never yield the satisfaction or the certainty of having been fulfilled.[81] All Leontes can do is present his hand and deny Hermione nothing, uncertain of what love might require. The assumption and the wager of the play is this: that the world becomes more livable and more joyous when faith is to a law that does not eliminate but instead induces, and even assures, such incertitude.

At stake in replacing the law of works with the law of faith is our apparatus for conceiving of ethical behavior. Espousing the law of works, Mark Johnson points out, clarifies one's ethical standing; either one has kept to the path of righteousness—in *The Winter's Tale*, the path set out by Paulina prior to the statue scene—or one has gone astray.[82] As Johnson puts it, according to this view, "moral character is conceived as being principally a matter of control"; moral laws are constraints and moral action is "movement that does not violate these constraints" (50, 18). Johnson would regard Leontes's loss of clearly demarcated moral ground as salutary, though for different reasons than Shakespeare. To think of ethical behavior exclusively in terms of keeping to constraints, Johnson argues, is to overlook the imaginative character of ethical decision-making, and is even "to overlook a conception of morality as a means of exploring possibilities for human flourishing—a conception that is primarily expansive and constructive" rather than constraining (31).[83] Johnson's new moral theory would allow us to reason creatively about ethical issues, to explore possibilities, to flourish. Ethics could then become a site for self-realization.

In *The Winter's Tale*, Shakespeare hardly imagines ethics as such a site. Again we see, as we did in the chapters on *Lucrece* and *Othello*, how the limited skepticism of cognitive science—its admission that our concepts are contingent and metaphorical rather than fixed—yields to a confident, pragmatic faith more difficult to locate in Shakespeare. When Shakespeare imagines ethical behavior not as keeping to the path of righteousness but as the offer of a hand, the self must always be divided, humble, and unsure of its abilities. Yet it is this uncertainty—not an increase in creative capacity—that makes it possible for us to flourish.

Conclusion

I want to end by illustrating one broader consequence of the resemblance, if not the identity, between the outlook evinced by *The Winter's Tale* and that delineated by Agamben and Badiou. Specifically, I want to highlight how the play either rejects outright or operates outside models of thinking available to Shakespeare. I have used Montaignean and Jacobean context primarily as support, as a way to ground my reading of the play and to help strengthen links between the early modern and the modern, but in a sense *The Winter's Tale* exceeds these contexts, showing how right Richard Strier is to claim that we sell literature short when we "mandate what a text (or a valuable text) from a particular period must or must not do or mean."[84] I want to highlight this point by comparing Shakespeare's skeptical practice not only to a fellow traveler such as Montaigne but also to Calvin and Luther.

Earlier in this chapter, I mentioned that Montaigne at times counsels submission to authority. In focusing on overlap between Montaigne and more radical aspects of *The Winter's Tale*, I have downplayed this conservative aspect of the *Essays*—one that, according to Christian Thorne, is crucial not to the Pauline, but rather to the Pyrrhonist quality of Montaigne's skepticism. Thorne claims that Montaigne, following the classical Pyrrhonist Sextus Empiricus, draws attention to human fallibility, the contingency of signs, and the pitfalls of presumption not in order to free subjects from the hold of law, but rather in order to "indentur[e] the subject to customary practices without having to offer up any justification for them."[85] While the classical Pyrrhonist assumes that we can find an equally-evidenced counter for every assertion we might make about the world, the proper end of philosophy nevertheless is *ataraxia* (or unperturbedness); and so rather than create discord, the Pyrrhonist will follow existing customs even though no longer convinced about their rightness. In Thorne's reading, Montaigne fits this pattern. If Montaigne demonstrates how "you do not in fact have the sound reasons you thought you did to believe what you do," he also— deliberately—demonstrates "that you have no sound reasons for believing *anything else*," and thus that "the *only* reason—the single, exclusive reason—you have to believe something is that you were born into it" (88). For instance, the vast discrepancies between the laws of one culture or period and another induce humility about how we can ground a given law's rightness; yet such epistemological weakness, Thorne argues, discourages actually abandoning positive law. Abandoning such law does not bring tranquility. Obeying it does.

Proving whether Montaigne is so straightforwardly a classical Pyrrhonist in the *Essays*—whether, that is, Thorne succeeds in overturning the long tradition of seeing a more liberating Montaigne—is well beyond the scope of this chapter. The very fact that Thorne is able to mount his argument with reference to the *Essays,* however, suggests a difference between Montaigne's thinking and Shakespeare's in *The Winter's Tale* (not to mention, as we will see in Chapter 5, Shakespeare's radical neo-Pyrrhonism in *Timon of Athens*). Montaigne can be taken to advance skepticism aimed at bolstering positive law in its given state. De-emphasizing positive law in favor of a law of faith, *The Winter's Tale*'s end takes a different aim and, in doing so, forges a distinctive connection between skepticism and faith—this, despite the fact that seeing a connection was quite common in the sixteenth and seventeenth centuries. Richard Popkin has displayed how many early modern thinkers sought solutions for how to put skepticism in service of systematic religion: for how to retain faith in religious code given the advent of Reformation doubt about Catholic doctrine.[86] Thorne argues that early modern skepticism in general leads to passive acceptance of the status quo and bolsters authoritarian structures.[87] But whereas both Popkin and Thorne cast skepticism's compatibility with faith in conservative lights, showing how the two can balance each other out in coherent normative systems, *The Winter's Tale* shows how entwining the two can lead to eschewing those systems.

As Popkin's account of the Reformation implies, the view evinced by *The Winter's Tale* also differs markedly from those of Calvin and Luther. For both, attending to law induces humility that is deep but also distinct from both Montaigne and Shakespeare. For these reformers, difficulty resides neither in knowing the grounding of the law (as in Montaigne), nor in knowing whether law has been fulfilled (as in Shakespeare's late romance). According to Calvin and Luther, we can know both of these things. Calvin, for instance, argues that the first purpose of moral law is that it "admonishes everyone of his own unrighteousness"; far from blurring our moral standing, as does the law of faith in *The Winter's Tale,* moral law is a mirror that reflects with perfect clarity the "infinite distances" separating us from holiness.[88] Luther argues for the necessity of moral law similarly; without the perspective that the law affords, "the corruption and blindness of human nature is . . . so great that it neither sees nor feels the magnitude of sin."[89] Calvin and Luther thus reject the antinomian notion that the justification of Christians by faith rather than by works (established in Romans 3:27–8) means that believers have been freed from Mosaic law's dictates. Believers are freed merely from ceremonial law, not from moral law. In other words, Calvin and Luther argue against a reduction—in this case, of the stipulations of the Decalogue to an unspecific law of neighborly love; they argue against the reduction that both Agamben and Badiou perform in their readings of Paul, and that Shakespeare implies at the end of *The Winter's Tale.*

Calvin and Luther, unsurprisingly, read the epistles in less selective a fashion than Agamben, Badiou, and Shakespeare. Considered in isolation, verses of the epistles do seem to urge the Decalogue's reduction. Most obviously, there is Galatians 5:14, "For all the lawe is fulfylled in one worde, which is this: Thou shalt loue thy neyghbour as thy selfe," and Romans 13:8, "Owe nothyng to no man, but to loue one another: For he that loueth another, hath fulfylled the lawe." Yet with the next verse of Romans, Paul specifies what he means: not that the law of neighborly love replaces the laws of the second table but merely that it encapsulates them: "For this: Thou shalt not commit adultrie, thou shalt not kyll, thou shalt not steale, thou shalt not beare false witnesse, thou shalt not lust: and yf there be any other commaundement, it is comprehended in this saying: Namelye, Thou shalt loue thy neighbour as thy selfe."

Paul hardly suggests that Christians have been freed from the moral law merely because they are justified by faith and enjoined to neighborly love. This is to say nothing of the first table's commands, the importance of which is evident throughout the epistles and evident hardly at all in Agamben, Badiou, or *The Winter's Tale.* To observe, as I do, that a play of Shakespeare's might not be Christian in outlook is hardly new.

As Peter Holbrook points out, such an idea has a long pedigree, one that includes André Gide, George Santayana, and A. C. Bradley.[90] If what I have argued is right, part of what makes *The Winter's Tale* distinctive in this regard is its offer of a Pauline, yet agnostic solution to the problem of cultivating virtue, a skeptical practice of turning from systems of politics and religion in favor of a law of faith that cannot be codified.

CHAPTER 4

Doubtful Freedom in *The Tempest*

"free as mountain winds"

*T*he *Tempest* is an unrelenting, even obsessive meditation on the theme of freedom. Virtually every scene explores what free existence is, how we might partake of it, how freedom feels or would feel. Shakespeare queries an array of ideals of freedom. He considers well-worn ideals— for instance, the self-government of individuals and states that we have seen in each chapter of this book. He also considers more uncommon ideals—for instance, liberty found in amorous enthrallment or sublime poetic rapture, liberty akin to Othello's quayside meeting with Desdemona and the statue-event in *The Winter's Tale*. The images of freedom that Shakespeare invokes, likewise, range from free movement to extreme enthrallment. Not one of these ideals escapes challenge; as David Norbrook puts it, "[a]ll of the play's utopian ideals . . . come up for ironic scrutiny."[1] Shakespeare's meditation on freedom is surely a skeptical one, in the common sense that he subjects different ideals of freedom to serious doubt, but also in the more philosophical sense that he balances them—seemingly to show, through ironic scrutiny, that they are equally promising yet equally uncompelling. In this, Shakespeare's skepticism would seem to shade into cynicism, were it not the case that Shakespeare suggests a way that every ideal he queries could become compelling and open a way to freedom. Skepticism yields to faith in *The Tempest*, I will argue, by allying freedom with self-transformation: by suggesting that self-government, amorous enthrallment, and sublime poetic utterance, though neutral in themselves, are liberating if selves are transformed through them, freed from their given, preexisting states. This thrilling liberty cannot be predicted or guaranteed, so faith in it requires epistemological weakness, openness to an experience of freedom that cannot be known in advance.

For an initial illustration of why this might be, let me begin by considering a freedom that supposedly is known in advance. One of the earliest figurations of liberty comes as act 1 draws to a close, when Prospero tenders his servant Ariel an initial promise to be set free, one that he reiterates:

> Thou shalt be as free
> As mountain winds; but then exactly do
> All points of my command. (1.2.499–501)[2]

Since Ariel is composed of pure spirit, Prospero imagines, his liberty can assume the form of wholly unimpeded movement, freed from every constraint imaginable. Prospero frames his image with a spatial structure, a mountain, but only so as to indicate liberty's unbounded character. If ever freedom is thought in terms of free movement, it is here.

Limited as we are by bodily dimensions and by forces in our natural, social, and psychological worlds, the liberty that Prospero imagines is not one that we might attain. Still, it could serve as a metaphor for an ideal worth trying to approximate: the ideal, later articulated by J. S. Mill and sometimes found in germinal form in Shakespeare, of pursuing one's own good in one's own way.[3] By enjambing the simile, Shakespeare infuses the freedom it describes with a seductive, breathless expansiveness. Given Ariel's earlier existence, immured in a pine, as well as his present existence, indentured to Prospero, it is hard not to conceive of freedom, first, simply as the ability to move, in whichever direction and fashion one decides. George Lakoff and Mark Johnson, departing from the flexibility they ordinarily urge, go so far as to say that all of our concepts of freedom—from the most conservative to the most radical—share a non-metaphorical core that consists in this ability. According to Lakoff and Johnson, our earliest childhood experiences—our negative reactions, more or less immediate, to being unduly restrained and bound—render inevitable the opposition between freedom and bondage.[4] "The idea of freedom," Lakoff writes, "is felt viscerally, in our bodies," and means "being able to achieve purposes, either because nothing is stopping you or because you have the requisite capacities, or both."[5] When we imagine the opposite of freedom, we naturally think of the following: "'in chains,' 'imprisoned,' 'enslaved,' 'trapped,' 'oppressed,' 'held down,' 'held back,' 'threatened,' 'fearful,' 'powerless'" (29).

Perhaps we do. In the end, though, Shakespeare casts the freedom that Prospero promises to Ariel in an unflattering and unreal light. First, being free as mountain winds might mean being unobstructed, but would also seem to mean being utterly empty, devoid of purpose. How, Shakespeare prompts us to ask, would freedom feel if it were comparable to mountain winds? Where would freedom lead and how would we arrive there? One difficulty inherent in this idea—that being free means being able to pursue one's own good in one's own way—is that the origins of the "good" and the "way" start to evaporate; the motives and pathways that shape freedom become as insubstantial as a change in drift.[6]

The more I seek to grasp Prospero's image for Ariel's liberty, the more it falls to pieces. Is wind itself, after all, really a figure for self-direction? Does it not instead conjure air impelled by a force outside itself? Is wind not a figure for being driven by fortune? Describing his unfreedom in *The Winter's Tale*, Leontes remarks that he is a feather for every wind that blows. Would he have been more free were he the wind?

Either way, Prospero's phrase draws attention to the emptiness at the center of self-direction. We can, if we wish, entertain his simile as apposite to *The Tempest* insofar as there are figures in the play who pursue self-interest—for example, Antonio and Sebastian—but they do so in a dastardly and destructive fashion, one that is not the least bit liberating. Antonio and Sebastian are stock figures of the Machiavel, slaves to hackneyed desire for power.

A final trouble with Prospero's formulation follows quickly upon the simile. He claims that Ariel must perform all that his master commands. Why? Prospero could simply mean that if Ariel desires to be totally free, he must first undergo total obedience. Yet the ambiguity of "but then"—which could mean either "but first" or "but when you are free"— might well suggest that to be free as mountain winds, from Prospero's perspective, is to perform all the points of his command.[7] If so, Prospero's words allude to the Christian concept of total freedom found in total servitude, a concept to which we will return further along. For now I note that if Prospero does allude to liberty found in servitude, Shakespeare may suggest, darkly, that such freedom is similar to—just as insubstantial as—being free as mountain winds.

Prospero's obscure initial formulation is, in any case, unusable as an image for understanding freedom. He is far from finished describing Ariel's freedom, of course, raising the issue again at the end of act 4 when Prospero tries to reassure his servant:

> Shortly shall all my labors end, and thou
> Shalt have the air at freedom. For a little,
> Follow, and do me service. (4.1.264–6)

Now, instead of being as free as the wind, Ariel will have the air at freedom. Liberty is less an experiential state than a possession, a form of dominion. Perhaps Prospero's thinking has changed. His airy descriptions of how freedom would feel might be inept, but at least he can give whatever liberty is to Ariel and is willing to contrast, rather than conflate, this provision with his tricksy spirit's earlier service. Still, it seems important that we cannot tell, from Prospero's point of view, what kind of experience his provision would enable. Such freedom—a property conferred upon Ariel by his erstwhile master—here calls to mind Jean-Luc Nancy's claim that " 'freedoms' do not grasp the stakes of 'freedom.' " At best, Nancy argues, 'freedoms' "sketch the contours of their common concept—'freedom'—as if these were the borders of an empty, vacant space."[8] Prospero's descriptions of Ariel's freedom leave me with such vacancy, and leave me wondering whether Prospero has much of a sense of freedom at all. At the least, he certainly fails to understand Ariel's own sense. After Prospero promises him liberty yet again, in act 5, Ariel imagines free existence:

> Where the bee sucks, there suck I;
> In a cowslip's bell I lie;
> There I couch when owls do cry.
> On the bat's back I do fly
> After summer merrily.
> Merrily, merrily shall I live now
> Under the blossom that hangs on the bough. (5.1.88–94)

When Ariel pictures freedom, he does not picture being unimpeded. Prospero's unending cycle of promise and deferral has made a pursuit of freedom like chasing after wind. Ariel, though, pictures being in a cowslip or under a blossom. Freedom, to him, means being enclosed, the enjambment of lines 93–94 imputing as much expansiveness to enclosure and passivity as Prospero imputes to openness and activity.

Ariel pictures freedom not with images of active, self-directed, or unobstructed movement but with images of rest, of freedom from work
and even from exertion altogether. Even when his vision of freedom involves movement—when he pictures flying on the bat's back—he
hardly moves on his own. Enjambment yet again seems important, as
the bat flies "after" summer and liberty itself seems adventitious, an ad-
venture unrelated to his own capacities.

But even Ariel's more complex vision ultimately crumbles. As we
will see, his vision of idle freedom resembles that of another discredited
figure: the "honest old counselor" Gonzalo. Shakespeare also presents
the speech itself in dubious terms. Ariel speaks of his liberty mostly in
the present tense, as if he already is free, as though life, henceforth, will
be no different from what it has been. Ariel clamors for freedom almost
the moment he appears, presumably unfree and hopeful that liberation
will bring about change. Yet, here, he cannot imagine his new life as
differing from the old. This inability of his provokes a question: if Ariel
cannot recognize, describe, or experience a distinction between his unfree past and his free future, can we understand him as capable of a free
existence? Put more generally, if Ariel cannot imagine or undergo
change, can he ever be free? I believe that he cannot, because freedom
in this play is inseparable not just from change but from genuine, unpredictable transformation. Since Ariel cannot undergo either, neither
he, nor Prospero, nor anyone else could describe the terms of his freedom. Ariel is incapable of freedom. This chapter explores what being
capable would mean, and how Shakespeare's skepticism about freedom
ends in faith.

In what follows, I address particular critical claims about *The Tempest*, but the more general question of Shakespearean freedom arises
often. The answer, frequently and understandably, can resemble Prospero's. Recently, Stephen Greenblatt has argued that in Shakespeare
"free" means "the opposite of confined, imprisoned, subjected, constrained, and afraid to speak out." Positioning freedom and constraint
as antitheses, Greenblatt details Shakespeare's fascination with physical, social, and mental autonomy, arguing that these ideals are just
that—unattainable, not quite real—but compel Shakespeare nevertheless.[9] Peter Holbrook, whose argument we encountered in this book's
introduction, advances an unreserved form of Greenblatt's argument,
maintaining that "Shakespeare is an author for a liberal, individualistic
culture"—that Shakespeare associates freedom with choice, self-

realization, and authenticity.[10] Greenblatt and Holbrook both celebrate autonomy, then, but not always in a rarefied form akin to mountain winds. Both critics, for instance, celebrate *Measure for Measure's* portrayal of the prisoner Barnardine, an inveterate drunkard and murderer who refuses execution. Greenblatt writes that Barnardine is possessed of "intense, unexpected, and irreducible individuality";[11] Holbrook, likewise, writes that "Barnardine is stubbornly, unswervingly, unapologetically himself," and that he serves as proof of "Shakespeare's deep attachment to freedom—even freedom of an unreasoning, unedifying, animalistic kind."[12]

The following account shares with Greenblatt and Holbrook insofar as Shakespeare, Ariel's example notwithstanding, sometimes presents the quest for freedom as a quest for self-sufficiency, though that sufficiency is more Stoic—and thus more circumscribed, more dependent on submission to principles—than is the proto-modern autonomy that we can see in Barnardine. I take exception to Greenblatt's and Holbrook's equations of freedom with the insistence on "being yourself." Barnardine, resistant to all forms of change, is himself exemplary. I cannot fathom how his stubborn insistence on remaining self-identical could constitute freedom, unless freedom begins and ends in doing what you want—regardless of what you are doing or how it shapes your existence. Barnardine is as incapable of change as is Ariel. The prisoner's pursuit of what he regards as good renders his form of life completely predictable, set within a daily cycle as determined as the dimensions of the cell he refuses to leave. He cannot be free if his actions are wholly conditioned in advance, in this case not by social expectation but by appetite.[13] In addition to this metaphysical claim about freedom, one also made in *The Tempest*, Shakespeare makes an aesthetic—though, importantly, not a moral—claim about Barnardine and his unfreedom: namely, that his stubbornness gives fixity to a distinctly ugly existence. The same, we will see, goes for Prospero's anger.

Greenblatt and Holbrook's accounts hardly exhaust the field of recent thinking about Shakespearean freedom. Other recent treatments of the theme focus on how liberty involves dependence, on others and on normative discourse, of the sort that Barnardine refuses. Joshua Scodel, to cite just one example, links freedom to dependence by emphasizing how liberty, in Shakespeare's view, might depend on Stoic reason or God.[14] This chapter shares with Scodel insofar as *The Tempest* also engages with Stoic and Christian notions of liberty without straightforwardly endorsing either. Scodel's concerns, though, are to establish what it takes, in Shakespeare, to acquire the agency or free will to speak and act freely.[15] In *The Tempest*, by contrast, freedom has no essential connection to the exercise of free will or even to ability. Freedom sometimes seems to require the cultivation of willed, rational self-control, yet sometimes seems to require that such control be utterly lost.

In this shifting, Shakespeare is again much like Montaigne, who will arise as often here as he did in the previous chapter. That chapter traced Montaigne's doubt about man's strength and capacity for control, but the skepticism of the *Essays* on the whole assumes the form of entertaining variable answers to this question. Taken together, the *Essays* are probably more akin to *The Tempest* than *The Winter's Tale*. And yet if *The Tempest* and Montaigne's *Essays* seem merely to suspend judgment on the question of freedom, they do not quite do so, a point I have suggested earlier in this chapter and show in the sections that follow. In both, though more blatantly in Shakespeare's play, skepticism gives way to faith and inconsistency to consistency in that all of freedom's possible forms are transformative, liberating the self from the automatism of life as it is given. Being able to experience liberty thus requires that we accept freedom's uncertain alterations of the self, that we not presume to know what the experience of liberty will be like.

Prospero and Rational Self-Government: The Care of the Self

By and large, *The Tempest* queries the theme of freedom within the bounds of a traditional field: that of how one stands in relation to passion. A chief difference between Ariel and the rest of the play's characters—a difference that helps explain his inability to imagine undergoing change—is his inability to have any relation to passion. Describing Gonzalo's tears over Alonso's imprisonment and distraction, Ariel tells Prospero that his "charm so strongly works 'em, / That if you now beheld them, your affections / Would become tender" (5.1.17–19), as would his own if he were human. Ariel certainly induces passion in others, for instance when singing to Ferdinand about his father's supposed death, but never feels passion himself. Freedom can be understood as restrained, rational self-government—often in Stoic terms deployed routinely, if also controversially, in early modernity—and if freedom is, or at least can be, the achieved triumph of reason over passions, then Ariel, with no passions to govern, could not be free.

   Shakespeare entertains the ideal of rational self-government through many of *The Tempest*'s characters and, as Holbrook points out, most fully through Prospero.[16] Put mildly, Prospero does often have little control over his passions and especially over his anger—a fact made painfully evident in the play's second scene. When Ariel requests his liberty, Prospero rages, his fury epitomized by a set of ejaculations: "How now? moody?"; "No more!"; "Thou liest, malignant thing!"; "If thou more murmur'st, I will rend an oak / And peg thee in his knotty entrails till / Thou hast howled away twelve winters" (1.2.244–57, 294–6). Slight provocations make Prospero wildly exclamatory, his threats worthy of Leontes in his jealousy's most vicious throes. Ariel's exit and Caliban's entrance fan the fire in Prospero's blood: "Thou poisonous slave, got by the devil himself / Upon thy wicked dam, come forth!" he cries, assuring the recalcitrant Caliban that tonight he "shalt have cramps" (1.2.319–325). Caliban responds crankily, and the slave-master explodes: "Hagseed, hence! . . . I'll rack thee with old cramps, / Fill all thy bones with aches, make thee roar / That beasts shall tremble at thy din" (1.2.365–71). For making him shriek, Prospero threatens to amplify his instigators' cries infinitely. Montaigne writes that "[t]here is no passion that so shakes the clarity of our judgment as anger" and that it "is a passion that takes pleasure in itself and flatters itself."[17] Remarks such as these, as we saw in the previous chapter, cast doubt on human capacity properly to see and judge. Shakespeare, likewise, shows how the prism of Prospero's anger makes torture look like a satisfactory response to small questionings of authority.

   Stephen Orgel writes that for much of 1.2, the sense we have of Prospero is "of a mind achieving full control of itself," and that there we see him "working out the last traces of bitterness and vindictiveness."[18] Another aspect of Orgel's argument, I suggest in my conclusion, helps us understand freedom in *The Tempest*; but in 1.2 we see passions far stronger than Orgel allows. Prospero's initial rage cannot be mistaken, and there exists real disagreement about whether Prospero ever undergoes change. Some critics, such as Harry Berger, Jr., claim that he does not, whereas others, such as Holbrook and Paul Cantor, assure us that he does.[19] Prospero's arguably most famous speech, bookended by stupendous passion, appears in act 4. During the masque that Prospero puts on for Miranda and Ferdinand, Prospero recalls the plot against his life that Caliban has hatched with the drunkards Stephano and Trinculo. Ferdinand sees how upset Prospero is, and the older man, perhaps noticing this, addresses the younger in these words:

> You do look, my son, in a moved sort,
> As if you were dismayed: be cheerful, sir.
> Our revels now are ended. These our actors,
> As I foretold you, were all spirits and
> Are melted into air, into thin air;
> And, like the baseless fabric of this vision,
> The cloud-capped tow'rs, the gorgeous palaces,
> The solemn temples, the great globe itself,
> Yea, all which it inherit, shall dissolve,
> And, like this insubstantial pageant faded,
> Leave not a rack behind. We are such stuff
> As dreams are made on, and our little life
> Is rounded with a sleep. Sir, I am vexed.
> Bear with my weakness: my old brain is troubled.
> Be not disturbed with my infirmity.
> If you be pleased, retire into my cell
> And there repose. A turn or two I'll walk
> To still my beating mind. (4.1.146–163)

The speech raises several questions, only one of which I want to pose now: why does Prospero urge cheerfulness on Ferdinand only to then dwell on the transience of all things under the sun? The train of thought seems especially odd because Prospero does not also claim, as certain Stoics and Christians would, that proper reflection on worldly transience leads to tranquil liberty from worldly attachment. Tranquility is a common goal for philosophical reflection in antiquity, and while a skeptic such as Sextus Empiricus believes that tranquility comes when we stop believing "that anything is by nature good or bad," Prospero's language here resonates most with Cicero or with a Stoic like Marcus Aurelius.[20] In the chapter on *Lucrece*, I attended to their practices of viewing the present in a wide temporal frame so as to weaken their susceptibility to, and achieve independence from, present troubles. In the middle of the speech, Prospero himself seems almost to have become unconcerned about the specific situation before him. And yet he fails to pry himself loose from the things of his world. Reflecting on the fact of transience actually magnifies his passion. Prospero's utterance, sublime in its majesty, seems only to deepen his own vexation. So he resolves to walk a turn or two, as though literal self-direction might help him direct his passions. He still lacks control but at least he now seems to wish for it.

In act 5, Prospero claims the control as his own. As noted earlier, Ariel relates the plight of those whom Prospero has afflicted, remarking that his master's affections would grow tender if he but beheld the sufferers. "And mine shall," Prospero asserts:

> Hast thou, which art but air, a touch, a feeling
> Of their afflictions, and shall not myself,
> One of their kind, that relish all as sharply
> Passion as they, be kindlier moved than thou art?
> Though with their high wrongs I am struck to th'quick,
> Yet with my nobler reason 'gainst my fury
> Do I take part. (5.1.21–27)

It is not, Prospero claims, that he has extirpated his passions, as might a Stoic, but that he selects from among them. Whereas rage simply overcame him just hours earlier, now he says that he will opt for tenderness, will employ "nobler reason" in order to experience virtuous rather than vicious affect. Prospero lays claim to an acute degree of achieved moderation. Is the claim justified? He at least manages to pardon his malefactors, and his speech lacks some of the exclamatory vitriol it had earlier. Ire, though, spills into his speech. Having solemn music played, Prospero declares it "the best comforter / To an unsettled fancy," yet when he thinks of his captives' brains, he bursts out that for now they remain "useless, boiled within thy skull!" (5.1.58–60). For someone whose passion is supposedly reined in, Prospero seems rather excited about boiling his enemies' brains.

The pardons themselves also arouse our doubt. While Prospero shows tenderness in his treatment of Alonso and Gonzalo, he cannot help but insult the fratricidal Sebastian: "I do forgive thee," he says, "Unnatural though thou art" (5.1.78–9). With his brother Antonio, contempt shades into anger:

> For you, most wicked sir, whom to call brother
> Would even infect my mouth, I do forgive
> Thy rankest fault—all of them; and require
> My dukedom of thee, which perforce I know
> Thou must restore. (5.1.130–4)

Still hatefully hyperbolic, Prospero is hard to picture as having achieved self-control. He does not exact vengeance, but the "virtue" he practices is of rather a bitter, vindictive sort. Intemperate anger counts among his most persistent flaws, leaving readers to wonder whether Prospero could have gained control over that anger, and what form control might have assumed. How would control be established to begin with? Would it result from diligent application, from carefully cultivated practices of the self, or could it have resulted instantaneously, in a sudden conversion?

The Stoic strain in Montaigne's earlier essays can be of help here. In those essays, Montaigne presents himself as a kind of anti-Prospero. "I am little subject to these violent passions," he writes. "My susceptibility is naturally tough; and I harden and thicken it every day by force of reason."[21] Montaigne's basic program, of using reason and discourse to temper passion, draws on classical practices of the self that Michel Foucault outlines in the later volumes of *The History of Sexuality* and related lectures, essays, and interviews. Foucault shifts focus, at his career's end, from how subjects form in relation to coercive discourses toward ways that the self might work upon itself. The "care of the self," in the form of physical, social, and intellectual exercises, emerges for Foucault as an important category, one that allows for practices of freedom—for the cultivation of an ethics that is also, and is inseparable from, an aesthetics. Insofar as self-mastery is good, and insofar as the good and beautiful are inseparable in classical frameworks, the care of the self allows for the incremental transformation of the self so that it comes to approximate a work of art.[22] In a range of these frameworks—whether Platonic, Stoic, or Epicurean—the care of the self involves triumphing over and mastering violent passions. Discourse, whether written or spoken, can be an effective means for this.

Prospero certainly would need to reform his current discursive regime in order to develop rational self-control. He generally uses words only to threaten, excoriate, or otherwise coerce. I can, thus, imagine benefits that he might reap from keeping the sort of notebooks, or *hypomnemata,* that Foucault describes and that promote the internalization of quotes, examples, and reflections.[23] Imagine—while forgiving, for the next couple of pages, the initial ridiculousness of what I ask—what might occur were Prospero to dwell on quotes transcribed from Marcus Aurelius's *Meditations*: "be at once entirely passionless and yet full of natural affection"; banish "every thought of the kind which leads you astray from close watch over your governing self"; "you may at any hour you please retreat into yourself."[24] Prospero by constitution seems so resistant to these achievements that a notebook's continual reminders might be required for even minimal absorption of Aurelius's injunctions.

Say Prospero were exposed to Seneca. Taking issue with the Aristotelian notion that well-used passions can be deployed as weapons, Seneca writes that passions "don't wait for the hand that wields them, they're not possessed, they do the possessing."[25] Montaigne, also confuting Aristotle, writes of anger as "a weapon whose use is novel. For we move other weapons, this one moves us; our hand does not guide it, it guides our hand; it holds us, we do not hold it."[26] Were Prospero in possession of a notebook in addition to a spell book, language might cease to be a vehicle for the anger that moves him and instead be a means by which he cultivates freedom. Foucault notes that for Plutarch, ameliorative discourse "silences the passions like a master who with one word hushes the growling of dogs."[27] The next time Miranda asks questions too quickly, Caliban fetches wood too slowly, or Ariel broaches the topic of his liberty wrongly, Prospero might retreat to his inner citadel rather than lash out. Prospero then might become less likely to blurt "Hagseed, hence!" and set spectral hounds on adversaries. He might be more likely to craft sublime utterances about the dissolution of cloud-capped towers and gorgeous palaces and to draw sensible conclusions from those utterances. In so doing, he might develop the aesthetics of his existence; in his freedom, Prospero might start to resemble a work of art. Seneca writes of the angry that they "have the repellent and terrifying features of people who are deformed and bloated"; "it would be hard to say," he concludes, "whether the vice is more abhorrent or disfiguring."[28] Prospero's anger is just as contemptible—and just as ugly. Given his appreciation for masques and majestic palaces, surely he believes in beauty. Surely he would be chagrined to see himself in anger's grips.

The idea that Prospero would benefit from keeping *hypomnemata* still may seem implausible. One of the first things we learn about Prospero, after all, is that he seems already to have devoted a significant portion of his life to the care of the self. Prior to being usurped and exiled, he had been "neglecting worldly ends, all dedicated / To closeness, and the bettering of my mind" (1.2.89–90). Prospero claims to have performed the classical operation described by Foucault—the turn away from the world and toward the self, and the dedication of oneself to the self—and yet, when we meet him he seems preternaturally susceptible to the world from which he supposedly has turned. Foucault writes that the inward turn effects a break "with regard to what surrounds the self . . . so that it is no longer enslaved, dependent and constrained."[29] Montaigne, too, claims that once we undertake to live solitary lives, we then can "make our contentment depend on ourselves." "[L]et us cut loose from all the ties that bind us to others," he enjoins readers; "let us win from ourselves the power to live really alone and to live that way at our ease."[30] Yet Prospero's solitude led not to the establishment of a tranquil back shop, inaccessible to others, but to total turmoil within and without.[31]

Why? Shakespeare may limit the degree to which any inward turn could effectively fortify the self against the shocks of outrageous fortune. Neglecting worldly ends might be feasible in a place of ease; maintaining self-control while exiled or left for dead is another matter. Seneca may impute more efficacy to practices of the self than Shakespeare will allow.[32] (*Lucrece*, we saw, certainly suggests as much.) Alternatively, the manner of Prospero's inward turn could account for his lack of self-mastery. What, exactly, was he up to when he turned from the world and commenced bettering his mind? Prospero describes the process as "being transported / And rapt in secret studies" (1.2.76–7). Presumably this refers to his study of magic; it does not sound like something that Seneca would recommend. Prospero's inward turn put him not on the path to self-knowledge but on a subterranean route to magical power. He was "rapt" on this path of secret study, which did not do for him what the care of the self does in Foucault's accounts: permanently fix a part of the self now inoculated against rapture. In a lecture that touches on Epictetus, Marcus Aurelius, Seneca and others, Foucault says that for these figures

> Wisdom consists . . . in never allowing ourselves to be induced to make an involuntary movement at the behest or through the instigation of an external impulse. Rather, we must seek the point at the center of ourselves to which we will be fixed and in relation to which we will remain immobile. It is toward ourselves, toward the center of ourselves, in the center of ourselves, that we must fix our aim. And the movement we must make must be to turn back to this center of ourselves in order to immobilize ourselves, indefinitely.[33]

Marcus Aurelius crystallizes this idea nicely when, praising the "sovereign power within," he says that we ought to "[b]e like the headland on which the waves continually break," just as Montaigne writes that in solitude, one might settle and limit one's cogitations so as to establish a fixed, unperturbed center to the self.[34] Prospero's inward turn, on the other hand, just does not involve cultivating any classical form of a free relation to passion. Instead of immobilizing his passions through devotion to the self, Prospero studies the occult, losing himself in secret raptures. Prospero turned inward for the wrong reasons and so adopted the wrong object, sought to master not himself but the natural world.

In this way, Prospero shows that free movement of the sort promised to Ariel only has meaning, if it has meaning, if one has already established self-mastery. Orgel writes that we as readers "are continuously aware of the extent to which this world is controlled by Prospero and is even at times indistinguishable from him."[35] Prospero is capable of an astounding degree of free movement insofar as the island is a thing over which he has dominion. In the absence of self-control, though, this dominion cannot bring freedom. For Prospero, the primary freedom would not be free movement but achieved immobility, the inner state in which one is not and cannot be moved by passion. When his book is drowned and his staff broken, Prospero notes, he will resume his dukedom and "Every third thought shall be my grave." Prospero, we sense, will think interment not to achieve inner peace but to deepen and extend his depression. He should have been reading Seneca and Epictetus and instead seems to have spent his solitude absorbed in Solomon's Key. Hence the passionate wreck that we find on the island. Prospero is a Stoic inverted, with near total control over the outer world, yet completely enslaved by life on the inside.

In order to be free, Prospero would have had to undergo change, to transform his relationship to passion. I have said that Ariel cannot be free because he cannot imagine change, a future that differs from his past, and Prospero for his part never desires such a future, a point that we have seen and that Shakespeare punctuates through Prospero's articulation of freedom in the epilogue:

Now my charms are all o'erthrown,
And what strength I have's mine own,
Which is most faint. Now 'tis true
I must be here confined by you,
Or sent to Naples. Let me not,
Since I have my dukedom got
And pardoned the deceiver, dwell
In this bare island by your spell;
But release me from my bands
With the help of your good hands. (1–10)

When Prospero imagines his own freedom, he imagines it in the same terms—as free movement—with which he imagines Ariel's. He depends on the audience for this freedom as Ariel has depended on him; they can confine him on his bare island or release him from his bands. But being set free does not open Prospero to a transformative future; rather, it allows him to reclaim his old identity, to ensure that his future is like his past, much as the actor in Prospero's role, after the play, reclaims the identity he had before stepping onstage. Prospero has no wish for transformation, and so the applause that he says will deliver him to liberty will merely transfer him to a predictable world, one where every third thought is fixed.

Prospero and Rational Self-Government 2: Good Orders Make Good Men

Prospero's conception of studiousness, we have seen, makes it hard to imagine him reading Seneca. The possibility remains that Shakespeare thinks it unlikely that any of us will choose to read about Stoic self-mastery rather than bone up on how to wake the dead. *The Tempest*, like other of our texts of focus, does not close the door on self-control but invites us to consider whether rational self-government is achievable only in the most limited sense, whether classical practices of the self are very practicable.[36]

One need not search with assiduity to find the same skepticism in Montaigne, his occasional assertions of Stoic optimism notwithstanding. The "Apology," as we saw in the previous chapter, probably casts the most resolutely skeptical eye on man's capacity for self-control. There, man is a "miserable and puny creature"; only by acts of tremendous presumption can we imagine ourselves as anything other than "the most vulnerable and frail of all creatures."[37] Montaigne even says that to think otherwise—to adopt the position taken in other of his essays—is to affect deity. "As long as he thinks he has some resources and power by himself," Montaigne writes, "never will man recognize what he owes to his master; he will always make chickens of his eggs, as they say." He thus "must be stripped to his shirt" (438). As a partial antidote to our inborn presumption and false claims to self-sufficiency, Montaigne in the "Apology" argues that we ought to "bridle and bind" ourselves "with religions, laws, customs," among other things (509–10). Here we see the potential conservatism that Christian Thorne sees in Montaigne; since

Montaigne himself is inadequate, he claims that "I accept other people's choice and stay in the position where God put me. Otherwise I could not keep myself from rolling about" (521).

The Tempest also engages the question of whether external constraints might succeed where self-imposed constraints fail. Typically, though, Shakespeare is not thought to champion adhering to the status quo. If self-government falls short as a practice of the self, perhaps it could measure up as the practice of a reformed English state, with political structures made to resemble republican ones. While Prospero fails to achieve self-mastery, Constance Jordan claims that at minimum "[h]is restorative actions imply a commitment to some kind of contractualism with respect to rule within the body politic, a commitment that further implies support, however qualified, for the subjects' liberties and liberty."[38] If Prospero never achieves self-control, he at least realizes this and (eventually) willingly cedes control to others, acknowledging, as a proto-republican thinker, that he needs an order to overrule him.[39] As James Harrington would put it much later, "'Give us good men and they will make us good laws' is the maxim of a demagogue . . . But 'give us good orders, and they will make us good men' is the maxim of a legislator and the most infallible in politics."[40] According to the long tradition of republican thinking in the British Isles, from George Buchanan to its full fruition mid-century, individuals by nature are simply too subject to tyrannical passion for absolutism to work. Unless checked by law, this tyranny will necessarily manifest itself in government, as we saw it manifest in *The Winter's Tale*'s Sicilia. Buchanan believes that any monarch's susceptibility to passion renders him unfit for absolute rule: "because we fear he be not firme enough against inordinat affections, which may, and for the most part use to decline men from truth," Buchanan writes, "we shall adjoyn to him the Law, as it were a Colleague, or rather a bridler of his lusts."[41]

All rulers, Prospero included, must be limited by legal structures that they cannot alter according to whim. Such structures help protect subjects from arbitrary interference—which, for those under Prospero's control, is more terrifying than Leontes's inept tyranny in extending indefinitely, such that one could be immobilized and totally controlled, body and mind utterly overthrown. For Buchanan, men will not respect each other's boundaries on their own. Stoic optimism about self-mastery being wildly unrealistic, Prospero needs someone like Buchanan to alter the island's government and, in time, its ruler's own inner order.

The Tempest may ratify not only the notion that absolute rule fails to bridle passion but also the idea that such rule actively incites uncontrollable affect. Elliott Visconsi, taking Jordan's lead, argues this point in examining the relationship between Prospero and Caliban. Shakespeare, according to Visconsi, reveals Prospero and Caliban's sovereign-subject bond as too personal, too driven by passion, and thus far too unstable compared to the more abstract bonds that preceded Shakespeare and that would succeed him in modern constitutions.[42] There is a charge internal to the bond between Prospero and Caliban that dooms it—and the Jacobean conception of monarchy—to failure. Visconsi thus contends that in this late romance Shakespeare seems "a skeptical political theorist engaged explicitly in what has been called 'popular constitutionalism'" (3).

Read in *The Tempest*'s light, legal safeguards for freedom look particularly appealing. Shakespeare does seem to long for something like a republican world and possibly even for a popular constitution. The play's world would be less treacherous if certain negative freedoms existed and were respected, especially those regarding the body: freedom from Prospero's tyrannical, arbitrary will, or from the bodily incursion that Caliban would make in raping Miranda. This line of thinking meets obstacles, though, when we consider that Shakespeare populates his dramatic world with characters that seem singularly incapable of elaborating or living under constitutions that would foster these freedoms. I cannot imagine that Prospero, his dukedom restored, would encourage liberty in the Antonios who are his subjects or, even if he did, that these Antonios would allow virtue to flourish. Caliban, presumably, will be left on the island—the bond between him and Prospero having been severed—and does Shakespeare expect readers to imagine any workable bond between the two?

We have to look far beyond the play—and do more than merely imagine how Prospero might respond to *hypomnemata*—in order to answer positively. One could suggest that the play is full of bad men because they live under bad orders, and that a good order—a republican one—would make good men, ones made incapable of dangerous passions, if not in Prospero's generation then perhaps in Ferdinand and Miranda's. While such transformation might be possible, and might indeed bring freedom, the play certainly does not mandate or even encourage such an interpretation. Prospero would be free if he were transformed and made master of his passions; his subjects would be free if law could transform men. Shakespeare remains skeptical about whether practices of the self or of the state could accomplish this, infusing the play with passions strong enough to burst apart even the most virtuous order. Freedom as rational self-government—at either level—is attractive but exceedingly hard to attain.

Liberty and Love: Ferdinand and Miranda

For *The Tempest*'s characters to be free, their relation to passion would need to be transformed, and so far no transformation has taken place. Ferdinand and Miranda, though, may stand as the exception to this rule. Their love, which institutes an overpowering, transformative passion, is innocuous and, at least arguably, more than a little liberating. It could be that the question, for Shakespeare, is not (or at least not only) about whether freedom might be achieved by subduing affect but also about sorting passion that liberates from passion that is tyrannical. We might be barred from freedom by anger and delivered to it by love. Love might realize the transformation that politics and classical practices of the self never could.

Newly reminded (in song) of his drowned father Alonso, Ferdinand beholds Miranda for the first time. He exclaims over her (1.2.426). Prospero, as is his wont, accuses Ferdinand of treason, then paralyzes him, and Ferdinand—despite declaring his resolve to resist just a moment before—seems suddenly to mind neither his paralysis nor his father's apparent death. Raptures free him from all worldly cares save one. Utter attachment to Miranda makes him otherwise Stoic, detached from and unperturbed by all else. She so enthralls his heart that being literally enthralled by Prospero becomes a matter of total indifference. "Come on, obey!" Prospero cries. "Thy nerves are in their infancy again / And have no vigor in them" (1.2.486–7). "So they are," Ferdinand agrees, his pugnacity all gone:

> My spirits, as in a dream, are all bound up.
> My father's loss, the weakness which I feel,
> The wrack of all my friends, nor this man's threats
> To whom I am subdued, are but light to me,
> Might I but through my prison once a day
> Behold this maid. All corners else o' th' earth
> Let liberty make use of. Space enough
> Have I in such a prison. (1.2.487–94)

Assuming Ferdinand speaks truly, he lodges major claims about love's power to liberate. Literally enslaved, newly burdened by grief, it is hard to imagine circumstances less conducive to the freedom he claims to have. Yet he claims that love lifts him out of the given, makes him anew, changes his outlook—his ways of perceiving, of creating value and meaning—completely. Here is freedom. Love brings it into being and does so in an instant, and not just for an instant, as when quayside ecstasies briefly free Othello from all cares. Love differs from practices of the self and state in its suddenness, its separation from the exercise of will, and its indifference to freedom as free movement. The freedom Prospero promises to Ariel conjures purely, freely willed movement, while the complex liberty of Stoic self-control conjures not only self-directed movement but also the stilling by the self of an unruly internal object. Ferdinand's freedom exists at an even further remove from free movement, freed as he is through an absolutely overpowering transformation. Ferdinand invites us to think of this instantaneous enchantment as liberty.

Shakespeare, however, induces caution about taking Ferdinand at his word. Though Ferdinand changes in being no longer enslaved by grief over Alonso's supposed death and even by literal slavery, he also changes in being newly inarticulate, unable to say just what he means.[43] His first words—ones we read before he meets Miranda—are relatively composed:

> Where should this music be? I' th' air or th' earth?
> It sounds no more; and sure it waits upon
> Some god o' th' island. Sitting on a bank,
> Weeping again the king my father's wrack,
> This music crept by me upon the waters,
> Allaying both their fury and my passion
> With its sweet air. Thence I have followed it,
> Or it hath drawn me rather; but 'tis gone.
> No, it begins again. (1.2.388–96)

Being led by Ariel's song allays Ferdinand's passion, and when we meet him, he is eloquent. When he encounters Prospero and Miranda, though, Ferdinand's speech becomes so tangled that what he utters runs contrary to what he tries to convey; his use of the negative *nor*—"nor this man's threats . . . / are but light to me" (ll. 489–90)—makes his misfortunes sound burdensome, not light, even though the next four lines make clear that Ferdinand meant to indicate just the opposite.

Those four lines themselves are peculiar. Ferdinand speaks of liberty in lines 492–3 as though it is a thing that makes use of space, rather than a capacity made use of by individuals in space. Yet lines 493–4 suggest that he considers himself a free agent; prison affords sufficient space provided that it permit a glimpse of Miranda. Ferdinand knows not what he says, whereas earlier he could qualify his speech and convey thought precisely ("Thence I have followed it, / Or it hath drawn me rather; but 'tis gone. / No, it begins again" [ll. 394–6]). We might be tempted to say that Prospero's spell, not Miranda's enchantment, induces these lexical difficulties, and we might be tempted to link them with sovereign power's perniciousness. Only the difficulties persist long after Prospero releases Ferdinand from his paralysis. In 3.1, he remains unable to express himself properly:

> I am, in my condition,
> A prince, Miranda; I do think, a king
> (I would not so), and would no more endure
> This wooden slavery than to suffer
> The flesh fly blow my mouth. Hear my soul speak!
> The very instant that I saw you, did
> My heart fly to your service; there resides,
> To make me slave to it; and for your sake
> Am I this patient log-man. (3.1.59–67)

Ferdinand (maybe) says that death is preferable to slavery, though the formulation itself ("flesh fly blow my mouth") is quite difficult. As editors suggest, he may be saying that if it were not for Miranda, he would rather his corpse be devoured by flies than endure servitude. But it is just as easy, and just as sensible, really, simply to be entangled by the language. Further along, Ferdinand—again, in words that call attention to themselves—describes falling in love as his heart flying to Miranda's service rather than to Miranda herself. Presumably Ferdinand intends the latter; after all, he says that he is a patient log-man for Miranda's sake, not for the sake of her service. His words, though, force us to consider what it might mean for Ferdinand to fly to another's service, and then to reside in that service. The unintentional sexual pun is hard to ignore. Here, Ferdinand makes Orlando's horrendous verse in Arden sound like Shakespeare's sonnets.

Ferdinand claims to have found freedom in and through captivity, in total servitude and through passion's throes. For some reason, Shakespeare conveys the claim in unintentional, inappropriate words. Despite this, David Evett and David Schalkwyk argue that Ferdinand and Miranda's love expresses an important freedom, one found in intentional, devoted service. Evett contends that Shakespeare is acutely concerned "to underscore the subjective phenomenology of this transformation of service into freedom—or perhaps, more accurately, the discovery of freedom in service."[44] When Ferdinand wills rather than opposes life as a log-man, he achieves an ideal not of Stoic or merely courtly but, supposedly, of Christian liberty, one articulated in the Pauline epistles. Can we reconcile this lofty interpretation of Ferdinand's love with the inept language that conveys it—with what Schalkwyk calls "very inattentive grasping for the most obvious cliché"?[45]

Evett remarks that establishing Christian liberty involves instituting "volitional primacy," the willed transformation of what happens to us into what we have taken on by choice. In Ferdinand's case, this means willingly allowing Prospero to injure him rather than merely enduring injury.[46] Ferdinand asserts that this has taken place: that he in fact prefers log-bearing servitude to the alternative. In his conversion narrative, the old self would throw off his chains, bludgeon Prospero, or perish in the attempt. Now, in the aftermath of Miranda's appearance, which has transformed him with idolatrous grace, he embraces his captivity. As Luther would put it, he is at once "a perfectly free lord of all, subject to none" except the one who has saved him, and "a perfectly dutiful servant of all, subject to all," able to willingly and even cheerfully accept any adversity thrust upon him.[47]

But if Ferdinand's failure to control his language is inseparable, as I think it is, from his attempt to establish volitional primacy, then the language serves to satirize the attempt. In love's grips, Ferdinand cannot even articulate ideas clearly, let alone establish control over what holds him. His wish to demonstrate free choice yields garbled, embarrassing clichés that seem evidence of internal struggle, not triumphant freedom. Ferdinand's will is the enemy of self-transformation rather than its instrument. The grab for volitional primacy—the will to remain sovereign and self-identical, to be the prince he has always been, even when enchanted and enthralled—puts liberty out of reach.

Ferdinand's obliviousness to this grows most flagrant just after Miranda proposes to him. When she asks if Ferdinand will be her husband, he says "Ay, with a heart as willing / As bondage e'er of freedom.

Here's my hand" (3.1.88–9). In offering his hand to Miranda, Ferdinand declares that it is by his will that he is and shall be bound to her, but we know that the bond is hardly voluntary. "At the first sight," Prospero observes earlier, "They have changed eyes . . . They are both in either's pow'rs" (1.2.441–2, 451). They have exchanged eyes, not hands, the suggestion being that each apprehends the world through the other's outlook, having undergone a drastic, unsettling re- and disorientation. Deprived of bounded, discrete self-conceptions, each exists in subjection to the other. Love, as we saw in *Othello*, is a phenomenon of non-sovereignty, and insofar as there is consent—here and elsewhere in *The Tempest*, for good and for ill—that consent cannot be reduced to the simple voluntarism claimed by Ferdinand. When Ariel puts Alonso, Gonzalo and others to sleep, Antonio remarks that "They fell together all, as by consent. / They dropped as by a thunderstroke" (2.1.202–3). This is an apt image of consent in this play, being as it is more akin to the strike of lightning than to the considered offer of a hand.[48]

Shakespeare's handling of Ferdinand carries one of two implications for the play: that Ferdinand has not found freedom in loving servitude, or that freedom cannot be found in such servitude. Relatedly, Shakespeare criticizes either Christian liberty, at least as Evett understands it, or the freedom offered by love, at least as Ferdinand understands it. I will say, first, that Ferdinand's situation seems to me like Christian liberty only in broad terms. We saw in the previous chapter how Christian liberty consists first and foremost in being freed from the curse of God's law, which, in the absence of grace, solicits its own transgression yet which also, after the inception of grace, fosters willing obedience. Early modern doctrines of Christian liberty depend on skepticism about the capacity of fallen humanity to achieve freedom either through classical practices of the self or through the institution of law, which on their own simply show the infinite distances separating us from righteousness. The foundation of Christian liberty consists not in free exercise of self-control, as it does for Stoics; such control is at best an effect of freedom, not its essence. Rather, freedom is first freedom from the automatism of selfhood in its given state of sinfulness, a state wherein life is defined by perceiving boundaries and automatically transgressing them. Christian liberty has at its core natality, being freed by being made new.[49]

While certain aspects of Ferdinand's situation fit the aforementioned description, his assertion of liberty fails to fit for a range of reasons.

Among them are the facts that (1) he is under Prospero's law, not God's; (2) that particular law solicits transgression immediately *after* the moment of "grace," understood here as his being enraptured by Miranda; (3) his willing, cheerful obedience, when it comes, comes because of Miranda's beauty, not because of the lawgiver's grace; and (4) if Ferdinand is freed from the old self and made new, he is freed not by God but by an idol. Within the world of *The Tempest,* the closer analogue to doctrines of Christian liberty could be found in Prospero's attempt to convict his malefactors' consciences and to then liberate them in an act of grace. As Berger points out, this attempt fails stupendously.[50] To understand the case of Ferdinand, we have to foreground that the inception of grace for him is not like that of Saul of Tarsus—of one arrested by God's voice on the road to Damascus—but that of a young man enraptured by his beloved. These forms of grace bear similar structure in that an event frees them from the determinants of a situation (Saul from his obsessive persecuting, Ferdinand from his grief-stricken state), but the similarities do not extend much further. Through Ferdinand and Miranda, Shakespeare explores whether terrestrial love has the power to liberate, not whether God does.[51]

Through his portrayal of Ferdinand and Miranda, Shakespeare seems skeptical about the grace of terrestrial love and especially about whether love can extinguish the willfulness that rules out transformative freedom for Ferdinand.[52] Other plays by Shakespeare might well evince more optimism about the transformative liberty of love, though not to the degree that Ferdinand suggests. In *Othello,* for instance, we glimpse the hero's relinquishment of his will in Desdemona's ("I will deny thee nothing!"), but this is neither transformative (Othello asks to be left to himself) nor liberating; it is felt as a burden. In *The Winter's Tale,* Shakespeare makes greater allowances: when the statue-event transports Leontes, his infinitizing offer of a hand does suggest the giving over of his will to another. Yet, as we have seen, the event of love divides the subject, depriving Leontes of the triumphant certitudes to which Ferdinand falsely lays claim. Love fails to turn Ferdinand from princeliness to true humility and from self-will to will lost in someone else. Instead, love frees him only from his grief; his will overrules, which leads to further self-assertion. Ferdinand stubbornly insists on preserving his pre-shipwrecked, sovereign self, such that his initial defiance of Prospero and subsequent paralysis come to symbolize the self-defeating nature of his self-will—its inability to achieve its aims and its ironic capacity to end in self-enslavement. Ferdinand, in some deep sense, will always be frozen, unfree, as unchanging and predictable in his willfulness as he is in the bearing of logs.

Sublime Freedom: Caliban's Dream

In its treatment of freedom, *The Tempest* elaborates a structure that alternates between slight satisfaction and major frustration. Shakespeare proposes a set of possibilities as to what freedom might be—pursuit of self-interest, Stoic self-sufficiency, republican self-government, the new life achieved in *eros*—but mostly so as to undermine them, to subject them to withering doubt. *The Tempest* is Shakespeare's broadest and most developed testing ground for freedom, yet the results thus far have been terribly inconclusive.

We have not yet considered Caliban, so it may be no surprise to read that the freedom most worthy of the name is one that can be found in him. He, like Ferdinand, like Prospero—like almost all of the play's characters—speaks with unmistakable passion. Unlike either Prospero or Ferdinand, his freedom is often understood to exist not in power over the external world, or in love's charmed circle, but simply in speech, in passionate utterances that he controls and uses to his advantage. Prospero fails completely to interpellate his slave, who, when we meet him, possesses clear linguistic facility. He seems at least Prospero's equal when they come to verbal blows, advancing claims for possession of the isle and for his mistreatment. In these moments, to be free he, unlike Prospero, need not eradicate passion, and unlike Ferdinand, need not merely give in to it. Caliban harnesses passion, uses it to clear a space for freedom. Norbrook encapsulates the arguments of many when he remarks that "Caliban's subjectivity is not just passively determined by discourse" and that his "exchanges with Prospero enact his resistance by means of a grammatical rebellion."[53] Here, to stand in free relation to passion is to achieve one's ends by way of that passion.

I also regard Caliban's freedom as one realized through words, though it is realized rather differently than in Norbrook's account. I want to focus not on Caliban's fearless, oppositional speech, which, for a reason set out below, Shakespeare does not present as particularly liberating. Rather, I want to focus on a freedom that manifests itself in a startling linguistic sublimity. This freedom emerges, so far as I can tell, in but a single speech. When Ariel frightens Stephano and Trinculo by playing a tune invisibly, Caliban comforts them:

> Be not afeard: the isle is full of noises,
> Sounds and sweet airs that give delight and hurt not.
> Sometimes a thousand twangling instruments
> Will hum about mine ears; and sometime voices
> That, if I then had waked after long sleep,
> Will make me sleep again; and then, in dreaming,
> The clouds methought would open and show riches
> Ready to drop upon me, that, when I waked,
> I cried to dream again. (3.2.134–42)

The speech describes extreme, exquisite subjection. Prospero encircles his slave with sound, exercising control over as basic a bodily function as sleep. Caliban's very dream—its agonizing offer and withdrawal of wealth—may be a function of Prospero's manipulations, and it may even be that the manipulations incite a desire to be coerced into sleep once more.

When we consider what Caliban says as a speech-act, though, it suggests liberty. After all, he opens by establishing that he is—and that Stephano and Trinculo ought to be—free from fear, and he urges his companions on to murder. The speech's first three words, urging bold fearlessness, thus are of a piece with Caliban's earlier acts of *parrhesia*. We know, from his fractiousness in 1.2, that Caliban is hardly servile—this, despite Prospero's extensive control over his slave's body and psychology. We now also know of Caliban's capacity for emotional sensitivity and sublime utterance, sublimity to which I will return in a moment.

First we must establish what the dream means, since the status of its sublimity depends upon this meaning. The first question to ask—in terms Shakespeare would have understood—is whether Caliban's dream is a true or a vain one. According to Thomas Hill, following many others, true dreams foretell future events, while vain dreams do not.[54] Classifying Caliban's dream at first seems easy. Hill details a lengthy list of dream-objects that could signify riches: stars, teeth, rain, bread, a father's head propped in a lion's mouth (!). He does not indicate what riches themselves signify, but we might say that for Caliban, riches signify riches. He wants and cannot have them, just as he wants and cannot ever have prosperity in waking life. If we extend to Caliban a minimal figurative capacity and speculate that riches signify Miranda's bare flesh, Prospero's books of magic, or something of that sort, the dream still seems vain. He is no more likely to obtain any of these things than to happen upon a chest brimming with wealth. In crying to dream again, and to lust after what he can never have, Caliban displays radical unfreedom, shows that he is, as some have argued, even more enslaved to passion than Prospero himself.[55]

And yet Caliban never sees riches in his dream. He sees clouds. He thinks that these clouds on opening will drop riches on him. The appropriate interpretive question, then, is probably not "How can we understand the riches in Caliban's dream?" but "How well did Caliban understand the clouds?" He sees clouds, expects treasure. We know that he never obtains this wealth, but we have to ask if his dreaming self glossed the clouds wrongly—if covetousness colors his mental process. Ought he, on the basis of their appearance, to have anticipated great cramps instead of gold coins?

Were we to prevail upon Thomas Hill for interpretive aid, he would require additional information. What, he would ask, was the hue of the clouds in question? Dark clouds "signifyeth . . . hindraunce of actions sorowes and heauines of mynde"; "white cloudes," on the other hand, "be signifyers of a happier estate."[56] Were Caliban's clouds dark or light? He does not say, and Hill, as Shakespeare would like, would be at a loss. Portraying a dream that seems at once terribly obvious and totally obscure, Shakespeare forecloses readerly ability to draw warranted conclusions about whether the dream foretells a future event, since he leaves unclear what sort of event would be foretold. By Hill's early modern standards, we cannot discern the dream's vanity or truth.

Perhaps Hill's terms are not the right ones for adjudicating Caliban's dream and thus for discerning whether or not passion makes him unfree. Not only Hill's, but also Montaigne's skeptical perspective on dream interpretation might have informed Shakespeare's portrayal. Montaigne writes that he would "rather regulate my affairs by the chance of the dice than by such dreams"; besides, he has "enough to do digesting the present" that he will not waste time "anticipating future things."[57] Montaigne dismisses the tradition of dream interpretation in which Hill works. Yet when Montaigne queries how we are tormented by our opinions of things rather than by things themselves, he remarks that the soul, "sovereign mistress of our condition and conduct," "profits from everything without distinction," which means that "[e]rror and dreams serve it usefully, being suitable stuff for giving us security and contentment."[58] Putting dreams at the soul's disposal—for safety and contentment rather than divination—allows us to follow nature rather than "abandon ourselves to the vagabond freedom of our fantasies" (46). We cannot divine truth with dreams, but with them we may induce peace of mind. Montaigne views dreams skeptically, but not cynically or dismissively.

Shakespeare's view of Caliban's dream resembles Montaigne's, with one important difference. Like Montaigne's dreams, Caliban's dream has non-predictive value. Recounting the dream brings not a promised future but present comfort, which Caliban means to extend to his new companions. Recounting the dream also frees Caliban from fear and from the reactivity—the interminable circuit of obedience and transgression—that defines his everyday life. Montaigne would, I think, admire relaying dreams as a practice of freedom. Freedom from fear and from a purely reactive form of life delivers Caliban to a new linguistic freedom, one distinguishable from the *parrhesia* described by other critics. *Parrhesia* is tactical invective, and, in this play (though certainly not in general), seems to me subsumed within a framework of subversion and containment so predictable as to bar Caliban from any profound freedom. Richard Strier reminds us, lest we forget, that when Caliban turns against Prospero in favor of Stephano and then sings of freedom, "his conception of freedom . . . seems to consist in getting a 'new master'"—seems, that is, simply to involve more slavery.[59] Caliban speaking of his dream, by contrast, seems to me a rupture in the text, one for which Shakespeare leaves readers, and even Caliban himself, wholly unprepared. Unlike the use of dreams that Montaigne counsels, then, Caliban's recounting seems beyond his control. Because the speech is so unlike his other discourse, I rather think Caliban, too, must be overcome by the surprising, sublime generosity of being that wells up in him.

The speech includes all five of what Longinus calls the "fountains" of sublime expression: "grandeur in the conceptions"; "emotion, of the vehement and uncontrollable kind"; "the appropriate molding of figures"; "the use of dignified language"; and "an admirable and majestic general structure or manner of composition."[60] The language of Caliban's dream "like a thunderbolt scatter[s] all in its way" (3). By the time I reach "I cried to dream again," Caliban seems not only free of fear but free even of his present machinations. As Jennifer Lewin puts it, "we are watching Caliban come as close as any Shakespearean character does to creating the very circumstances he describes."[61] The intent with which he begins, to steel his companions in their quest for power, is swept up and washed away. So whereas the speech begins in the domain of willed self-control—and yet arguably is determined by Caliban's circumstances—by the time he speaks of his cries, the whole of existence outside the speech, and perhaps even outside the line, has dissolved.[62] Caliban seems freed not only from fear or from predictable reaction, but from the given world altogether.[63] This eruption of poetic language, far beyond Caliban's grasp, liberates him from the elements of his situation, scatters those elements as would a thunderbolt.

Caliban cannot plan for this as he can for Prospero's demise. He cannot guarantee this freedom, nor could anyone else. For a moment such as this can never be guaranteed; the moment it could, it would cease to be freedom in that it could be foreseen, would reinforce, and be conditioned by, the speaking self in its given, preexistent, predictable state. The freedom evident in Caliban's speech can exist only if it simply arrives, independent of calculation.

Montaigne, if infrequently, acknowledges the existence of moments such as these. For all that he advises the use of discourse in order to cultivate self-control, Montaigne is aware not only that discourse can operate otherwise, but that it should. Montaigne writes of Cassius Severus, for example, that "he spoke better without having thought about what he was going to say . . . he owed more to fortune than to diligence."[64] Montaigne claims that he is of a similar disposition and even connects the event of unpremeditated speech to the experience of self-discovery. "I do not find myself in the place where I look," he writes; "I find myself more by chance encounter than by searching my judgment" (31). Caliban, likewise, finds himself—no different, for Montaigne, from finding his freest and best self—by chance.

Paradoxically, Caliban is freest (from the misery Prospero intends for him, from his own reactive responses) when he loses control over his language, when it no longer serves as the instrument by which he seeks to realize his designs. He finds himself, to borrow from Gonzalo and Montaigne, when he is not his own—when he is not Prospero's or Stephano's Caliban, nor even Caliban's Caliban; he becomes himself and is delivered to freedom when the event of sublime language creates him anew. In juxtaposing Caliban with his master, Shakespeare distinguishes between two forms of lost control: one that enslaves and another that liberates. When Prospero is in the grips of anger, he is an automaton, determined in the sense that Richard III is determined to play the villain, both resolved to act and unable to act except predictably. When Caliban is overcome by sublime raptures, though, he is beside himself in the best sense, given over to unpredictable ecstasy, surprised by joy, freed from his otherwise fixed existence.

Taken together, the cases of Caliban, Ferdinand, and Prospero show that freedom, for Shakespeare, is best—because first—understood as natality rather than as sovereignty. Freedom, in this play, is always a question of how one stands in relation to passion, and Shakespeare seems not to advocate any one such relation. With Prospero, classical practices of the self, aimed at reining passion in, would have brought freedom—however impossible the reining in seems—whereas Ferdinand thwarts his own freedom by insisting on sovereignty over passion. Caliban's moment of freedom comes from being overwhelmed by sublime emotion. What these otherwise disparate cases share is this: that the relation to passion is or could be liberating when that relation transforms the self. We have also encountered seemingly contradictory practices of freedom in Montaigne—for example, toughening the self as a Stoic from within and being bridled by custom from without. While I will not hazard any definitive pronouncement about so complex a thinker, Montaigne's practices also seem to involve change, whether by hardening one's susceptibility against the outside of self, or being stripped down, brought to realize one's dependence on that outside. Freedom's changes are perhaps less dramatic in Montaigne than Shakespeare suggests in *The Tempest*, but changes they remain.

The central point, the point at which Shakespeare's skepticism gives way to faith, is hard to avoid: that freedom from the given self—not mere freedom to self-direction—forms liberty's core in *The Tempest*. Freedom is being made new, whether through the work of the will, unlikely though this work seems, or irrespective of it. So Shakespeare casts doubt not only on the achievability of freedom as self-mastery but also, and more deeply, on the idea that freedom would preserve and protect the given self. This is why Shakespeare severs freedom not from will, entirely, but from self-assertion, the attempt to remain selfsame. Prospero seeks to preserve himself and his world by acting as he has acted. Passion prompts him; inconstancy is his constant, his core. Ferdinand, we have seen, is prompted by princeliness. Both remain unfree, determined by and enslaved to already existing wishes and structures of self. Only transformation would bring freedom. So the most apt image for freedom in *The Tempest* is not the image put forth by cognitive science—that of a stable self moving through space—but that of selves destabilized, undergoing drastic change. Freedom arrives, if it arrives, in this change. Such freedom cannot be perfectly predicted. Since freedom involves our noncoincidence with our preexistent self, it is intrinsic to freedom that its exact parameters and effects be unknown in advance.

In this commitment to what cannot be known, this fidelity to skepticism, *The Tempest* resembles our other texts of focus. In *Lucrece*, we best negotiate the mind-body problem when we regard it as finally insoluble. Othello loves best when acknowledging that he cannot say what he should expect of it, while Leontes behaves best when he embraces unclear ethical standing. In *The Tempest*, freedom is likeliest not as a possession or even as an ability but in openness to suffering change, to the self's uncertain future.

In his own account of suffering's meaning, Orgel perceptively reads Ariel's song to Ferdinand about his father's alterations on the ocean floor. Orgel argues that the song gives us a way to understand *The Tempest*'s central dynamic, and the crucial lines of Ariel's are these:

> Full fathom five thy father lies;
> Of his bones are coral made;
> Those are pearls that were his eyes;
> Nothing of him that doth fade
> But doth suffer a sea change
> Into something rich and strange. (1.2.397–402)

Orgel writes of Ariel's song what seems to me an insightful, even staggering paragraph about what Shakespeare's late romance tries to accomplish. "His song," Orgel writes,

> is about nature becoming art; and in it, disaster and death involve not decay and loss, but a transformation into something wonderful, something almost directly opposite to loss, tremendous richness. And the word for that transformation is *suffer* . . . In Ariel's song we begin to be aware that the whole concept of *suffering* is now undergoing a sea-change. It is not being diminished at all, but we are seeing it from a different viewpoint, whereby the endurance of violence and destruction leaves us infinitely richer. That richness has

been taken perfectly literally by the song; the drowned man has become a work of art, and the transformation has been effected by the art of the figure who has suffered most, and whose very name conveys the richness he embodies: Prospero.[65]

I differ with Orgel in his characterization of Prospero, and the difference affects my thinking about freedom. Orgel is crucially right, though, to observe that suffering change and transformation, in *The Tempest*, can mean being left infinitely rich. What the above account has sought to add, in part, is the insight that to suffer such change is to experience freedom. We like to—indeed, perhaps cannot help but—think of freedom as the movement of a stable, sovereign self through a space over which the self has mastery, as Prospero has over his island. Shakespeare, by contrast, attends not to how freedom is action of the self on the world, but to how it can be action on the self, working on oneself and, even more so, being worked upon until a new self emerges.

To the extent that Shakespeare privileges natality over sovereignty, he might be said to share with Hannah Arendt, the preeminent theorist of natality, and even Foucault. For Arendt, seeking sovereignty thwarts freedom; doing so not only turns the question of freedom into a mere question of free will but also equates freedom with the power to impose one's will.[66] Arendt argues that freedom once consisted and should consist in action, activity that interrupts life's automatic processes, an inception of the genuinely new. Foucault's account of certain forms of Cynic *parrhesia*, on which I have not dwelt here, shares with Arendt in its emphasis on action's creative dimensions, but even the Stoic freedom outlined by Foucault identifies freedom first with natality in that Stoic practices aim for a conversion to self; the inward turn is a striving to be gradually transformed, to approach one's best self step by disciplined step.[67] Indeed, will and natality, despite Arendt's devaluing of the former, connect both in her work and in the later Foucault. Both, like Shakespeare, deny that free will is the essence or true end of freedom; both, unlike Shakespeare, nevertheless imagine natality that always depends upon willed effort—for Arendt, the willed disclosure of the self in public space, and for Foucault, the willed approach to the self in inner space.

In *The Tempest*, the connection between freedom and will is more tenuous than in Arendt or Foucault's accounts, however much care both take to forge connections that are less than ironclad. This tenuousness in *The Tempest*, it should be said, makes freedom seem especially ephemeral and impossible to guarantee. Realized freedom in the play is but brief, when it exists at all. Arendt herself observes that if freedom is natality and consists in action, then freedom lasts only as long as action itself. The way to make this freedom possible—to give it any guarantee—is to keep public space open and so foster opportunities for interrupting automatism, for beginning again. *The Tempest* offers no such guarantee and evinces a less determinate sense of freedom's conduits. One could only hope to see what freedom is, to be skeptical of the given self and open to alteration, to finding one's way to free existence or being simply delivered to liberty. Shakespeare goes no further.

Conclusion: Gonzalo, Imagination, and Autonomy

The Tempest would seem to resist the preceding account on at least one point. The problem might be formulated as follows: if freedom is first freedom from the given, what is Gonzalo's thoroughly discredited speech about utopia doing in Shakespeare's text? After all, Gonzalo's utopian vision is full of liberation from life as it was given in Shakespeare's England. It is utterly unlike life on the island or in Milan, and even only somewhat like what we find in Shakespeare's source, Montaigne's "Of cannibals."[68] "I'th commonwealth," Gonzalo explains,

> I would by contraries
> Execute all things; for no kind of traffic
> Would I admit; no name of magistrate;
> Letters should not be known; riches, poverty,
> And use of service, none; contract, succession,
> Bourn, bound of land, tilth, vineyard, none;
> No use of metal, corn, or wine, or oil;
> No occupation; all men idle, all;
> And women too, but innocent and pure;
> No sovereignty. (2.1.147–56)

Freedom from the given, as imagined by Gonzalo, conjures the vacuous conceptual world of Prospero's mountain winds. Gonzalo would eliminate an array of limits that inhibit literal and figurative freedom of movement: boundaries that establish possession and right-of-way; structures of authority signified by magistracy; constraining demands of occupation. Gonzalo would even exclude the limits imposed by language. If having "no sovereignty" denotes freedom from old forms of life, the new form's purely negative terms make idleness the only life imaginable. To be freed from the given world, Gonzalo shows us, can mean to go nowhere.

That Gonzalo pictures a world without sovereignty is especially odd in light of his strongly hierarchical worldview. In the opening and closing scenes alike, Gonzalo hopes to see the boatswain hanged for his insubordinate outburst, unable as he is to brook the boatswain's question: "What cares these roarers for the name of king?" (1.1.16–17, 57, 5.1.217–18). Gonzalo only articulates his vision of a world without sovereignty in order to enlighten his sovereign's drooping cheer, speaking in the hope that he will reinforce, not undermine Alonso's rule. Before outlining his utopia, Gonzalo remarks that "It is foul weather in us all, good sire, / When you are cloudy" and has just reprimanded Sebastian for speaking ungently—for "rub[bing] the sore / When you should bring the plaster" (2.1.138–42). For whatever reason, Gonzalo tries to free his king from overwhelming grief by picturing a kingless world, but he does not actually advocate—nor does Shakespeare quite satirize—freedom from the given. Gonzalo deploys an inept vision of such freedom so that Alonso might again feel kingly.

While we know that Shakespeare has borrowed from Montaigne, Gonzalo claims to have conjured this world on his own. Within the dramatic world, there exists no reason to think that he did not. Shakespeare's portrayal of Gonzalo is as much about, and as skeptical about, the power of autonomous imagination as it is about freedom in an imaginary state. Along these lines, I want to end by claiming that Gonzalo's vision of an idle world, an evacuated version of Montaigne's own account, is the product of an idle mind, more akin to what we see at work through Ariel than what we see through Caliban. Criticism often focuses on Shakespeare's erasure of the source for Gonzalo's utopia as evidence of the playwright's surreptitious appropriation and cultural cannibalism. To me, Shakespeare's aim seems not so much to arrogate imaginative autonomy to himself as to interrogate whether such autonomy has worth.

Montaigne's essay on cannibalism is the text most frequently taken up to highlight the otherwise dim outlines of Gonzalo's utopia, but the essay on idleness is equally illuminating. There, Montaigne writes that minds ought to be kept "busy with some definite subject that will bridle and control them"; otherwise "they throw themselves in disorder

hither and yon in the vague field of imagination." Montaigne contends
that idleness—and the totally unbounded thought it affords—leads not
to self-transformation but to the worst sort of self-loss. "The soul that
has no fixed goal," Montaigne insists, "loses itself; for as they say, to be
everywhere, is to be nowhere." In Gonzalo's case, nowhere is the world
elsewhere that his unencumbered mind extrudes. After remarking on
the appeal of being idle, Montaigne denounces how it begets in him
"many chimeras and fantastic monsters, one after another, without order or purpose."[69] In the "Apology," Montaigne catalogues imaginative
autonomy's costs for humankind:

> if it is true that he alone of all the animals has this freedom of
> imagination and this unruliness in thought that represents to him
> what is, what is not, what he wants, the false and the true, it is an
> advantage that is sold him very dear, and in which he has little cause
> to glory, for from it springs the principal source of the ills that
> oppress him: sin, disease, irresolution, confusion, despair.[70]

Gonzalo's idle mind draws the contours of a chimerical, insubstantial
commonwealth that nevertheless oppresses those around him. *The
Tempest* hardly advocates the mind's free play or the imagination's unconstrained generation of worlds. Shakespeare's reservation is not
with freedom from the given but with such freedom when it emerges
out of free (in this case, inner) movement. Shakespeare here extends
the skepticism evident in his presentation of Prospero's vow to Ariel, here
figured through Gonzalo's unbounded yet empty flight of imagination.
In this, Shakespeare eschews the imaginative autonomy celebrated by
Sidney in his *Defence of Poesy*. Sidney writes that the poet, "lifted up
with the vigor of his own invention,

> doth grow in effect another nature, in making things either better
> than Nature bringeth forth, or, quite anew, forms such as never were
> in Nature, as the Heroes, Demigods, Cyclops, Chimeras, Furies, and
> such like: so as he goeth hand in hand with Nature, not enclosed
> within the narrow warrant of her gifts, but freely ranging only within
> the zodiac of his own wit.[71]

Whereas Sidney celebrates imaginative freedom as the wit's freely rang-
ing, Shakespeare—at least in *The Tempest*—regards it as specious, empty.
Where Sidney sees an autonomous imagination "making things" either
better than those in nature or wholly absent from nature, in total freedom from the given, Gonzalo in his autonomy makes nothing but

trouble, and nothing of aesthetic merit. I mentioned earlier that in cultivating freedom, Prospero might become more like a work of art, and with Ferdinand and Caliban there also is a link between freedom and aesthetic existence. In being freed from his quotidian existence Caliban becomes, for a moment, nothing other than sublime utterance. If not for his willfulness, the same might have occurred for Ferdinand; his log-bearing might have become a thing of beauty. Exploring the point in depth would be distracting now, but I should at least note that in this play, freedom—true freedom—would not confer the ability to create art autonomously, a mere glimpse of which Prospero's masque affords us. Rather, being steeped in an unknown liberty turns the subject into an aesthetic object wondrous to behold.

In considering Gonzalo's imagination, Shakespeare could not help but also consider his own. We sometimes think of Shakespeare as a—even the—truly autonomous artist, limited neither by early modern censorship nor by early modern forms of thought. He does what we cannot, makes something out of nothing, makes being free as mountain winds into a productive enterprise. Yet Shakespeare doubts the power of autonomous imagination to effect the uncertain transformations that he associates with freedom and with an aesthetic existence. Autonomy in this play is another word for emptiness, the curse of being free as mountain winds, whether in the outer world or in the domain of imagination. The aesthetic dominion we ascribe to Shakespeare would, in the world of *The Tempest*, make him a king most unfree, sovereign over nothing.

CHAPTER 5

Looking Two Ways at Once in *Timon of Athens*

I n this book I have considered how, in reading Shakespeare, there emerge skeptical practices that pertain to issues of living: of love, of ethics, and freedom, of body and mind. I want to end, though, by thinking more directly about reading practice itself and about the cognitive value of reading Shakespeare. In particular, I show how the skepticism of *Timon of Athens* induces a wrenching yet rewarding disorientation, a distinctly readerly humility. Much as loving well, being free, and behaving ethically become most possible when our openness means that we lack mastery, so reading Shakespeare becomes most valuable when we lack mastery of the text and accept how the text masters us.

It seems strange to ground the value of reading Shakespeare by way of *Timon*. Though recent scholarship tends not to focus on aesthetic merit, William Empson speaks for many critics in remarking that "[n]obody pretends that *Timon* is a very good play."[1] Nobody pretends this, partly, because *Timon* is full of flat characters, none of whom have the complex interiority of even Richard II, let alone that of Hamlet;[2] if, as Anthony Dawson claims, a character needs to project a "feeling of depth and inscrutability" in order truly to be a character, then no figure in the play, Timon included, really qualifies.[3] *Timon* itself falls short in being structurally disjointed—"strikingly bipolar"—as Coppélia Kahn puts it,[4] lacking the cohesion of the mature tragedies; even an apologist such as A. D. Nuttall admits that "*Timon of Athens* is not, to put it mildly, a polished piece."[5] To worsen matters, Shakespeare likely wrote *Timon* in collaboration with Thomas Middleton. So: in a book that treats canonical masterpieces such as *Hamlet*, *Othello*, and *The Tempest*, why vindicate reading Shakespeare with recourse to a collaborative, psychologically shallow, and aesthetically poor work?

First, as Nuttall points out, *Timon* is a particularly "readerly" text, one "which exists, most crucially, on the page, rather than—say—in the implied stage performance" (3).[6] *Timon*, as far as we know, was not staged while Shakespeare lived and is fitting for an approach centered on reading experience.[7] Despite the play's lack of polish, Nuttall avers that *Timon's* "intellectual movement is indeed almost Euclidian . . . The play," he remarks, "is like a procession, sculptured in relief, to be apprehended serially before the underlying intellectual structure is realised in the mind" (xxii). I agree with Nuttall that *Timon* is readerly in nature and serial in design, but I will argue that the play's movement is hardly Euclidean, is instead exceedingly difficult to picture in "the mind's eye." *Timon's* two major sections (the first in Athens, the other in the wild) do not fit together like two sides of a triangle that the reader, having reached the end of the text, can connect. If the structure that Nuttall describes could be pictured as we picture a geometrical figure, to me the play's two parts compose a whole that—to *Timon's* credit—cannot be comprehended with clarity. To achieve clarity would be like superimposing the semi-transparent image of one world upon another and losing central features of both. Resisting frames that bring the play into focus, *Timon* casts doubt on whether the understanding that reading brings can be captured best by metaphors of clear vision.

Second, the "strikingly bipolar" aspect of the play is precisely the aspect that makes *Timon's* skepticism most interesting and cognitively rich. This bipolarity prompts me not so much to pathologize Timon (or diagnose *Timon*) but to be open to reading experiences that feel considerably twisted. Whether or not *Timon* is unfinished or a collaborative work, the play's divided structure creates two challenges for the skeptical self: one about whether reading skeptically means seeing through doubtful appearances to concealed truths, and another about whether reading should strengthen the reader's sense of his or her interpretive ability.

Timon, the next two sections show, presents opposed worlds—an Athenian one defined by scarcity and a wild one defined by superabundance. In each world, Shakespeare seems to urge a specific form of doubt. In Athens, that doubt is of the trustworthiness of others, suggesting the need to be possessive, calculating, and insistent about boundaries. In the wild, doubt shifts to boundaries themselves, to whether they have value and whether possessiveness is at all necessary. In the end, however, the play urges a third, distinctly skeptical—and largely a

Pyrrhonist—form of doubt. The play is Pyrrhonist, we will see, in placing these visions in equipollence (*isothenia*) as well as in prompting suspension of judgment (*epochē*), but departs from Pyrrhonism in yielding just the opposite of unperturbedness (*ataraxia*). Reading *Timon* elicits a disorienting attempt to look two ways at once, an attempt that leaves the reader feeling incapacitated but that nevertheless repays time and attention.

The value I derive from reading *Timon*, then, does not count among the values often attributed to reading literature in general and to reading Shakespeare in particular (described more fully later in this chapter): that his work clarifies our sense of ourselves, of others, and of the world; heartens us about human capacity for insight and invention; sharpens our ability to appreciate and solve complex problems of ethics and politics; and furnishes us with aesthetic satisfactions that compensate for quotidian existence. While other Shakespearean texts might offer some, most, or even all of these things, *Timon* offers me none, save in a degraded sense. The experience of reading *Timon*—of trying to look two ways at once—offers only the most vexed pleasure. The play's skepticism scrambles my sense of myself, unsettles grounds for ethical action, and impairs my capacity for insight rather severely. Indeed, *Timon* yields cognitive frustration that is more total than my other texts of focus, yet it is just this frustration that makes the play worth reading. Other texts I treat might not yield certainties that increase our proficiency at living, but since these texts offer ways to cope with problems of living, they may smuggle a certain pseudo- or semi-practicality beneath a layer of impracticality. Reading *Timon*, by contrast, permits as stringent a test of epistemological weakness as I can imagine.

An Empty Coffer: Doubt in Athens

Shakespeare's portrayal of Athens makes a strong case for doubt about others and for a guarded, possessive relation to one's resources—a relation that Timon himself cannot fathom. The play's first act catalogues Timon's insane generosity—his lavish gatherings and his willingness to lend, unquestioningly, to all who ask. Of Timon's own excesses and total lack of possessiveness, an Athenian Senator says this:

> Still in motion
> Of raging waste? It cannot hold, it will not.

> If I want gold, steal but a beggar's dog
> And give it Timon—why, the dog coins gold;
> If I would sell my horse and buy twenty moe
> Better than he—why, give my horse to Timon;
> As nothing, give it him, it foals me straight
> And able horses. (2.1.3–10)[8]

Dogs coin gold; a male horse "foals." The economy of Athens, as Jody Greene points out, seems to be one "where things which ought not to procreate reproduce themselves, and do so exponentially."[9] Timon enables this illusion by being always—willingly—on the losing end, by choosing to lose as extravagantly as a thriving usurer might gain (176). Unlike life within a more moderate order, Timon's giving (until there is nothing left to give) and others' taking (all that he gives) produce a paradoxical, tragic economy, excessive consumption that is somehow never enough.[10] This economy is threatening—its waste so dire—because the Athenian world is one of limited resources, which everyone, except Timon, knows but does nothing to respect, instead taking advantage of his generosity in bloodthirsty fashion. Timon cannot keep giving, his "friends" cannot keep taking; resources run out, his generosity has no chance. He fails to listen to those (Flavius, his steward, and Apemantus, a cynic) who insist that the Athenians around him exploit, at his expense, the distinction between surfaces of friendship and depths of indifference, current prosperity and the poverty to come.

In portraying Athens, Shakespeare seems to endorse a doubt—hardly a thorough skepticism, but a doubt nevertheless. As critics often point out, credulity and extravagance such as Timon's caused definite concern at the time of the play's writing, early in the reign of James I—so much so that critics regard the king as *Timon*'s target. David Bevington and David Smith, for instance, note several qualities shared by Timon and James, among them "the epic scale of the giving" and "the lack of awareness on the part of the giver that disaster is lurking."[11] Other like-minded critics imagine Timon as an exaggerated James. Theodore Leinwand notes that James, unlike Timon, at least "was ready and able to deal, to negotiate, to work the economy."[12] Andrew Hadfield, similarly, reads *Timon* as an open critique of James's credulity and as a call to a more prudent political approach—a call to which James himself may well have been open were he exposed to the play.[13]

When critics set *Timon* in a Jacobean context, they regularly invoke an instructive episode in which Robert Cecil tempered James's extravagance toward Robert Carr, his favorite. To dissuade the king from lavishing twenty thousand pounds upon Carr, Cecil set out the sum in a chamber that James was sure to enter. Upon seeing the sum, James collapsed on the heap, claimed he never meant to give Carr nearly so much, then "scrabled" around to collect a small fraction of what he saw.[14] While the episode is possibly apocryphal, James's letters reveal repeated calls for a tightened household economy, suggesting that he could discern the truth of his situation. Carr's mere request for so great a sum might have concealed the request's enormity, but once Cecil sets the sum in front of him, James acknowledges folly. He does what Timon initially could not but what *Timon*'s readers can: he sees the flatterer lurking within the friend, sees how loving care could shade into recklessness.[15]

Timon himself fails to see through anything until it is far too late, and Flavius best captures the nature of the failure.[16] "'Tis pity bounty had not eyes behind," he laments, "[t]hat man might ne'er be wretched for his mind" (1.2.168–70). "What will this come to?" he continues,

> He commands us to provide, and give great gifts,
> And all out of an empty coffer.
> Nor will he know his purse or yield me this—
> To show him what a beggar his heart is,
> Being of no power to make his wishes good. (1.2.201–7)

If Timon could see the empty coffer his bounty has left him, he would know that he cannot make something out of nothing, cannot give from a void. He refuses to be shown what Flavius wants him so desperately to see but cannot entirely articulate: that he has given disastrously.

If Timon possessed doubt, he, like a doubtful reader, would soon also possess knowledge. After all, Flavius frames his criticism of Timon with a common metaphor for a rather confident epistemology. "'Tis pity bounty had not eyes behind" figures a pervasive metaphor described by cognitive scientists: "knowing is seeing." The metaphor's pervasiveness, in their accounts, derives from early childhood, when seeing and knowing often occur together and are therefore conflated. The example that George Lakoff and Mark Johnson use is " 'Let's see what's in the box,' " where seeing what's in the box correlates with knowing what's in the box.[17] (As Flavius sees it, Timon himself needs only a child's discernment: "Let's see what's in the coffer.") Early experience makes the "knowing is seeing" metaphor almost inevitable, and whatever its flaws as a frame for knowing, that metaphor has shaped the Western epistemological tradition from Plato through Descartes and beyond (77).

"'Tis pity bounty had not eyes behind" contains two peculiarities that help specify both Timon's particular inability to see as well as an initial notion of the play's cognitive value. Flavius may mean only what I have already suggested: that he wishes his master had considered giving's consequences, had pictured in advance the nothing that would be left behind. Yet the phrase "eyes behind"—rather than, say, a metaphor of eyes opening—conjures a counterfactual mental state: Timon with eyes in the back of his head. It seems odd that he should have needed them there simply to give sustainably. The Athenian economy depends heavily on credit, so grasping one's financial state might be more complex than Flavius assumes; all the same, we lack reason to believe that Timon's ruin results from his incomprehension of financial complexities.[18]

Why Timon requires eyes in the back of his head to see the painfully obvious is less puzzling when we remember that "bounty," not simply the man Timon of Athens, lacks "eyes behind." Though Flavius no doubt means for his criticism to apply beyond his master to all those who give bounteously, his diction also highlights how Timon has sought to become bounty, to be other than a calculating—or a doubting—human being. Through his ceaseless stream of gifts Timon seeks the impossible: to become inhuman, to become the principle of giving.[19] To become a principle, he must dispense with everything, which includes all aptitude for doubt. One whose mind is void save a single imperative—*Give!*—would require something like eyes in the back of his head to see that in giving to others he gives himself to tragedy.

Timon's impulse to turn himself into a principle drives out any impulse to conjecture about others' minds. At the play's opening, Timon seems unaware that others even have minds distinct from his own, minds he might want to distrust.[20] Unlike the play's reader, Timon is immune to a training that, according to critic and cognitive theorist Lisa Zunshine, constitutes one of literature's cardinal values: training in effective mind-reading, in honing our ability to calibrate trust and distrust, credulity and suspicion.[21] Timon cannot undergo this education until it is too late, but *Timon* can drill readers, encouraging scrutiny and sorting of characters' utterances according to the degree of their reliability. Flavius should perhaps be trusted; most other characters should be distrusted; still others, for instance Alcibiades, should be trusted on occasion but not always. *Timon* provokes scrutiny of possible discrepancies between what appears on the surface and what actually is. Prompting us to take virtually all utterances under serious advisement, the play makes us more discerning, more discriminating in our ability to sift through illusions that shape social life.

Why Want? Doubt in the Wild

Critics such as Bevington and Smith capture life in Athens quite well. The Athenian world, though, is not the only world that *Timon* presents. Indeed, one of *Timon*'s economies resembles Georges Bataille's general economy, wherein the world is defined not as in Athens—by scarcity—but by surplus, by resources that must be wasted.[22] Early in the play, Timon holds the seemingly childlike belief that his world is itself inexhaustible, and though we can read the play as Timon's painful correction on this point, he banishes himself to a wilderness that offers him far more than he requires, a place where exorbitance would be anything but unwise. "Why should you want?" Timon asks.

> Behold, the earth hath roots.
> Within this mile break forth a hundred springs.
> The oaks bear mast, the briars scarlet hips.
> The bounteous huswife Nature on each bush
> Lays her full mess before you. Want? Why want? (4.3.469–73)

Even the gold which ran out in Athens, Timon discovers, is everywhere out in the wild. Suddenly the notion of the precious, scarce object seems an Athenian invention, as empty a fabrication as Apemantus's claim that the "bleak air" and "cold brook" cannot possibly sustain Timon, cannot serve as the page and chamberlain that could attend him in the human world. For out here matter is superabundant and resources cannot possibly be exhausted. It is people who fabricate scarcity—people who create the need for calculation, dividing the world into sets of subjects and objects to be manipulated and stockpiled.

Now it seems that Timon's extravagance can be pathologized only within fabricated social space, only within the walls that he would have "dive in the earth / And fence not Athens," only when we impose an economy not dictated by the resources of the nonhuman world (4.1.2–3). The play suggests that waste—now in a context of plenitude—loses its appeal only when we insist that that world is essentially ungenerous.

To the extent that surplus, not scarcity, defines the world outside Athens, the play opens onto a second terrain of doubt, on which we might find Bataille's sovereign man.[23] Sovereign man refuses basic distinctions (between subject and object, surface and depth, human and animal, present and future) on which the acquisitive, rapacious figures of *Timon*'s Athens depend. In Bataille's account, the experience of sovereignty offers a therapeutic exit from the world of precious things easily lost, freedom from the anguish that is anticipation—of what we do not have, of what we are not yet. Unlike the self-possessed sovereignty that Shakespeare often entertains, in Bataille's model of sovereignty we no longer cling to ourselves as possessive subjects with protected interiors, stop dividing life into a present and a dreamed for (or dreaded) future, stop longing for missing objects and distant self-fulfillments. Whereas classical self-sovereignty hems in such wishes with a well-fortified inner citadel, Bataille's sovereign self stops thinking in terms of separations between subject and object, self and world. This requires just the opposite of bounded selfhood: an embrace of useless expenditure, existence in a pure present that excludes the wish for life and the fear of death alike.[24]

In the wild, Timon finds a kind of sovereignty. The social does intrude on him time and again (to name a few, Apemantus, the Painter and Poet, bandits, Alcibiades, and Flavius all turn up). Still, by the close he finds a possible exit from the world of duplicity, the monstrous world of humankind. Apemantus may be right to say that Timon "has cast away [him]self, being like [him]self," but by the end of the play this self-loss is not a problem (4.3.247). "My long sickness / Of health and living now begins to mend," Timon says; "And nothing brings me all things" (5.1.213–15). Bataille writes of a "miraculous moment when anticipation dissolves into NOTHING," a "negative miraculous" that can manifest itself in death.[25] Timon, soon to die, views moving toward the nothing of death as moving from fear toward sovereignty. He even claims that his present state is not anticipatory: the nothing that brings him all things has already arrived and is not the same as death, or not yet. As Timon "mends" toward that end, he exhibits an abandon free of features that Bataille associates with the consciousness that he reviles: ponderous individual affirmation, reflection, "the unhappy gravity of human life"

(219). Timon abolishes limits that these features impose, and in their place there opens a world, one that arrests readers left to wonder how nothing, here, brings Timon all things.

In destitution's "nothing," it is true, Timon discovers ostensibly infinite riches. But for him, gold is without value. Timon severs himself from the world of precious objects easily lost, pushing himself to the threshold of a world clear of objects. "Destruction fang mankind!" Timon exclaims, longing throughout act 4 for "large confusion" and "planetary plague," urging Alcibiades to "swear against objects" (4.3.24, 144, 122, 138). If objects mediated all his relations in Athens, now he wants for there to be no objects at all. On desiring destruction, the experience of objectlessness, and how both relate to thought, Bataille writes this:

> My thought loses its point of support if objects cease to obsess me, if my interest in destroying them at once prevails over the consideration I had for them, over the anxiousness I had to acquire them, over the seriousness they possess by themselves . . . My thought then passes from one world to the other, from the objective one where it constructs itself to the subjective one where it is undone, but in the time it takes to come undone, before it is completely undone, I can still externalize its content.[26]

Bataille believes that insofar as thought finds coherence through stable object relations, thought takes shape in an objective world. If, on the other hand, the subject enters an objectless world—in Timon's case, if his thought passes from Athens to the world of nothing, the obliterated world—subjectivity deepens not despite but because of thought's undoing. I have mentioned Anthony Dawson's contention that Timon fails to project either a "feeling of depth and inscrutability" or "inner doubt or conflict."[27] For Dawson, this makes Timon a " 'pre-character' . . . one that flames with a brilliant, black light," one whose "poetry of surface" at best creates an illusion of depth (211, 199). Yet in its withdrawal from objects, Timon's externalized thought—however narrow, however lacking in the complexity of Othello, Prospero, or Hamlet—takes on a depth of intensity that cannot be called an illusion. Timon's thought, in fact, gathers its intensity precisely by being devoid of the nuance it might develop in relation to an intricate object-world. Timon's withdrawal delivers him, and invites readers, to a short-lived richness beyond their usual imaginings.

Having said this, Dawson's description of Timon as a figure who "flames with a brilliant, black light" is entirely apt. Leo Bersani writes that for a range of thinkers and artists,

> the sign of beauty is a certain brilliance or shining—as if the disappearance of the material world as object and event were best figured by an unnatural lighting (one that in Caravaggio is not projected on objects but seems to come from within objects), a lighting that signifies a withdrawal from the visible world into the superior visibility of what has been derealized.[28]

When nothing brings Timon all things—as Athens recedes from him, as the material world dissolves as an object and he draws near to death—he is perhaps most easily pictured in the unnatural lighting of a Caravaggio, a figure becoming derealized.

Having refused human relations, Timon imagines death as entrance into a form of relation without clearly defined objects. Of his death, he asks Flavius to say that

> Timon hath made his everlasting mansion
> Upon the beached verge of the salt flood,
> Who once a day with his embossed froth
> The turbulent surge shall cover . . .
> Graves only be men's work, and death their gain.
> Sun, hide thy beams. Timon hath done his reign. (5.1.246–55)

When sovereign man erodes distinctions, Bataille writes, he develops a peculiar relationship to death. Sovereign man may still die, but he does not die humanly inasmuch as he does not die in anguished anticipation (whether of dissolution or of final fulfillment).[29] For Timon, similarly, to be "done his reign" is to do himself in sovereignly. On the verge between land and sea, Timon imagines himself as a human subject becoming nonhuman, indistinct from natural process. Bersani charts the shattering of selves who become "shifting points of rest in a universal and mobile communication of being"; creating sameness and eliminating depth, the shattered self might enter a state in which he "is, briefly, the contact between himself and the world."[30] Timon, too, becomes imprecisely located (does he exist in the mansion that will be covered by the tide? Is he the embossed froth itself?), his grave marked not with a name or span of life but with repeated pounding, a place defined by its flux. He imagines himself always returning, existing nowhere precisely, instead within a cycle without end. Anticipating nothing, Timon does not, cannot, die humanly. We might even regard this, as Hugh Grady does, as Timon's "transition into art," a transition that brings him a brief tranquility.[31]

Given Athenian life, Shakespeare sensibly leads readers to yearn for a world elsewhere, one free of distinctions that allow subjects to conceive of themselves as bounded, discrete, and delineated. Enforcing the distinction between surface and depth, having (in Hamlet's famous phrase) "that within which passes show," does good only for the most repellent characters (1.2.85). That distinction does not delineate and protect a positive interior space—of reflection and salutary freedom from outside incursion—but instead merely enables deceit and manipulation, subjects divided from the world and from each other in ways that are only ever lamentable.[32] As Timon's servant remarks, "The devil knew not what he did when he made man politic"—when he made man cunning enough to feign friendship (3.3.30–1). As Timon himself remarks after his transformation into Misanthropos, "There's never a one of you but trusts a knave / That mightily deceives you" (5.1.103–4). "Each man apart, all single and alone" becomes a consummate villain to anyone in his company (5.1.119–20). So from the vantage of the wild, *Timon*'s relationship to doubt appears quite different than it does in Athens. Doubt there had to do with what lurks behind the boundaries that separate Timon from other Athenians; now doubt shifts to personal boundaries themselves, and whether those boundaries have value.

Timon of Athens, *Timon of Phlius, and Improving Reading*

When I was first writing this chapter, my thinking about the play terminated somewhere in the previous section. Accounts such as Bevington and Smith's are partial; mine moves beyond the threatening Athenian world to describe the abundant economy that the play privileges and urges on its audience.

The trouble is that I can no longer advance this argument. I have stopped believing that the play really warrants accepting one consideration of *Timon*, my account over Bevington and Smith's, the world in the wild over Athens. The skepticism of our other Shakespearean texts more easily allows me to accept one reading over another, whether through the synthesis of seemingly opposed possibilities or through one possibility displacing another. But not *Timon*. Athens is an unhappy, unappealing place; arguably Timon ought to have seen this and, still more, ought to have adjusted to the imposition of an economy of scarcity, the structuring distinctions that separate subjects from, and should make them wary of, each other. Besides, while Timon seems to have found in the wild a place of salutary excess, the Athenians who show up over and over cast doubt on whether a world of surplus and dissolved selfhood is actually obtainable. The play presents a pair of worlds at odds with each other: in one, distinctions exist that can and should be acknowledged insofar as they mask a dangerous excess, a rapacity that should be unmasked, and in the other, these distinctions can and should be undone. The play supplies no reason to want to live in the first world, nor does it give full realization (or full plausibility) to the second. Shakespeare seems confused.

But "confused," if it carries negative valences, may be the wrong term to describe the play's competing economies. At least two other frames might aid in understanding the play, and both involve not just doubt but definite skepticism. Forget the practice of Lucian's *Timon the Misanthrope* (the most commonly cited source of the play);[33] forget, more crucially, the logic that views opposition in terms of antagonism, that would oppose argument to counterargument, Bevington and Smith's to mine, as Timon opposes himself to the city that he would like to split apart with his spade. For another Timon informs the play—Timon of Phlius, pupil of Pyrrho, part of the skeptical tradition that led to Sextus Empiricus and his *Outlines of Pyrrhonism*. "Skepticism," Sextus writes, "is an ability to place in antithesis, in any manner whatever, appearances and judgements, and thus—because of the equality of force in the objects and arguments opposed—to come first of all to a suspension of judgement."[34] We suspend judgment and become unable to dogmatize, according to classical skepticism, by setting things in opposition. Skeptics such as Sextus and Timon of Phlius believe that this is always possible; no given argument, no one account of the world, lacks a strong, equally-evidenced counter, one that forces us to suspend judgment, unable to dogmatize.[35]

The opposing of worlds in *Timon of Athens* conduces to this. In defining the modes of doubt, Sextus writes that nothing "appears to us singly but in conjunction with something else," just as Athens appears to us alongside the wild beyond.[36] Sextus also emphasizes the effect of positions and perspectives on how the world looks to us; depending on where we find ourselves in *Timon*, similarly, we see a world defined by scarcity or by surplus, by excess that is dangerous on the one hand and salutary on the other.[37] In opposing worlds, and in equipping us with no sure method to adjudicate between them, the play holds those worlds in irresolvable equipollence. The play thus urges us to suspend judgment about which world is true.

This being so, *Timon* develops a skepticism that, I will argue, is exceedingly disorienting. Initially, though, the idea that Shakespeare presents opposed, balanced viewpoints may seem part of a normative humanism or of earlier readings of Shakespeare treated in this book's introduction. I may, for instance, be reiterating Coleridge's idea that Shakespeare is myriad-minded,[38] or T. S. Eliot's idea—later repeated, albeit differently, by figures such as Harold Bloom and Stephen Greenblatt— "that about anybody as great as Shakespeare, it is probably that we can never be right."[39] The turn we have just taken could merely echo what Greenblatt wrote thirty-five years ago, that Shakespeare simply "*explores* the relations of power in a given culture,"[40] or Bloom's sense that Shakespeare's brilliance precludes adopting any particular position.[41]

If *Timon* is an exercise in and inducement to myriad-mindedness, the play would fit quite well within the humanistic frameworks that Bataille detests. In these frameworks reading renovates the mind, sharpening mental tools and even, according to some, enhancing our fitness as human beings—an enhancement well beyond the course in "mind-reading" detailed by Zunshine. Reading *Timon* could, to begin, yield the two central benefits of literature that John Carey sets out. The first is literature's ability, alone among the arts, to criticize; "it is the only art capable of reasoning" and can do so without dogmatizing.[42] "Literature," Carey argues,

> gives you ideas to think with. It stocks your mind. It does not indoctrinate, because diversity, counter-argument, reappraisal and qualification are its essence. But it supplies materials for thought. Also, because it is the only art capable of criticism, it encourages questioning, and self-questioning. (208)

Carey's argument is like Bloom's in *How to Read and Why*, which exhorts its audience to read "not to believe, not to accept, not to contradict" but "to find what truly comes nearest to you, that can be used for weighing and considering."[43] *Timon*, like my other texts of focus, encourages readers to question, weigh, and consider, to appraise and reappraise; it evinces what seems like an argument strongly in favor of a calculating form of life, followed by an argument strongly against it.

The play does not indoctrinate us because it does not ask us to favor a principle about the world's abundance, and perhaps helps instill one of Bloom's principles of good reading: *"Clear your mind of cant"* (23–4).

The second benefit that Carey attributes to reading literature derives from its ambiguity—what he calls "indistinctness"—and how ambiguity fosters our imaginative capacities. Carey's exemplar here is Shakespeare; indistinct Shakespearean phrases such as "wilderness of monkeys" (*Merchant of Venice*) and "broken tears" (*Macbeth*) can only make sense—can become distinct in readers' minds—by way of "private, individual imagining."[44] Literature's indistinctness, for Carey, helps us cultivate not just our critical habits, but also our creativity. Bloom, too, includes *"One must be an inventor to read well"* among his principles of good reading.[45] Even a lesser work like *Timon* prompts readers to read creatively in puzzling through how nothing could bring all things; in opposing worlds without adjudicating between them, likewise, *Timon* makes less sense unless we fill conceptual gaps.[46]

For Carey and Bloom, reading's critical and creative features enable us. According to Carey, literature stimulates imaginative exercise, instills a sense of ownership, and so "empowers the reader."[47] "The reader creates," he writes, "and feels a creator's possessiveness" (213). Carey nominates this "sense of ownership" as "literature's unique gift," one that works "to strengthen one's sense of selfhood and individuality" (247, 213). Bloom advances a kindred claim, one in accord with his version of Western tradition: "[u]ltimately we read—as Bacon, Johnson, and Emerson agree—in order to strengthen the self, and to learn its authentic interests."[48] In reading *Timon*, and in gravitating to one of its worlds or to a third, absent world, we might make the text ours, learning our true interests in the process. Positioning ourselves with respect to deceit and scarcity, excess and abundance, we could emerge from *Timon* with clearer, firmer self-conceptions. All of the texts treated in this book, if read differently than I do, could serve a similar purpose—*The Tempest* could prompt us to think of whether freedom is sovereignty or natality, while *Othello* could help us weigh and consider the values of union and separation in love. We could even—I will argue that we have reason to doubt, but we could—say that in *Timon* Shakespeare returns to the situational pragmatism endorsed in the early *Lucrece*. Just as a unified self might be sensible in some circumstances and a dualistic self in others, so a possessive relation to objects might be sensible in *Timon's* Athens but not in the wild.

Humanists like Carey and Bloom might not welcome being linked, as I believe they are linked, to the group of literary critics known as "Literary Darwinists," who argue that the enhancements of reading actually serve adaptive purposes. Carey's account of literature's power to transform prisoners, for example, suggests that literature has survival value in enabling offenders to find their way in the world—to elevate self-esteem and become socially functional.[49] In this way, Carey's account of literature's value resembles that of Joseph Carroll, who, accounting for literature's adaptive value, recounts how David Copperfield's reading allows him to escape "from an impoverished reality into the larger world of healthy human possibility" and "to adapt successfully to this world."[50] Bloom and Carey also imagine that literature in general, and Shakespeare in particular, offers us entry to such a healthy world. While they might not care for Carroll's Darwinism, in their humanism they cannot help but conclude that literature conduces to our advancement.[51]

Reading's humanistic benefits, which dovetail with those identified by literary Darwinists, might derive not only from our other texts of focus but even from *Timon*. Denis Dutton's summary of how literature could serve adaptive purposes, for instance, includes the fact that fictions "encourage us to explore the points of view, beliefs, motivations, and values of other human minds."[52] *Timon*, populated by characters who act according to single principles—giving, and taking—might not yield sophisticated conceptions of other minds, but it could, as we saw earlier, inspire curiosity about others' inner workings. Dutton also notes that literary texts "provide low-cost, low-risk surrogate experience," allowing us to explore "what if" scenarios without putting ourselves at risk (110). *Othello* and *The Winter's Tale*, arguably, give us the surrogate experience of possessive jealousy—allow us to see inside, and to learn from, its most dangerous instantiations—without the fallout of sons that die spontaneously, smothered wives, or suicide. Criticism of *Timon* that reads the play as an admonitory text for James I fits with Dutton's paradigm similarly, so even one of Shakespeare's less humanistic texts might provide benefits identified by humanists. One of his least "evolved" plays might still play into evolutionary psychology.

Looking Two Ways at Once

I do not mean to deny that *Timon's* Pyrrhonism, when approached a certain way, enhances critical and creative intelligence, or could be thought to have adaptive value. I myself, however, cannot adopt this view, since my experience reading *Timon* has not brought encouragement of this kind. The play has not honed my ability to criticize anything because it has initiated an inner criticism that has no outcome. And while the play does, at points, lead me to compose distinct readings from indistinct formulations, composing has not felt like establishing ownership of the text or like becoming situated in a way that bolsters my sense of myself. For me, *Timon's* Pyrrhonism is too unsettling to be empowering. My reading experience thus is significantly more twisted than the experience of literature is in a view such as Carey's. The play's opposed worlds are disorienting, not reorienting. I cannot craft a frame within which they both would fit.

Comparison with *Lucrece* helps explain this disorientation. Shakespeare's early poem prompts us to suspend judgment about the structure of selfhood, much as *Timon* prompts us to suspend judgment about the structure of the world. *Lucrece* also allows us to imagine alterations that would improve its world and ours—if, for instance, Tarquin were open to Lucrece's pleas at the right moment, or able to gain distance on himself as he verges on atrocity—an aspect of the poem that, I argued, lends it to pragmatic skeptical practice. *Timon*, for its part, forbids what *Lucrece* allows. I struggle to imagine Timon learning suspicion in Athens and struggle still more, had he learned this, to imagine his life in Athens—awful as the city is—in terms of healthy possibility. Life in the wild, likewise, is so extreme, in its abundance and in Timon's fatal response to this abundance, that it feels unalterable, diamond-hard. *Timon* presents two opposed worlds, each of which is reduced to one principle and neither of which is livable. Shakespeare constructs adamantine worlds from which readers are excluded, forced instead to behold how these worlds rule each other out.[53]

Encountering such contradiction draws me near to the state that, according to Timon of Phlius, the otherwise accomplished Xenophanes wanted to enter but could not. "Would that I had attained my share of shrewdness," Xenophanes declares,

> To look two ways at once; on a treacherous path
> I was led astray, an old man, and still innocent
> Of Doubt! For wherever I turned my mind,
> All was resolved into one and the same, and all that exists,
> However weighed, was always of one same nature.[54]

The wish to "look two ways at once" accounts for the principal differ-ence between Xenophanes's thinking and that of the humanists and lit-erary Darwinists described earlier. Carey and Bloom value how Shakespeare permits us to consider multiple perspectives, to look one way, then another—to weigh and consider and so, in the end, see our-selves and our worlds more clearly. In gaining clarity, literary Darwinists argue, we gain in fitness. Looking two ways at once forbids this. Dras-tically different from normal embodied experience—from looking in one direction, as we are constituted to do—looking two ways figures scrambled cognition; it induces incapacity and blurs what could be clear.

In drawing me toward Xenophanes's ideal, reading the play drives me far from both the humanism described earlier as well as the vision offered by Bataille. The play's interest comes to reside not only in an unveiling—in seeing through deception, or in seeing through the illu-sions of possessive individualism to the true worth that comes from ex-ceeding that sort of subjectivity. The play also urges readers to accept the disorientation of looking two ways at once and so to exceed both the strengthening and the exceeding of subjectivity. This is not just a matter of entering a state of non-assertion, of neither affirming nor de-nying, of appreciating difference and distinction between forms of life without imputing final value to one over another. Nor is it a matter of acknowledging, in life outside the play, the different worlds that we in-habit and move between, and of admitting that there is no reliable way to order or make full sense of them, to choose one over the other. The play suggests that to begin to think adequately about my experience—of texts and of the world—I would need to thwart my usual forms of cognition, eschewing two basic assumptions drawn from human per-ception: first, that things which are concealed can be uncovered, and, second, that to "look" at a given moment is to look along one vector.

This is as vexing as it sounds. Classical skeptics, we have seen, claim that the suspension of judgment entailed by trying to look two ways at once, coming after great frustration about the world's resistance to uni-fied views of it, opens onto an experience of tranquility or "unpertur-bedness" (*ataraxia*).[55] I myself leave *Timon* feeling frustrated that its world seems to contain bounded subjects and scarce objects, but also sovereign, open subjects and superabundance, excess and waste that are pathologized as well as excess and waste that are praised. It frustrates me that the world appears one way at one moment but not the next. I remind myself that the question of what the world is, for this play, matters less than its contradictory appearances. I try to inhabit the contradiction rather than argue my way out of it. Does *ataraxia* arrive? Not usually, and not for long.

The play's Pyrrhonism does, at least, counter the dogmatic thinking that often seems like second nature, and affects how I read. It has made me consider whether producing compelling readings can mean producing incoherent ones—incoherent not in being meaningless but in being surcharged with meaning, in stretching cognition to its limit.[56] As I try to think as the play seems to want me to, norms grow obscure, lost in gaps of understanding about how selves and worlds are composed. I confront a blurred normativity (if I do not know how the world is, nor do I know how I should behave), while strong theories of selfhood's emergence (of psychoanalysis, say, or social construction) seem built on hazy foundations. True difficulty presents itself, from without and from within, and this alters my sense of Pyrrhonism's possibilities.

I have said that for Sextus Empiricus, skepticism promotes tranquility and keeps perturbation at bay. So when faced with decision, the skeptic will calm himself and others by acting in accord with common opinion; Christian Thorne, as we have seen, points this out in a recent attack on Pyrrhonism's radical potential.[57] *Timon*, though, shows that we cannot reach Sextus Empiricus's conservative conclusion when looking two ways at once is taken seriously. I cannot, for instance, think that Timon should have conformed with Athenian custom and favored a clutching, deceptive form of life. Reading *Timon* shows how looking two ways at once is, in its structure, a radically destabilizing enterprise. In *Timon*, as in *The Tempest*, we see that Shakespeare's skeptical practice departs from, even as it deploys, Pyrrhonism. *The Tempest* exceeds Pyrrhonism by adding to its methods, synthesizing, rather than only balancing, seemingly opposed conceptions—using the concept of transformation to bring together freedom as working upon oneself and freedom as being worked upon. *Timon* exceeds Pyrrhonism by altering its ends, replacing *ataraxia* with disorientation.

That disorientation, I can safely say, has not elevated my self-esteem or boosted my epistemological confidence. I would wager that it has not enhanced my fitness for survival, much as Shakespeare's conceptions of love, ethics, and freedom fail to enhance such fitness—though *Timon*, it should be said, thwarts mastery more comprehensively than other

Shakespearean texts. *Lucrece, Hamlet, Othello, The Winter's Tale,* and *The Tempest* might not allow mastery of ethics, liberty, or love—might not encourage us to think we know where we stand ethically or amorously, or think we know, exactly, how freedom would feel—but they do allow for a limited mastery of the text itself. *The Winter's Tale,* for instance, encourages us to think of ethics as the offer of a hand rather than as treading the path of righteousness. *The Tempest* encourages us to think of freedom as transformation, not sovereignty. *Timon,* on the other hand, not only disallows conceptual mastery—denying us a sense of whether the world's resources are scarce or superabundant—but also prohibits mastery of the text, keeps us from synthesizing opposed interpretations or choosing one interpretation over another. What value can reading *Timon* have, given how forbidding it is?

Timon *and Reparative Reading*

Trying to look two ways at once has had rewards; reading *Timon* does not constitute the minor tragedy of wasted time. Stanley Cavell, we have seen, offers the most prominent instance of how skepticism can produce real ruination, dwelling on figures whose skepticism is conditioned by the wish for knowledge and who cannot live their skepticism except in and through catastrophe.[58] As Anita Gilman Sherman and Ellen Spolsky point out, though, Shakespearean skepticism is not always an affliction.[59] Even if accepting a skeptical condition fails to increase our fitness, such acceptance need not require or even call for recovery—if skepticism can be disarticulated from the desire to know. *Timon* does this; allow me to explain how.

Timon's outlook is never skeptical. He falls by assuming that knowledge is his: that he can discern the world's essence and a principle by which to live. Initially, he puts his faith in dishonest "friends," with no regard for doubt. Out in the wild, similarly, Timon ignores the potential pleasures of the abundant world that appears before him, spending most of his time railing against man and the meager Athenian world. Never does he consider contrary possibilities. If the skeptic does not dogmatize, Timon accelerates his unraveling by his inability to be anything but dogmatic, by the presumption that makes *Othello* a tragedy and nearly makes *The Winter's Tale* one. Belief, not doubt, undoes him. And while Timon may be beyond repair, readers of the play are not.[60] *Timon* can, in us, help disarticulate skepticism from the desire to know.

It can incite the desire for knowledge—the wish for a definitive reading—then release the reader from this desire by driving home its futility.

Such a release has valuable consequences for reading practice, and comparison with Cavell again yields insight. Cavell has regard for how we cannot possess texts, or knowledge of them, as we possess things. We cannot say that we have even truly read a text unless we think of it as in some way having read us, exposed us to a questioning that changes us fundamentally.[61] Cavell does not believe in the "mastery" of definitive reading, and though this seems a turn toward the openness urged by Shakespeare's *Timon*, in practice it is not. Since we cannot master the text, Cavell argues, we simply must admit it. Cavell acknowledges that his reading of Shakespeare "is nothing if not partial" even as he frets that some will, wrongly, take his "claim to partiality as more arrogant than the claim to judiciousness."[62] The point is to content ourselves with avowedly partial readings.

Cavell's modesty is akin to the epistemological humility that *Timon's* skepticism would encourage, though his solution—to admit partiality—is not. His modesty, at least, also shares with Eve Kosofsky Sedgwick's in her brilliant critique of what she calls immodest "paranoid" reading (even as one of Sedgwick's own alternatives, I will suggest, is like Cavell's and unlike Shakespeare's). Sedgwick lists five central characteristics of paranoia that—by contrast—help specify some reading practices implied by *Timon*:

> Paranoia is anticipatory.
> Paranoia is reflexive and mimetic.
> Paranoia is a strong theory.
> Paranoia is a theory of negative affects.
> Paranoia places its faith in exposure.[63]

Paranoia is anticipatory in that the paranoid reader aims to avoid all bad surprises and thus is unstintingly suspicious, expecting to find hidden evils. While *Timon* cultivates comprehensive doubt, such doubt is emphatically unsuspicious. The global project the play sets before me—as opposed to the project it seems to set in portraying Athens—is not to see through false appearance to hidden truth; rather, that project is to avoid presuming to see through the play's contrasting appearances to its truth.

Paranoid readings are reflexive and mimetic, according to Sedgwick, in that "[p]aranoia seems to require being imitated to be understood" and "seems to understand only by imitation." "Paranoia," Sedgwick argues, "proposes both *Anything you can do (to me) I can do worse*, and *Anything you can do (to me) I can do first*" (131). Paranoia, that is, is a strong theory that organizes all information around basic, underlying facts prepared for by the paranoid reader. In *Timon*, that fact could be— and often is taken to be—humankind's hidden cupidity and one's consequent need to be suspicious. We know, having read the play once, that Athens will break our trust, so we approach the text having already broken that trust on our own. What the text might do to us we can do first, and do worse. *Timon* as a whole, though, cannot be organized around this dark "truth" and dares to be read in the absence of such organization.

Unsurprisingly, paranoia makes for stringently negative affect. From the paranoid perspective as Sedgwick describes it, all appearances are bad, even—especially—those that seem good, so all things, including all positive affects, should be distrusted, resisted, and, if possible, eliminated. *Timon's* skepticism is not so extreme. The play opens the reader to an affective spectrum—profound irritation about Athens, strange exultation about Timon's approach to an objectless world, perplexity about the play's entirety.

Sedgwick's paranoid reader justifies negative affect, last of all, by placing faith in exposure, in truths beneath surface appearances that not only should, but also can, be brought to light. Quite apart from whether deep truths exist or can be discovered, Shakespeare in *Timon* does not attribute any inherent value to searching for them. Shakespeare gives us no sense, for instance, that Timon would have been better off had he been suspicious from the outset. He may have retained his wealth, but that wealth, kept, would have had no value for a man who wants to be the principle of giving. If *Timon* asks us to place faith in anything, it is in not presuming beyond what appears.

In favoring non-dualistic, non-algorithmic, and reparative practices over paranoid ones, Sedgwick goes further than anyone has in thinking through reading's possibilities. Yet Sedgwick, in one sense like Cavell, quotes Joseph Litvak to argue that taking a reparative outlook means taking "the terror out of error," means making "the making of mistakes sexy, creative, even cognitively powerful."[64] However valuable being unafraid to make mistakes may be, *Timon* does not encourage this fearlessness. Sedgwick and Litvak endorse making the "mistake" of reading texts one way, only with humility, acknowledging that there may be two, or three, or thirty ways to look at that text. One can readily see how this emerges in critical practice. When we produce a reading, inevitably readings counter to our own occur to us, and in response we either suppress those counter-readings or make certain concessions to them, adjusting our own arguments accordingly. This is harmless enough and, admittedly, is what I have done in this book's first four chapters, with (I hope) a higher incidence of concession than suppression. What Shakespeare's *Timon* might have us do is begin from the skeptical premise that we can always find a contrasting account, one as strong as our own—that if we look hard enough, these balancing arguments will emerge. When a position is manifested to us, its opposite may be manifested as well, and we may have no way to decide between them. This undecidable moment will not always arise—it certainly does not for me in reading other Shakespearean texts—but *Timon* would open us to the possibility that it will. So open, I would work first not to take a stand but to not take a stand. Rather than working around or finessing the voices that tell me that my readings do not quite work, I would seek to thwart those readings myself.

Timon of Phlius and *Timon of Athens* may, I admit, put us on a route that we cannot see to its end. These Timons ask for what seems nearly impossible but what is worth taking seriously: they ask us to look two ways at once—to not only (as I have done in this chapter) consider in turn two sides of a contradiction, two parts of a play, but to consider both at one and the same time: to feel, and perhaps learn to respect, the full import of this incoherence and the suspension of judgment to which it leads. These Timons ask us to yearn for the sudden illumination that this "confusion"—if we choose to call it that—could yield, though the illumination would be one that discourse, unfolding over time, could not fully bear.

Can readers withstand this experience? Can it be anything other than vexing, and can the vexation ever also be a pleasure? I think so.[65] Reading *Timon* is neither quite a horror nor a joy. I would hazard, though, that the play excites when we consider whether its disorientations might be vital—when, in other words, the orientation we bring to disorientation is not already negative. In asking readers to hold incompatible worlds in mind, to look two ways at once, *Timon* forces us into awareness of the contestable contours of the extra-textual world—of the contortions required to make it make sense. If I myself try to look two ways at once at any length, I seem to enter, or in me there seems to emerge, a world elsewhere, one without normal coordinates, one where everyday perception cannot occur. Soon I feel overwhelmed, fatigued by mental exhilaration that has gone on too long. I feel almost irrecoverable, enlarged, and also lost.

Epilogue: Shakespeare as a Way of Life

R eading *Timon*, for me, is not a self-strengthening enterprise. Lisa Zunshine, whose own account of literature's empowering aspects can serve as a final contrast, compares reading to weight lifting, using detective novels as a specific example. Like other literature though more intensely, such novels help perfect our aptitude for suspicion, fashioning "our ability to store representations under advisement" as we search for truth, much as working with weights fashions muscles and increases the degree of resistance that muscles can overcome.[1] Reading novels also makes readers want to undergo further training, much as lifting (for some) makes weight lifters want to work out again. As lifters gradually improve their form and add to their maximums, so readers gradually improve at suspecting everyone and at identifying guilty parties. If this link between intellectual and physical activity seems inadmissibly post-Darwinian in a study of an earlier period, we need only remind ourselves, as Pierre Hadot does, that the link is ancient, that "the notion of philosophical exercises has its roots in the ideal of athleticism and in the habitual practice of physical culture"; physical and philosophical exercises of antiquity often occurred in the same space and to the same end, "to shape the true person: free, strong, and independent."[2]

My encounters with *Timon* are not like this. Trying to look two ways at once does not make me want to try again sometime soon. My ability to read the play has not improved, certainly not in the sense of improved ability to apportion guilt among the tragedy's characters or among social forces of the early seventeenth century. I struggle with *Timon* nearly as much now as I did a decade ago. Reading the play, for me, is not like lifting weights, or, if it is like lifting weights, it is like lifting them for the first time, every time. I leave the text with a humbled sense of my interpretive ability, mentally spent, more than a little giddy. I feel the cognitive equivalent of what I felt the day after my first experience, more than twenty years ago, with free weights. When I tried to raise my hand, to answer a question in Geometry, I needed my left arm to support the one struggling up. After class, it took effort to extract myself from my desk and shuffle off to lunch. I ached. The extent of the ache embarrassed me but it, like the ache I feel when I leave *Timon*, was exquisite.

Looking two ways at once, I have said, is the most impractical of the skeptical practices described in this book. Practices found in other chapters yield to faith more swiftly: about what makes ethical behavior or freedom possible, or about what allows us to abide in love. This faith, to be sure, resides in the elusiveness of the object and yields cognitive discomforts: an insoluble problem of body and mind in *Lucrece*, and freedom's uncertain transformations of the self in *The Tempest*; endlessly shaky ethical standing in *The Winter's Tale*, and a love in *Othello* whose demands might well prove infinite. I leave these texts without a more muscular sense of ethics, love, or liberty, without enhanced proficiency at living. Shakespeare leaves no path of righteousness along which I might mark my progress, no idea of liberty that allows me to measure my true range of motion. If these texts differ from *Timon* in degree rather than in kind, reading them nonetheless has more obvious value than *Timon* because they outline stances—of openness, perseverance, and patience—which render more manageable the discomforts that they require and which open possibilities for hope: that mind and body might come into saving configuration, or that freedom might arrive again; that love might again be ecstasy, or that the unending offer of a hand might have its satisfactions. The openness urged by *Timon* offers only to intensify discomfort, asking readers not just to accept cognitive frustration but also to seek that frustration out. In *Timon*, Shakespeare asks for epistemological humility that exhausts as much as it exhilarates us.

In no chapter of this book, really, have I meant to nominate Shakespeare as a lost path to perfect contentment. Shakespeare as a way of life is not literary self-help or cognitive-behavioral therapy. Michel Foucault's point in turning to classical practices of the self, likewise, is not

to say, 'We have unfortunately forgotten about the care of the self; so here, here it is, the key to everything.' Nothing is more foreign to me than the idea that, at a certain moment, philosophy went astray and forgot something, that somewhere in its history there is a principle, a foundation that must be rediscovered.[3]

At the same time, Foucault does believe that modern notions of self-cultivation, unlike their classical counterparts, are rather vacuous. He sees an "almost total absence of meaning" in expressions "which continue to permeate our discourse—like getting back to oneself, freeing oneself, being oneself, being authentic, etcetera." "I do not think we have anything to be proud of," Foucault writes, "in our current efforts to reconstitute an ethic of the self."[4]

Shakespeare is not the key to everything any more than classical texts are. Shakespeare is not, as Bloom maintains, a secular scripture, and it was ridiculous for Emerson to write, even if in half-jest, that one day Shakespeare would be called the final cause of the Earth's creation.[5] I am not, like Keats, "very near Agreeing with Hazlitt that Shakespeare is enough for us."[6] I do, though, agree with Foucault that we lack a fully developed ethic of the self, and I think that Shakespeare's skeptical practices can help reconstitute that ethic. These practices have political dimensions, as we have seen, but also aesthetic ones, ones that ask for further attention in appraising Shakespeare. In my chapter on *The Tempest*, I mentioned that for Foucault, practices of the self help us cultivate an aesthetics of existence. The poverty of our self-conceptions, according to Foucault, derives partly from the loss of this idea, from the fact that we no longer seek "to build our existence as a beautiful existence."[7] "In our society," Foucault laments, "art has become something that is related only to objects and not to individuals or to life" (261). While classical figures obsess over the aesthetics of existence, "we have hardly any remnant of the idea in our society that the principal work of art which one must take care of, the main area to which one must apply aesthetic values, is oneself, one's life, one's existence" (271).

We have seen that moments when characters become like works of art fascinate Shakespeare, even if they seem not the explicit or the primary aim of Shakespearean skeptical practice: when Othello imagines waves Olympus-high and Leontes starts to approach Hermione's statuesque existence, when Timon imagines his everlasting mansion and Caliban cries to dream again. A key difference between these moments and those described by Foucault is that Shakespeare's seem largely unrelated to the control and calm of the classical, well-sculpted self, unmoored from *autarkeia* and *ataraxia* alike. Life's problems, for Shakespeare, do not admit of such definitive solutions; care for the self can be palliative but not curative. He offers no program, as a classical Stoic, Epicurean, or Skeptic might, to guarantee that we advance from our given self to our best self, that we have left an ugly existence and now approach, however asymptotically, a personally or politically beautiful one. In Shakespeare's plays that approach happens, when it happens, in receptivity and almost by accident. An aesthetic existence arrives in a way that conjures the conversion to Pyrrhonism but that resists this skepticism's full program.[8] "The Sceptic," Sextus Empiricus writes,

> in fact, had the same experience as that related in the story about Apelles the artist. They say that when Apelles was painting a horse, he wished to represent the horse's foam in the painting. His attempt was so unsuccessful that he gave it up and at the same time flung at the picture his sponge, with which he had wiped the paints off his brush. As it struck the picture, the sponge produced an image of the horse's foam. So it was with the Sceptics. They were in hopes of attaining mental tranquility, thinking that they could do this by arriving at some rational judgement which would dispel the inconsistencies involved in both appearances and thoughts. When they found this impossible, they withheld judgement. While they were in this state, they made a chance discovery. They found that they were attended by mental tranquility as surely as a body by its shadow.[9]

A last difference between Shakespeare and Sextus Empiricus can be found in this notion of conversion and its aftermath. Although the Pyrrhonist converts to skepticism by chance, the skeptic then has a definite path—aphorisms to keep in mind, habits of thought to employ, a reason to act in accordance with custom—to promote indifference and ensure *ataraxia*. After conversion, the skeptical program becomes the sponge that cleanses and the gift that allows precise use of the brush, willed cultivation of a beautiful existence. For the reader of Shakespeare, by contrast, frustration and adventitiousness would persist almost undiminished after conversion to skeptical practice. One could only hope, in committing to the disorientations of love, ethics, and liberty, to have a moment like that of Apelles, when beauty appears amid the frustrations spread across life's canvas.

Shakespeare asks that we approach our central enterprises—love, ethics, liberty—with humility, with an admission that we cannot know exactly what to expect from them. This makes Shakespeare as a way of life hard to encapsulate in helpful precepts. Hadot writes of how classical philosophies were, by contrast, "reduced to a theoretical, systematic, highly concentrated nucleus, capable of exercising a strong psychological effect, and easy enough to handle so that it might always be kept close at hand."[10] An illustrative example that Hadot cites—in addition to the skeptical example we encountered in the introduction—is the Epicurean fourfold remedy:

> The gods are not to be feared,
> Death is not to be dreaded;
> What is good is easy to acquire,
> What is bad is easy to bear.[11]

Shakespeare offers nothing of this order, though it is tempting to believe that he does. David Bevington ends a recent book with a half-serious Shakespearean "credo," in which he imagines what the bard might have said were he asked to offer "some ideas that we human beings should strive to live by." The ideas that Bevington offers include "Be generous"; "Learn to forgive the unforgivable"; "Honor thy father and thy mother"; "Church-going is generally a good thing"; "Worldly possessions can be deadening to the soul"; and "Our scepticism needs to be tempered by faith in something we can call Providence."[12]

Some of these ideas—the call to generosity and forgiveness, for instance, or the injunctions against possessive individualism and unrelenting skepticism—bear a relation to ideas explored in this book. But Bevington's credo form makes Shakespearean precepts sound like a more sensible version of the "few precepts" that Polonius offers Laertes in *Hamlet*. I am not objecting on the old-fashioned grounds that Bevington's offer involves a heresy of paraphrase, but on the grounds of skepticism. There is an unsettling, disruptive quality about some of the scenes we have encountered—of Leontes's perpetually offered hand, for example, or of Othello's promise to deny Desdemona nothing. So unsettled, we are refused the assurance inherent in the credo form. Shakespearean texts are pitched at shaping readers' ways of living and being, but the aphorisms that might arise when his skepticism yields to faith ("ethics is the offer of a hand," "freedom is transformation," "love is non-sovereignty") fail to form a concentrated nucleus by which to live, by which, cured of anguish, we might craft our selves and our worlds as things of beauty. At times, Shakespeare seems to wish for clearer solutions: to solve the mind-body problem with pragmatism; to erase love's volatility by way of generosity; to establish self-government with a fixed center for the self or a stable constitution for the state. But Shakespeare never quite seems to believe in these solutions. A belief his texts instead evince is this: that while we cannot state the precise terms of obligation, love, or liberty, we can still cling to them, in the hope that our experience of them might, and that we ourselves might, become beautiful, for a time if not once and for all.

Acknowledgments

This project began in 2007, when Madhavi Menon invited me to write about *Timon of Athens*. I am grateful for her timely invitation as well as her comments on an early version of the *Timon* chapter. In its early stages, the book received indispensible support from my former intellectual home, Case Western Reserve University, and I would like to thank my colleagues there, especially Kurt Koenigsberger, Chris Flint, Athena Vrettos, Gary Stonum, and Michael Clune, who has served as intellectual model for years. So has Aaron Kunin of Pomona College. I am especially delighted to acknowledge my new colleagues at Brown. Amanda Anderson, Jacques Khalip, Karen Newman, Coppélia Kahn, and Stephen Foley deserve special mention; so does Rick Rambuss, who has been exemplary as a mentor and friend. This book would be far from completion were it not for research leaves granted by Case Western Reserve and Brown, for the resources of both institutions as well as those of the University of Auckland. Thanks also are due to my students at Pomona, Case Western Reserve, and Brown, who helped me formulate and refine the ideas in this book—more, I think, than they can know or I can say.

Several portions of the project have been presented in one venue or another, and I am indebted to those who have listened to my attempts to articulate ideas. I am grateful to audiences at meetings of the Modern Language Association, in panels organized by Laurie Shannon and Anita Gilman Sherman; of the Shakespeare Association of America, in seminars organized by Joseph Loewenstein and Randall Martin; and of the Renaissance Society of America, in a panel organized by Julia Lupton. Parts of this project were also presented to audiences at Cornell University; Pomona College; the University of York; King's College, London; and the University of Auckland.

Friends have been generous and forbearing enough to read parts of the manuscript, including Tom Bishop, Michael Clune, Bradin Cormack, Barbara Correll, John D. Cox, Jonathan Crewe, Kevin Curran, Simon During, Lars Engle, Marcie Frank, Carla Freccero, Jonathan Goldberg, Patrick Gray, Jody Greene, Richard Halpern, Coppélia Kahn, Jacques Khalip, Aaron Kunin, Joseph Loewenstein, Madhavi Menon, Nichole Miller, Karen Newman, Rick Rambuss, Bill Sherman, Richard Strier, Steven Swarbrick, and Steven Zwicker. Julia Lupton, whose intellectual generosity seems to know no limit, has supported my work from the beginning and continues to do so today. Katherine Eggert, Laurel Flinn, and Daniel Juan Gil read the entire manuscript, which is much improved because of their time and care. Tom Lay has been an ideal editor.

A small portion of the Introduction appears in *This Distracted Globe: Worldmaking in Early Modern Literature* (Fordham University Press, 2016). Part of Chapter 3 appeared in *Exemplaria: A Journal of Theory in Medieval and Renaissance Studies* 24.3 (2012): 260–281, while a small part of Chapter 5 appeared in *ShakesQueer*, ed. Madhavi Menon (Durham: Duke University Press, 2010). I am thankful for permission to reprint those portions of the manuscript here.

Last, I want to thank Richard and Lesley Flinn, who fashioned a space so that I might finish this book; my parents, David and Magreta, who made it possible for literature to form something like a way of life; a pair of teachers, Richard McDonough and Elizabeth Tringali, who gave that way appeal; and two who make it possible for the way to be sustained: Jonathan and Laurel. This book, though, is for two who are new to life, Celia and Edith.

Notes

INTRODUCTION: SHAKESPEARE'S SKEPTICAL PRACTICE
AND THE POLITICS OF WEAKNESS

1. *Selected Letters of John Keats*, ed. Grant F. Scott (Cambridge, MA: Harvard University Press, 2002), 61.

2. Li Ou, *Keats and Negative Capability* (London: Continuum, 2009), 2, 5.

3. *Selected Letters*, 380.

4. See Trilling, "The Poet as Hero," in *The Opposing Self* (London: Secker and Warburg, 1955), 37. Ou covers Trilling's reading of Keats on pp. 13–14.

5. For a few interesting overviews of Keats's relationship to Shakespeare, see John Middleton Murry, *Keats and Shakespeare: A Study of Keats' Poetic Life from 1816–20* (Oxford: Oxford University Press, 1925); R. S. White, *Keats as a Reader of Shakespeare* (London: Athlone Press, 1987); and William Flesch, "The Ambivalence of Generosity: Keats Reading Shakespeare," *ELH* 62.1 (1995): 149–69.

6. See Hadot, *Philosophy as a Way of Life: Spiritual Exercises from Socrates to Foucault* (Malden, MA: Wiley-Blackwell, 1995), and *What Is Ancient Philosophy?*, trans. Michael Chase (Cambridge, MA: Belknap, 2004). For Hadot's critique of Foucault, see *Philosophy as a Way of Life*, 206–13.

7. Hadot, *What Is Ancient Philosophy?*, 3.

8. The demand, we will see, arises not only from variation across plays but from the fact that, in single plays, Shakespeare's relation to skeptics is unstable. Though Shakespeare explores Pyrrhonist suspension of judgment in plays such as *The Tempest* and *Timon of Athens*, for example, he is never so thoroughly Pyrrhonist as to believe that the outcome of suspended judgment is tranquility and passive acceptance of the given situation. And while we can regard a play such as *Othello* as proto-Cartesian

in the sense that Desdemona occupies the place of Descartes's God and then the place of his evil genius, Shakespeare does not assign as sinister a quality to doubt as Descartes later would. In my view, any attempt to identify Shakespeare's skepticism as Academic, Pyrrhonist, or proto-Cartesian requires that we suppress other elements of his skepticism.

9. Charles B. Schmitt, in his careful study of the reception of Cicero's *Academica*, defines ancient skepticism—rightly—without terrible precision. Such skepticism was "marked by a cautious, non-dogmatic philosophical approach, characterized by refusing to make definitive statements on any particular issue, and by 'suspending judgement.' Moreover, the skeptics held that, if any knowledge could be obtained, it would be only 'probable knowledge' and not 'certain knowledge.'" See Schmitt, *Cicero Scepticus: A Study of the Influence of the* Academica *in the Renaissance* (The Hague: Martinus Nijhoff, 1972), 7. Of skepticism's appropriation in the Renaissance, Schmitt writes that "[c]ertain elements of the original source are blindly retained, others are subtly transformed, while still others are radically changed" (4). Something like this is at play in Shakespeare, though "blindly retained" is more pejorative than I would hazard.

10. Hamlin, *Tragedy and Scepticism in Shakespeare's England* (Basingstoke: Palgrave Macmillan, 2005), 5.

11. For a concise account of how Pyrrhonist modes of skepticism manifest themselves in Shakespeare, see Robert B. Pierce, "Shakespeare and the Ten Modes of Scepticism," *Shakespeare Survey* 46 (1993): 145–158.

12. Hazlitt, *Characters of Shakespeare's Plays* (Boston: Wells and Lilly, 1818), 71. For a preliminary sense of the range of philosophies engaged in relation to Shakespeare, see John J. Joughin, ed., *Philosophical Shakespeares* (London: Routledge, 2000).

13. For the possibility that Shakespeare might not have read much philosophy, see David Bevington, *Shakespeare's Ideas* (Hoboken: John Wiley & Sons, 2009), 1.

14. Hadot, *What Is Ancient Philosophy?*, 145.

15. Nor is what I describe the "conditional, tentative, and skeptical" faith in theater outlined by Richard McCoy and often attached to *The Winter's Tale*. McCoy, *Faith in Shakespeare* (Oxford: Oxford University Press, 2013), 4.

16. For a drastically different account of the conjunction of skepticism and faith in Shakespeare, see John D. Cox, *Seeming Knowledge: Shakespeare and Skeptical Faith* (Waco: Baylor University Press, 2007).

17. See Lakoff and Johnson, *Philosophy in the Flesh: The Embodied Mind and Its Challenge to Western Thought* (New York: Basic Books, 1999), especially parts 1 and 2.

18. Lakoff has discussed cognition's political ramifications, showing how the metaphors by which we understand politics can be both enabling and constraining, and how simple awareness of the contingent, metaphorical nature of political thinking presents us with a broadened range of political possibility. I agree with Lakoff in this, to the point that Shakespeare as a way of life consists largely in the commitment to a set of metaphors by which to live. But whereas Lakoff advances a resolutely liberal program for the reformation of neural pathways—in which we emphasize metaphors of nurturing and interdependence over those of strict discipline and independence—Shakespeare's program is more disorienting. See Lakoff, *The Political Mind: A Cognitive Scientist's Guide to Your Brain and Its Politics* (New York: Penguin, 2008).

19. Popkin, *The History of Scepticism: From Savonarola to Bayle*, 3rd edition (Oxford: Oxford University Press, 2003).

20. Thorne, *The Dialectic of Counter-Enlightenment* (Cambridge, MA: Harvard University Press, 2009).

21. Holbrook, *Shakespeare's Individualism* (Cambridge: Cambridge University Press, 2010).

22. Coleridge, *Biographia Literaria: Or, Biographical Sketches of My Literary Life and Opinions* (London: Bell and Daldy, 1817), 151.

23. Bate, *The Genius of Shakespeare* (London: Picador, 1997), 324. Bate adds to this characterization the importance of performativity, "[t]he performative truth of human 'being,'" but this is equally vague (332).

24. Garber, *Shakespeare After All* (New York: Pantheon, 2004), 7.

25. Nuttall, *Shakespeare the Thinker* (New Haven: Yale University Press, 2007), 24.

26. Bloom, *Shakespeare: The Invention of the Human* (New York: Riverhead, 1998), 10.

27. As Hamlin points out, however, even for Montaigne skepticism is not always a source of tranquility but can also be a source of torment. Hamlin, *Tragedy and Scepticism in Shakespeare's England*, 6.

28. Descartes, *Meditations on First Philosophy*, trans. Laurence J. Lafleur (New York: Macmillan, 1951), 23.

29. Cavell, *Disowning Knowledge: In Six Plays of Shakespeare* (New York: Cambridge University Press, 1987), 3.

30. Engle, *Shakespearean Pragmatism: Market of His Time* (Chicago: University of Chicago Press, 1993), 9.

31. Cavell, *Disowning Knowledge*, 5. The best we can do to make our skepticism a bit more livable is not to disown knowledge completely but to achieve an "acceptance of a repetition," one "that includes endless specific succumbings to the conditions of skepticism and endless specific recoveries from it, endless as a circle, as a serpent swallowing itself" (36).

32. For two other examples that resemble Cavell's, see Millicent Bell's *Shakespeare's Tragic Skepticism* (New Haven: Yale University Press, 2002); and David Hillman's brilliant *Shakespeare's Entrails: Belief, Scepticism, and the Interior of the Body* (New York: Palgrave Macmillan, 2007), which I take up in subsequent chapters.

33. Kuzner, "Unbuilding the City: *Coriolanus* and the Birth of Republican Rome," *Shakespeare Quarterly* 58.2 (2007): 174–199.

34. Rossiter, *Angel with Horns: Fifteen Lectures on Shakespeare* (New York: Longman, 1989), 292. Rossiter considers how the bard employs comic relief not as a release valve for an otherwise overtaxed audience but rather to achieve what Rossiter calls "comprehensiveness." Rossiter writes that Shakespeare "takes the contrast and collision of opposites to extreme lengths . . . every risk is taken in using discord or clash . . . the most heterogeneous *moods* are yoked by violence together" (280). Though he conjures the language of Johnson's denouncement of Donne, Rossiter celebrates Shakespeare's complexity.

35. Rabkin, *Shakespeare and the Common Understanding* (London: Collier-Macmillan Limited, 1967), 7. "Each value, or set of values," Rabkin writes, "is a total way of seeing which excludes the other. There can be no compromise; we are not allowed to believe optimistically, as Hamlet does in contemplating Horatio's mixture of blood and judgment, that the opposed goods can coexist in one value system or one universe. The play says to us: choose one or the other, and in doing so you will see how it rules out the other. And yet each makes equally compelling claims on us; at any given moment we feel ourselves drawn irresistibly to one or the other total view of things" (7).

36. "[I]f we consider what *Hamlet* has been saying to us," Rabkin writes, "we see that it does not make us see a world in which nothing is valid. We see a world in which reason and civilization are absolute values even though they are contradicted by other values that paradoxically turn out to be equally absolute . . . It is not as if neither of these sets of values is based on reality—the cynical response; for better or for worse, both of them are. Thus this tragedy whose 'theme' as stated in cold prose is nihilistic is strangely affirmative" (9). More recently, Graham Bradshaw has made a sophisticated version of this point. Bradshaw isolates two visions in Shakespeare, a "sustaining humanistic vision" on the one hand and an "utterly amoral" vision on the other. In the humanistic view, "Nature itself provides a sanction for human values, which then appear to be discovered, or recognised" whereas the "opposed view of Nature allows no such affirmation." According to Bradshaw, in *Hamlet* and in Hamlet himself we see a "terrifyingly extensive" "collision between opposed views of Nature and value." And yet, as in Rabkin,

Shakespeare does not urge audiences merely to throw up their hands. Again, though Shakespeare does not urge a set of values on the audience, he does suggest in plays such as *Hamlet* that a decision must be made. See Bradshaw, *Shakespeare's Scepticism* (London: The Harvester Press, 1987), 4–6, 37.

37. Hamlin, *Tragedy and Scepticism in Shakespeare's England*, 5. In this, Hamlin recalls not just Montaigne but Bertrand Russell who, in estimating the value of skepticism, remarks that it eliminates passion's influence. See Russell, "Introduction: On the Value of Scepticism," in *Sceptical Essays* (London: Routledge, 2004). See Anita Gilman Sherman's fascinating account of "countermonuments" in Shakespeare for an argument mostly congenial to Hamlin's. Sherman, *Skepticism and Memory in Shakespeare and Donne* (New York: Palgrave Macmillan, 2007). In a sense, Hamlin and Sherman both build on Joel Altman's discussion of "the thoroughgoing pluralism of the Elizabethan mind." See Joel B. Altman, *The Tudor Play of Mind: Rhetorical Inquiry and the Development of Elizabethan Drama* (Berkeley and Los Angeles: University of California Press, 1978), 97.

38. *Northrop Frye on Shakespeare* (New Haven: Yale University Press, 1988), 101–2.

39. I am interested, as is Julia Reinhard Lupton, in Shakespearean moments "in which certain political questions come up against problems of life and living." See Lupton, *Thinking with Shakespeare: Essays on Politics and Life* (Chicago: University of Chicago Press, 2011), 8

40. Unger, *The Self Awakened: Pragmatism* (Cambridge, MA: Harvard University Press, 2007), 135. Unger elaborates his use of negative capability in *False Necessity: Anti-Necessitarian Social Theory in the Service of Radical Democracy*, new edition (New York: Verso, 2001), esp. 277–311.

41. Even more, negative capability "is a direct manifestation of our godlike power to outreach the established settings of action and thought" (134).

42. See Engle, *Shakespearean Pragmatism*, passim.

43. This, despite the fact that Margreta de Grazia, in a well-known recent study, has shown how Hamlet can be and has been likened to the roustabout clown of the medieval folk tradition. See de Grazia, *'Hamlet' without Hamlet* (Cambridge: Cambridge University Press, 2007). For a compelling argument that Hamlet gives too much thought to ideas long understood, at least on a philosophical level, as "poppycock"—that, in particular, "Hamlet takes transubstantiation and alchemy far too seriously" to be as "[s]keptical and *de la mode*" as readers often take him to be—see Katherine Eggert, "Hamlet's Alchemy: Transubstantiation, Modernity, Belief," *Shakespeare Quarterly* 64.1 (2013): 45–57, esp. 57.

44. Bloom, *Shakespeare: The Invention of the Human*, 12.

45. Kuzner, "Hamlet and the Truth About Friendship," forthcoming in *This Distracted Globe: World Making in Early Modern Literature* (New York: Fordham University Press).

46. Adelman, *Suffocating Mothers: Fantasies of Maternal Origin in Shakespeare's Plays*, Hamlet *to* The Tempest (New York: Routledge, 1992), 29. Hamlet's attempt at a solution to this boundary panic, for Adelman, is to recuperate Gertrude: to change her from a source of contamination (and of blurring boundaries that should be secure) to a "benign maternal presence" (33). This more salutary vulnerability to her, in Adelman's account, is for Hamlet the only way of "making safe the boundary-permeability that had been a source of terror" (33). I, like, Adelman, trace how boundaries of identity break down in the play, but in looking to Horatio's friendship with Hamlet, rather than Hamlet's relationship with his mother and father(s), we can distinguish the skeptical practice that I describe from Hamlet's struggle for certainty, and in doing so can glimpse a more politically-robust account of vulnerability. For Hamlet, being sure of Gertrude's benign maternal presence allows him to commence "repairing the boundaries of his selfhood" in masculinist fashion (31). We will see that for Horatio, by contrast, being unsure where he stands or what is to be done unsettles his sense of himself irreparably, and his willingness to practice this uncertainty allows for a minimal, skeptical politics free of Hamlet's masculinist fantasies. In general, there are several points where Adelman's arguments and my own overlap—usually having to do with identity and the uncertainty surrounding it—and one critical difference. Adelman's readings often chart male fantasies of self-sufficiency and separation from a contaminating female, the failure of those fantasies, and—in some cases—their replacement by faith in female generativity. Another way of putting this is that Adelman's readings detail how male characters shift between faiths, some less salutary than others. I, by contrast, focus more on potentially salutary aspects of a skeptical way of life—a way that, as I point out in the following chapter, offers a way out of masculinist fantasies.

47. See Kuzner, *Open Subjects: English Renaissance Republicans, Modern Selfhoods and the Virtue of Vulnerability* (Edinburgh: Edinburgh University Press, 2011), esp. 44–47.

48. Quotations of the play are from *Hamlet*, ed. R. B. Kennedy (London: Harper Press, 2011).

49. "To judge by this summary," David Lucking writes, "the tale that Horatio intends bears little resemblance to what the prince has in mind," a tale in which Hamlet is likely to be "an agent of destruction swept up in a whirlwind of fortuitous happenings." While I think

Lucking overstates the case a bit here, his point has merit. See Lucking, "*Hamlet* and the Narrative Construction of Reality," *English Studies* 89.2 (2008): 152–65, esp. 155.

50. Of lines 373–78, James Shapiro writes that "Horatio's words underscore much he has failed to grasp about his friend." That Horatio is incapable of presenting a full or even an accurate account of his friend's story I would never deny. The question is whether he intends to aspire toward such an account. See Shapiro, *1599: A Year in the Life of William Shakespeare* (London: Faber, 2005), 299.

51. *Oxford English Dictionary, Online Edition.* Accessed 24 May 2013.

52. Engle argues that Horatio does embody a balance of this kind, that he is possessed of a "detached attachment": that Horatio is "able to take a disinterested, nonstakeholder's attitude toward what one is thinking about," not in any absolute sense but as a "relative virtue." See Engle, "How Is Horatio Just?: How Just Is Horatio?," *Shakespeare Quarterly* 62.2 (2002): 256–62, esp. 259 and 262.

53. Timothy Wong argues that "Horatio ends up as the most sovereign character in the kingdom when the curtain falls," because he "take[s] charge of the only remaining sovereign right at the end of the play, the dying voice of the prince." This formal sovereignty may exist, but I would maintain that Horatio feels nothing of it. See Wong, "Steward of the Dying Voice: The Intrusion of Horatio into Sovereignty and Representation," *Telos* 153 (Winter 2010): 113–31, esp. 113.

54. Francis G. Schoff, in something of an overstatement, calls Horatio a "nobody"; see "Horatio: A Shakespearean Confidant," *Shakespeare Quarterly* 7.1 (1956): 53–57, esp. 55.

55. See, for instance, Christopher Warley, "Specters of Horatio," *ELH* 75.4 (2008): 1023–50. See also Warley's *Reading Class through Shakespeare, Donne, and Milton* (Cambridge: Cambridge University Press, 2014).

56. In our own context Judith Butler writes that vulnerability is friendship's inevitable—but also its potentially valuable—outcome. We are, she writes, "attached to others, at risk of losing those attachments, exposed to others, at risk of violence by virtue of that exposure"; "[w]e're undone by each other . . . [a]nd if we're not, we're missing something." Butler, *Precarious Life: The Powers of Mourning and Violence* (New York: Verso, 2004), 20, 23.

57. Holbrook, *Shakespeare's Individualism*, 1. Holbrook, outlining Shakespearean possibilities for self-cultivation, has reacted against those—grouped under the title of "Theory"—who have discredited "the common-sense notion of a 'self' existing outside . . . linguistic, cultural and social networks" (57).

58. For Lupton as for her book's model, Hannah Arendt, such sovereignty is not only an unsupportable concept but a dangerous one. Consider Arendt: "Politically, this identification of freedom with sovereignty is perhaps the most pernicious and dangerous consequence of the philosophical equation of freedom and free will. For it leads either to denial of human freedom—namely, if it is realized that whatever men may be, they are never sovereign—or to the insight that the freedom of one man, or a group, or a body politic can be purchased only at the price of freedom, i.e., the sovereignty of all others . . . If men wish to be free, it is precisely sovereignty they must renounce." Arendt, "What Is Freedom?," in *Between Past and Future: Eight Exercises in Political Thought* (New York: Penguin, 1977), 164–5.

59. Lupton, *Thinking with Shakespeare*, 24.

60. Lupton is avowedly, if not single-mindedly or programmatically, Arendtian in her approach, so while her account is nuanced and textured in its conception of agency, she focuses on how we might "summon chances for action in every corner" of existence (12).

61. Gil, *Shakespeare's Anti-Politics: Sovereign Power and the Life of the Flesh* (New York: Palgrave Macmillan, 2013). For Gil all Shakespearean states—from the most republican to the most tyrannical—expose subjects to extralegal sovereign power, reducing them to what Agamben calls bare life, opening them to the unlimited capacity to be killed. For Gil, the plays "launch a nihilistic critique of state power" (2).

62. Once the state strips selves of the identity it is supposed to secure, selves can enter into what Gil calls "the life of the flesh": a "luminous fleshliness," an experience of extreme vulnerability but also of intense connectedness, evident in the cannibalistic intercorporeality figured by prostitution in *Measure for Measure*, in the riots of *Othello*, and in the wilderness of *King Lear* (9).

1. CICERONIAN SKEPTICISM AND THE MIND-BODY PROBLEM IN *LUCRECE*

1. This is not to say that these two problems overlap perfectly in early modern texts or in *Lucrece*, given the unstable, unsystematic nature of early modern self-conceptions; they are, however, synonymous enough in Shakespeare's poem to warrant the terminological slippage that others have employed in discussing *Lucrece* and that I employ as well.

2. Belsey, "Tarquin Dispossessed: Expropriation and Consent in *The Rape of Lucrece*," *Shakespeare Quarterly* 52.3 (2001): 315–35.

3. See Carla Mazzio and David Hillman, eds., *The Body in Parts: Fantasies of Corporeality in Early Modern Europe* (New York: Routledge,

1997); Victoria Kahn, Neil Saccamano, and Daniela Coli, eds., *Politics and the Passions, 1500–1850* (Princeton: Princeton University Press, 2006); Gail Kern Paster, Katherine Rowe, and Mary Floyd-Wilson, eds., *Reading the Early Modern Passions: Essays in the Cultural History of Emotions* (Philadelphia: University of Pennsylvania Press, 2004); Paster, *Humoring the Body: Emotions and the Shakespearean Stage* (Chicago: University of Chicago Press, 2004); and Michael Schoenfeldt, *Bodies and Selves in Early Modern England: Physiology and Inwardness in Spenser, Shakespeare, Herbert, and Milton* (Cambridge: Cambridge University Press, 1999).

4. On the distribution of thought, see Scott Manning Stevens, "Sacred Heart and Secular Brain," in *The Body in Parts*, 263–84.

5. See Patterson, *Reading Between the Lines* (Madison: University of Wisconsin Press, 1993), 297–312; Dubrow, *Captive Victors: Shakespeare's Narrative Poems and Sonnets* (Ithaca: Cornell University Press, 1987), 160–162; and Donaldson, *The Rapes of Lucretia: A Myth and Its Transformations* (Oxford: Oxford University Press, 1982), 43–44, 116–17. For some other influential readings that do not regard the poem as republican in any useful sense, see Coppélia Kahn, "The Rape in Shakespeare's *Lucrece*," *Shakespeare Studies* 9 (1976): 45–72, and Stephanie Jed, *Chaste Thinking: The Rape of Lucretia and the Birth of Modern Humanism* (Bloomington: Indiana University Press, 1989).

6. Hadfield, *Shakespeare and Republicanism* (Cambridge: Cambridge University Press, 2005), 130–53.

7. All references to *Lucrece* are to *The Narrative Poems*, ed. Jonathan Crewe (New York: Penguin Books, 1999).

8. Marcus Aurelius writes that "you may at any hour you please retreat into yourself," but Tarquin's structure does not quite allow for this. Aurelius, *Meditations*, trans. A. S. L. Farquharson (New York: Oxford University Press, 1989), 23.

9. And if so, constraint would be required, since Tarquin's desire is too unruly ever to exist as part of a harmonious reason-passion complex.

10. On this point, the text is not clear; the soul does seem to have extension, which suggests, but does not necessitate, property dualism.

11. For more on this, see Genevieve Lloyd, *The Man of Reason: "Male" and "Female" in Western Philosophy* (Minneapolis: University of Minnesota Press, 1993), 22–37.

12. Epictetus, *Discourses and Selected Writings*, trans. and ed. Robert Dobbin (New York: Penguin, 2008), 69.

13. *De Oratore*, 21.

14. *On Moral Ends*, ed. Julia Annas, trans. Raphael Woolf (New York: Cambridge University Press, 2001), 102. For Cicero's criticism of Stoic thought more generally, see *On Moral Ends*, 90–116.

15. *Cicero's Tusculan Disputations, Treatises on The Nature of the Gods, and On the Commonwealth*, trans. C. D. Yonge (New York: Harper and Brothers, 1877), book I, especially sections xx–xxxi.

16. *On Academic Scepticism*, trans. Charles Brittain (Indianapolis: Hackett, 2006), 72–3.

17. See, for example, *On Academic Scepticism*, 82.

18. Epictetus, *Discourses*, 141.

19. *De Oratore III*, in *De Oratore III, De Fato, Paradoxa Stoicorum, De Partitione Oratoria*, trans. H. Rackham (Cambridge, MA: Harvard University Press, 1982), 49.

20. *De Oratore II*, in *De Oratore I and II*, trans. E. W. Sutton (Cambridge, MA: Harvard University Press, 1948), 285. Cicero goes so far as to claim that being won over is more often a matter of passion than of deliberation. "Nothing in oratory," he writes, "is more important than to win for the orator the favour of his hearer, and to have the latter so affected as to be swayed by something resembling a mental impulse or emotion, rather than by judgement or deliberation." See *On the Orator* in *On the Good Life*, trans. Michael Grant (New York: Penguin, 1971), 255; and *De Oratore I and II*, 325.

21. In a reading of the poem in Ovidian and Lacanian contexts rather than republican and Ciceronian ones, Lynn Enterline details both how Shakespeare seems to long "for a truly performative rhetoric, a language powerful enough to change the world rather than merely represent it," and how "the failure of a merely instrumental (or merely representational) use of language is the positive condition for her [Lucrece's] emergence as a subject." See Enterline, " 'Poor instruments' and unspeakable events in *The Rape of Lucrece*," in *The Rhetoric of the Body from Ovid to Shakespeare* (New York: Cambridge University Press, 2000), 152–97, esp. 186 and 176.

22. *De Inventione, De Optimo Genere Oratorum, Topica*, trans. H. M. Hubbell (Cambridge, MA: Harvard University Press, 1949), 7.

23. *On Duties*, 21.

24. *De Oratore I and II*, 223.

25. *De Oratore I and II*, 331; *On the Orator*, 246, 307.

26. As I have noted elsewhere, a similar moment also occurs in *Titus Andronicus*, when Lavinia pleads with Tamora just before Chiron and Demetrius rape her. See Kuzner, *Open Subjects*, 109–11.

27. *On the Good Life*, 188.

28. *Brutus/Orator*, trans. G. L. Hendrickson and H. M. Hubbell (Cambridge: Harvard University Press, 1939), 217.

29. *De Oratore*, 41.

30. Cicero, *On the Commonwealth and On the Laws,* ed. James E. G. Zetzel (New York: Cambridge University Press, 1999), 101.

31. For more on *anacyclosis* and republican virtue, see *Open Subjects,* 13–23.

32. Aurelius, *Meditations,* 20.

33. For another reading of how the "*contrapposto* energy, the resistance to resistance" present here, and in the poem's very rhetoric, accounts for rape, see Joel Fineman, "Shakespeare's *Will*: The Temporality of Rape," *Representations* 20 (1987): 25–76, esp. 42.

34. For more on this, from the perspective of Stoicism, see Hadot, *Philosophy as a Way of Life* (Malden, MA: Blackwell, 1995), ch. 8, 217–37.

35. According to Epictetus, "[t]he gods have released you from accountability for your parents, your siblings, your body, your possessions—for death and for life itself. They made you responsible only for what is in your power—the proper use of impressions" (*Discourses,* 37).

36. Quoted in Hadot, *What Is Ancient Philosophy?,* 128.

37. Melissa Sanchez figures the paradoxical nature of agency and resistance in the poem around not *askēsis* but active rebellion. The poem, through its portrayal of Lucrece, suggests that "the failure actively to resist tyranny bespeaks a quiet collusion with the abuse of power" while at the same time "emphasizing the self-destructive nature of active rebellion," suggesting both the need for, and the impossibility of, rebellion that preserves the rebel. Sanchez, *Erotic Subjects: The Sexuality of Politics in Early Modern English Literature* (Oxford: Oxford University Press, 2011), 95.

38. For perhaps the most prominent argument still being made in favor of dualism—in this case, property dualism—see David J. Chalmers, *The Conscious Mind: In Search of a Fundamental Theory* (New York: Oxford University Press, 1996), esp. 93–171.

39. See Lakoff and Johnson, *Philosophy in the Flesh,* especially 267–89.

40. Taylor, *Sources of the Self: The Making of the Modern Identity* (Cambridge, MA: Harvard University Press, 1989), 188–9. For a compelling and contrasting account—of how Cartesian thinking was subject to immediate critique, and of how dualism has not held nearly the sway attributed to it—see Christopher Braider, *The Matter of Mind: Reason and Experience in the Age of Descartes* (Toronto: University of Toronto Press, 2012).

41. For more on these assumptions, see Lakoff and Johnson, *Philosophy in the Flesh,* esp. 290–336, as well as Lakoff, *Whose Freedom? The*

Battle Over America's Most Important Idea (New York: Picador, 2007); and Lakoff, *The Political Mind.*

42. See Johnson, *Moral Imagination: Implications of Cognitive Science for Ethics* (Chicago: University of Chicago Press, 1994).

43. For one example of an argument that separates Descartes himself from Cartesian dualism, see Gordon Baker and Katherine J. Morris, *Descartes' Dualism* (New York: Routledge, 1996).

44. For Johnson and Lakoff's account of Descartes and his influence, see *Philosophy in the Flesh*, 391–414.

45. Crane, *Shakespeare's Brain: Reading with Cognitive Theory* (Princeton: Princeton University Press, 2000), 16–17.

46. Paster, *Humoring the Body*, 10.

47. Schoenfeldt, *Bodies and Selves in Early Modern England*, 1. See p. 15 for Schoenfeldt's explanation of how he differs from Paster. See *Humoring the Body*, 20–21, for Paster's explanation of where she departs from Schoenfeldt.

48. Augustine writes that "it must be firmly established that virtue, the condition of right living, holds command over the parts of the body from her throne in the mind, and that the consecrated body is the instrument of the consecrated will; and that if will continues unshaken and steadfast, whatever anyone else does with the body or to the body, provided that it cannot be avoided without committing sin, involves no blame to the sufferer." See *The City of God*, trans. David Knowles (Harmondsworth: Penguin Books, 1972), 1.16: 26.

49. Belsey, "Tarquin Dispossessed," 331.

50. For a few representative accounts, see Luce Irigaray, *Speculum of the Other Woman* (Ithaca: Cornell University Press, 1985), 180–90; Genevieve Lloyd, *The Man of Reason: 'Male' and 'Female' in Western Philosophy* (Minneapolis: University of Minnesota Press, 1993); Victor J. Seidler, *Rediscovering Masculinity: Reason, Language and Sexuality* (New York: Routledge, 1989); Naomi Scheman, *Engenderings: Constructions of Knowledge, Authority, and Privilege* (New York: Routledge, 1993); and Elizabeth A. Foyster, *Manhood in Early Modern England: Honour, Sex and Marriage* (New York: Longman, 1999), esp. 28–31. For a range of essays on the topic of Descartes and gender, see Susan Bordo, ed., *Feminist Interpretations of Rene Descartes* (University Park: Pennsylvania State University Press, 1999).

51. Quoted in Kate Aughterson, ed., *Renaissance Woman: A Sourcebook: Constructions of Femininity in England* (New York: Routledge, 1995), 144.

52. *On the Commonwealth*, 82.

53. Cicero writes this in "De Amicitia." See *On the Good Life*, 201.

54. For an account of Cicero's rhetoric, see Nancy Myers, "Cicero's (S)trumpet: Roman Women and the *Second Philippic,*" *Rhetoric Review* 22.4 (2003): 337–52.

55. Cicero mentions Lucrece twice in *On the Commonwealth*, to draw attention to how her death galvanized the establishment of the republic, and to make the point that although there was no law against sexual assault under the Tarquins, Sextus Tarquinus nonetheless violated eternal law in raping Lucrece (47, 133).

56. See, for instance, *Letters to Atticus, Books I–VI*, trans. E. O. Winstedt (Cambridge, MA: Harvard University Press, 1980); *Letters to Friends*, vol. 1, trans. D. R. Shackleton Bailey (Cambridge, MA: Harvard University Press, 2001); and Anthony Everitt's biography, *Cicero: The Life and Times of Rome's Greatest Politician* (New York: Random House, 2001).

57. Belsey puts this point, particularly when it comes to Tarquin, in psychoanalytical terms: that Tarquin, "slave to an insatiable desire beyond the reach of Law, is strangely Lacanian three hundred and fifty years *avant la lettre*," that he "closely resembles Jacques Lacan's doomed, desiring subject." "[D]issatisfied with what he already possesses," Tarquin "wants precisely what, because it is forbidden, will destroy him and all he already has" (323).

58. Belsey, Kahn, Fineman, Enterline, and Dubrow all attend to such issues. See also Mark Breitenberg, "Publishing Chastity: Shakespeare's 'The Rape of Lucrece,'" in *Anxious Masculinity in Early Modern England* (New York: Cambridge University Press, 1996), 97–127

59. Hillman, *Shakespeare's Entrails*, 1, 2, 4–5.

60. See Chalmers, *The Conscious Mind*, 93–122.

61. Maus, "Taking Tropes Seriously: Language and Violence in Shakespeare's *Rape of Lucrece,*" *Shakespeare Quarterly* 37.1 (1986): 66–82, passim.

62. "Nor is the conviction that body and soul are inseparable merely a whim of the protagonists," Maus writes. "Shakespeare's rhetoric asserts it constantly" (74). Indeed, it is sometimes said that it is only by importing a modern, post-Cartesian perspective that we can regard the metaphoric embodiment of mental events as mere metaphor at all. Schoenfeldt, for example, writes that "Whereas our post-Cartesian ontology imagines psychological inwardness and physiological materialism as necessarily separate realms of existence, and thus renders corporeal language for emotion highly metaphorical, the Galenic regime of the humoral self that supplies these writers with much of their vocabulary of inwardness demanded the invasion of social and psychological realms by biological and environmental processes." See Schoenfeldt, *Bodies and Selves in Early Modern England*, 8.

63. This concept is so ubiquitous that comprehensive citation is not possible. For a preliminary sense of the importance of masculine self-control, see Foyster, *Manhood in Early Modern England*, 28–48; and Alexandra Shepard, *Meanings of Manhood in Early Modern England* (Oxford: Oxford University Press), 21–89.

64. Kahn writes that "[b]ecause Shakespeare has 'given tongue' to a heroine who hardly speaks at all in Livy or in Ovid, because he has endowed her with such keen insight into the patriarchal meanings of the rape, her 'bleeding body,' understood by the Romans as an icon of their newly won republican liberty, must also be a disturbing after-image of how patriarchy—whether in monarchical or republican form—configures the feminine." See Kahn, "Publishing Shame: *The Rape of Lucrece*," in *A Companion to Shakespeare's Works*, ed. Richard Dutton and Jean E. Howard (Malden, MA: Blackwell, 2003), 4:259–74, esp. 271.

2. "IT STOPS ME HERE": LOVE AND SELF-CONTROL IN *OTHELLO*

1. Cavell, *Disowning Knowledge*, 35. As Norman Rabkin writes earlier, "his love for Desdemona is a version of Christian faith." Rabkin, *Shakespeare and the Common Understanding*, 63.

2. Kövecses, *Metaphors of Anger, Pride, and Love* (Philadelphia: John Benjamins Publishing Company, 1986), 88. The "[i]nability to function normally in love involves a lack of control over love," Kövecses writes, and thus "[w]e have to decide whether we want *love* (together with a lack of control) or whether we want *control over love* (in which case, however, there is no room for 'real' love as it is defined by our culture)" (88).

3. *The Philosophical Writings of Descartes,*trans. John Cottingham, Robert Stoothoff, and Dugald Murdoch (Cambridge: Cambridge University Press, 1985), 1:348.

4. All references to the play are to *Othello*, ed. Russ McDonald (New York: Penguin Putnam, 2001).

5. For a detailed account of the gardening metaphors, see E. K. Weedin, Jr., "Love's Reason in *Othello*," *SEL: Studies in English Literature, 1500–1900* 15.2 (1975): 293–308, esp. 296–7.

6. Which is to say that I find overstated readings, at least as old as A. C. Bradley and at least as new as Raphael Lyne, in which "[t]he hero's all-in-all sufficiency . . . degenerates as the play progresses." While Othello becomes increasingly dependent, he is never self-sufficient. Lyne, *Shakespeare, Rhetoric, and Cognition* (Cambridge: Cambridge University Press, 2011), 163, 171. Janet Adelman, similarly, writes that "Othello has the presence, the fullness of being, that Iago

lacks" and that "Othello is everywhere associated with the kind of interior solidity and wholeness that stands as a reproach to Iago's interior emptiness and fragmentation." See Adelman, "Iago's Alter Ego: Race as Projection in *Othello*," *Shakespeare Quarterly* 48.2 (1997): 125–44, esp. 127–8. This belief (or lack thereof) in Othello's self-sufficiency has consequences for how we read the play. Consider, for instance, Adelman's *Suffocating Mothers*, in which Adelman reads *Othello* as a play about its eponymous hero's exchange of a martial identity defined by "self-sufficiency and isolation" for dependence on Desdemona (65). Othello's "love-language," Adelman writes, "is infused with the intensity of infantile need for the maternal presence that orders its world" (65). Unfortunately, Othello struggles between two intensities—the "desire for fusion with the woman he idealizes as the nurturant source of his being" and the "conviction that her participation in sexuality has contaminated her" (66–7). The latter intensity gains the upper hand, such that Othello, in imagining Desdemona's betrayal, recovers (in fantasy) the male identity that he had lost (71). As will become increasingly clear, Adelman and I both read *Othello* as a play about the negotiation between union and separation; we both also read the play's tragedy as driven by certainty. But there are also important differences. In Adelman's reading, separation and union belong to the spheres of battle and love (respectively), but I see Shakespeare working out a dynamic between separation and union *within* the sphere of love, in the quayside meeting and when Othello and Desdemona first quarrel. By considering the themes of union and separation within love, we are thus able, temporarily, to glimpse something other than the all-or-nothing situation in which Othello is either a self-sufficient war hero or utterly infantile in his dependence.

7. That passion tampers with common-sensical notions of causation in *Othello* is a point also made by Joel Altman; see " 'Preposterous Conclusions': Eros, Enargeia, and the Composition of *Othello*," *Representations* 18 (1987): 129–57. Altman shows how, in *Othello* as well as the Elizabethan period more generally, being "under the sway of passion" makes it possible to imagine that "effects precede causes (rationally construed)" and that "ends precede means" (132–3).

8. G. Wilson Knight, in a similar vein, writes that Desdemona is Othello's divinity, and that Iago's accomplishment is to turn her from a benevolent God into a devil. "During the action, as Iago's plot succeeds," Knight writes, "her essential divinity changes, for Othello, to a thing hideous and devilish—that is to its antithesis." Knight, "The *Othello* Music," *The Wheel of Fire: Interpretations of Shakespeare's Tragedy* (New York: Meridian, 1964), 97–119, esp. 114.

9. Without question, Othello's dependence has not only to do with how he conceives of love but also with his more general sense of social dependence. Very early in the play, upon hearing that Brabantio means to oppose his union, Othello says of his social life something quite similar to what he says of his intimate one: "I fetch my life and being / From men of royal siege" (1.2.21–2). Othello, that is, conceives of his existence as radically dependent almost as soon as we meet him, and in the broadest sense his story involves replacing men of royal siege with his wife. There are two crucial differences between how he conceives of Desdemona and of men of high rank, though, one that seems to strengthen the notion of Othello's radical social dependence, and another that shows how this dependence takes a specific form in love. First, Othello depends on men of royal siege both for life and for being, whereas in relation to Desdemona he can exist, in however impoverished a way, without her. In a sense, then, his dependence on men of royal siege is more total than his dependence on his wife. Surely, *Othello* is also a play about how the social field limits possibilities for agency and self-control. In another sense, however, his dependence on these men is far more limited compared to his dependence on Desdemona. In saying that he fetches his life and being from them, Othello assumes an active role in his creation and conservation; while he might depend on others for his place in Venetian society he, not men of royal siege, is the responsible agent. It thus makes sense that Othello makes this remark in a speech that registers self-confidence that he can "out-tongue" Brabantio's complaints against him (l.19). It is only in Othello's metaphors for love that he effaces his status as agent. So while Othello is hardly inclined to conceive of selfhood in terms of atomistic self-direction, it is only in love, only in relation to his deity, that that direction is altogether relinquished.

10. Descartes, *Meditations on First Philosophy*, trans. Laurence J. Lafleur (New York: Macmillan, 1951), 47.

11. For the definitive account of Descartes and causation, one that argues that Descartes not only allows for the causal efficacy of created beings but even evinces a position compatible with that of "mere conservationism," which grants fairly wide scope for individual agency, see Tad M. Schmaltz, *Descartes on Causation* (Oxford: Oxford University Press, 2007). The view of agency that Othello adopts, and that some Cartesians develop, is closer to "occasionalism," the view that God (in Othello's case, Desdemona) is the only real causal agent. For more on this in Cartesian, rather than Shakespearean contexts, see Steven Nadler, *Occasionalism: Causation Among the Cartesians* (Oxford: Oxford University Press, 2011).

12. Newman, "'And wash the Ethiop white': Femininity and the Monstrous in *Othello*," in *Essaying Shakespeare* (Minneapolis: University of Minnesota Press, 2009), 38–58, esp. 56.

13. J. Middleton Murry makes this point: "Because she loved it," Murry writes, "she forgot it only in the moment when it was right to forget it: when Othello was sick and her concern for the man she loved drove out all concern for the token of their love." See Murry, "Desdemona's Handkerchief," in *Othello: Critical Essays*, ed. Susan Snyder (London: Garland Publishing, 1988), 91–9, esp. 94.

14. In a fascinating account of causation in the play, Katharine Eisaman Maus articulates other, related problems with Othello's thinking about cause and effect and particularly with Othello's powers as an observer: "Either Othello must accept a degree of uncertainty in his relation to Desdemona," Maus writes, "or he must repress his awareness of his own limitations as an observer." Maus, "Proof and Consequences: Inwardness and Its Exposure in the English Renaissance," *Representations* 34 (1991): 29–52, esp. 42. See also Maus, "Horns of Dilemma: Jealousy, Gender, and Spectatorship in English Renaissance Drama," *ELH* 54.3 (1987): 561–83.

15. *Meditations*, 51.

16. In his famous treatment of *Othello*, Stephen Greenblatt, rather differently, identifies lust as the idolatrous aspect of Othello's love, one that, in the seventeenth century, can destroy the Christian's love for God and the marital relationship alike. See Greenblatt, "The Improvisation of Power," in *William Shakespeare's Othello*, ed. Harold Bloom (New York: Chelsea House Publishers, 1987), 37–59. This chapter formed part of Greenblatt's *Renaissance Self-Fashioning: From More to Shakespeare* (Chicago: University of Chicago Press, 1980).

17. As Kenneth Burke puts it, Othello is a "possessor possessed by his very engrossment." See "Othello: An Essay to Illustrate a Method," *The Hudson Review* 4.2 (1951): 165–203, esp.167. For a more recent essay that addresses the problem of a husband's "possession" of his wife in *Othello* and the status of woman in early modernity as "a *property* category" more generally, see Peter Stallybrass, "Patriarchal Territories: The Body Enclosed," in *Othello: Critical Essays*, 251–77. Stallybrass, as well as Alan Sinfield, see Emilia as offering a potential way out of patriarchal thinking. See Sinfield, "Cultural Materialism, *Othello*, and the Politics of Plausibility," in *Faultlines: Cultural Materialism and the Politics of Dissident Reading* (Berkeley and Los Angeles: University of California Press, 1992), 29–51, esp. 38. For more on the issue of possession, see also Maus, who writes that Othello "laments an arrangement

that grants men ownership of women but which cannot grant them the usual correlatives of possession, knowledge and control." Maus, "Horns of Dilemma," 578.

18. In a fascinating reading of Iago's role in this, Daniel Juan Gil argues that the villain wants two things: "to force more and more people to recognize themselves as abjectly and inescapably subject to sovereign power, and thereby to force them to interact with each other and then also with Iago himself at the level of the flesh and its perverse vulnerabilities when exposed to raw state power." See Gil, *Shakespeare's Anti-Politics: Sovereign Power and the Life of the Flesh*, 89.

19. Roland Barthes puts this doubleness the following way: "Subjection, though, is my business: subjected, seeking to subject the other, I experience in my fashion the will to power, the *libido dominandi*." Barthes, *A Lover's Discourse*, trans. Richard Howard (New York: Farrar, Straus, and Giroux, 1978), 121.

20. *The Passions of the Soul*, 389.

21. As readers often point out, his self-loathing does take this status as a source, most dramatically when he compares his self-killing to his killing of "a malignant and a turbaned Turk" and "circumcised dog" (5.2.353–5).

22. For perhaps the most engaging account of Desdemona's own flaws, see Harry Berger, Jr., "Impertinent Trifling: Desdemona's Handkerchief," *Shakespeare Quarterly* 47.3 (1996): 235–50.

23. F. R. Leavis, in his famous denunciation of Othello—mainly a reaction against A. C. Bradley and others who read Othello in sympathetic terms—diagnoses the general as prone to "self-preoccupation," "self-pride," and "ferocious stupidity." Leavis also remarks that Othello's love for Desdemona must involve "ignorance of her," "must be much more a matter of self-centered and self-regarding satisfactions." I certainly agree that Othello is ignorant of Desdemona, but if what I have argued is right, Othello cannot be as straightforwardly self-centered as Leavis suggests. See Leavis, "Diabolic Intellect and the Noble Hero: or The Sentimentalist's Othello," in *Othello: Critical Essays*, 101–26, esp. 116, 112, 111.

24. Much criticism of the play makes a version of this claim. For an insightful recent example in which the portrayal of Othello is a portrayal of erotic refusal, see Tzachi Zamir's chapter on the play in *Double Vision: Moral Philosophy and Shakespearean Drama* (Princeton: Princeton University Press, 2006). Zamir argues that "[t]he play is about the happy, painless destruction of a person that is conducted within the clasp of a loving embrace," and that Othello ultimately finds *eros* intolerable (160).

25. *Meditations*, 33

26. Of the end, Neill writes that it is "conspicuously shorn of the funereal dignities that usually serve to put a form of order upon such spectacles of ruin." See Neill, "Unproper Beds: Race, Adultery, and the Hideous in *Othello*," *Shakespeare Quarterly* 40.4 (1989): 383–412, esp. 383.

27. Murry sees the tragedy primarily in terms of the impossibility of total union in love, the fact that "[l]ove seeks between two total human beings a complete fusion of identity, and it cannot be" ("Desdemona's Handkerchief," 95). Othello's alternation between feelings of being possessed and wishing to possess could certainly be read as symptomatic of this tendency in love.

28. Menon, "Of Cause," *English Studies* 94.3 (2013): 278–90, esp. 281.

29. Gross, "Slander and Skepticism in *Othello*," *ELH* 56.4 (1989): 819–52, esp. 827.

30. Donald C. Freeman makes a similar point with specific reference to the 'understanding is seeing' metaphor. Freeman argues that Othello is ruled by an absolutist version of this metaphor, which Iago exploits. "Othello and the 'Ocular Proof,'" in *The Shakespearean International Yearbook* 4 (Aldershot: Ashgate, 2004), 56–71.

31. Indeed, in recent years there have emerged a number of manuals that advance the use of metaphor for a therapeutic repaving of the neural pathways that shape how we conceive of love. For just a few of these, see David Buss, *The Dangerous Passion: Why Jealousy Is as Necessary as Love and Sex* (New York: Free Press, 2000); Helen Fisher, *Why We Love: The Nature and Chemistry of Romantic Love* (New York: Henry Holt & Co., 2005); and Barbara L. Fredrickson, *Love 2.0: How Our Supreme Emotion Affects Everything We Feel, Think, Do, and Become* (New York: Hudson Street Press, 2013).

32. Lakoff and Johnson, *Philosophy in the Flesh*, 174–5.

33. Causation, for Lakoff and Johnson, thus "is a multivalent radial concept," such that any "theory of the one true causation becomes not merely false, but silly" (226). Lakoff and Johnson's account of causation in an earlier book, *Metaphors We Live By* (Chicago: University of Chicago Press, 1980), is arguably less nuanced than the account in *Philosophy in the Flesh*, or in books such as Johnson's *Moral Imagination*, and Lakoff's *The Political Mind*.

34. Turner points out that our first experiences of cause and effect include not only "*direct manipulation*"—but also "[t]he power of the sun to heat us, of the wind to chill us, of others (especially parents) to touch or hurt us, of the empty stomach to make us unhappy." Turner, "Causation," in *Death Is the Mother of Beauty: Mind, Metaphor, Criticism* (Chicago: University of Chicago Press, 1987), 139–83, esp. 161.

35. Lakoff and Johnson, *Philosophy in the Flesh*, 209.

36. Snyder, *The Comic Matrix of Shakespeare's Tragedies* (Princeton: Princeton University Press, 1979), 74.

37. See Kövecses, "The Concept of Romantic Love," in *Metaphors of Anger, Pride and Love*, 61–105. See also Kövecses, *The Language of Love: The Semantics of Passion in Conversational English* (Lewisburg: Bucknell University Press, 1988). Kövecses draws some of his examples from Lakoff and Johnson, *Metaphors We Live By*.

38. In a consideration of *Othello*, Richard McCoy makes a similar point about romantic love: that "[r]omantic love repeatedly blurs the distinction between religious faith and romantic fidelity, and the beloved is routinely idealized if not deified." McCoy, "*Othello* and the Stakes of Tragedy," in *Faith in Shakespeare*, 82–112, esp. 84–5.

39. Gibbs, *The Poetics of Mind: Figurative Thought, Language, and Understanding* (Cambridge: Cambridge University Press, 1994), 148.

40. Gibbs, *Embodiment and Cognitive Science* (Cambridge: Cambridge University Press, 2005), 120–1.

41. In a reading focused on Iago, Paul Cefalu also argues against reading the play as advancing cognitive therapy, as espousing the notion that "through mindful exercises—consciously turning irrational into rational beliefs—and aversive conditioning and habitual training, one can reconstruct one's cognitive architecture." Cefalu, "The Burdens of Mind Reading in Shakespeare's *Othello*: A Cognitive and Psychoanalytic Approach to Iago's Theory of Mind," *ELH* 64.3 (2013): 265–94, esp. 281.

42. Bloom, *Shakespeare: The Invention of the Human*, 435.

43. For a complex, fascinating consideration of Iago's dependence on Othello, one that reads Iago in Kleinian terms, see Adelman, "Iago's Alter Ego."

44. Bishop, *Shakespeare and the Theatre of Wonder* (Cambridge: Cambridge University Press, 1996), 7.

45. *The Passions of the Soul*, 353.

46. For an interesting account of wonder not dissimilar from the one offered here, see Luce Irigaray, "Wonder: A Reading of Descartes, *The Passions of the Soul*," in *An Ethics of Sexual Difference* (London: Athlone Press, 1993), 72–82. Irigaray is interested in wonder as what might prompt us to be "faithful to the perpetual newness of the self, the other, the world," and while this glosses Cartesian wonder nicely, there is quite a lot else at play in *The Passions*, for example, when Descartes focuses on self-mastery (82).

47. G. Wilson Knight argues that "[w]hen Othello is represented as enduring loss of control he is, as Macbeth and Lear never are, ugly, idiotic." One point I am making here is that Knight's assertion about the

connection between loss of control and ugliness is only sometimes true. See Knight, "The *Othello* Music," 103.

48. Bataille, *Death and Sensuality: A Study of Eroticism and the Taboo* (New York: Walker and Company, 1962), 17.

49. Greenblatt, "The Improvisation of Power," 48.

50. Snyder, *The Comic Matrix of Shakespeare's Tragedies*, 74.

51. May, *Love and Will* (New York: W. W. Norton & Co., 1969), 109, 100.

52. Julia Reinhard Lupton points out that this is a fantasy about which *Othello* evinces ambivalence. Lupton argues both that "[a]s Gentile barbarian, the black Othello enters the play as a living symbol of Christian universalism" and that we should be careful to avoid loving "this vision of Christian humanism not wisely but too well." Lupton, *Citizen-Saints: Shakespeare and Political Theology* (London: University of Chicago Press, 2005), 109, 111.

53. As T. S. Eliot puts it in his reading of Othello's final speech, "[h]umility is the most difficult of all virtues to achieve; nothing dies harder than the desire to think well of oneself." See "Shakespeare and the Stoicism of Seneca," in *Shakespeare's* Othello: *A Casebook*, ed. John Wain (London: Macmillan, 1994), 70.

54. In an essay that is mostly about patriarchy's deformations in the play, Edward Snow reads "I will deny thee nothing" in a radically different way. Snow claims that "Othello's reply sounds like the adolescent's attempt to appease this figure, and suggests how precarious and pathetic the sense of manhood wrested from it is." I agree that the reply comes from within a patriarchal structure, but Snow's reading strikes me as ungenerous in seeing Othello's reply as adolescent. Edward A. Snow, "Sexual Anxiety and the Male Order of Things in *Othello*," in *Othello: Critical Essays*, 213–50, esp. 234.

55. *The Passions*, 345.

56. Paul Kottman, for instance, argues that love is about "two individuals *who actively claim* their separate individuality, their own freedom, in the only way that they can—through one another." Typically we read *Romeo and Juliet* as dramatizing friction between lovers' desires and those of the community, but for Kottman this is to miss Shakespeare's insight. Romeo and Juliet do not establish a union that dissolves their individual identities in a new self with boundaries set in opposition to Verona. Rather, they accomplish individual separateness through each other. Love's bonds, in other words, ultimately deepen separation and individuation. In love, according to Kottman, we react against the fact that existence is just the opposite of what Bataille says it

is: that "nothing, not even mortality, separates or individuates us abso-lutely." Love lets us claim our lives as our own, to be discontinuous, to have greater degrees of control. In this, love makes possessive individual-ity possible. Kottman reads *Romeo and Juliet* ingeniously, but this is not Shakespeare's position in *Othello*, where he dramatizes loss of control in love, taking such loss—and the retention of only enough control to bear that loss—as necessary for love's success. Kottman, "Defying the Stars: Tragic Love as the Struggle for Freedom in Romeo and Juliet," *Shake-speare Quarterly* 63.1 (2012): 1–38, esp. 6, 37–8.

57. Fromm, *The Art of Loving* (New York: Open Road Media, 2013), 8, 17. We wish to ward this off, so much so that man's "deepest need" "is the need to overcome his separateness, to leave the prison of his alone-ness" (9).

58. Fromm does acknowledge some limits to our mind-reading ability: "We know ourselves and yet even with all the efforts we may make, we do not know ourselves. We know our fellow man, and yet we do not know him, because we are not a thing, and our fellow man is not a thing. The more we reach into the depth of our being, or someone else's being, the more the goal of knowledge eludes us" (27).

59. Badiou (with Nicholas Truong), *In Praise of Love*, trans. Peter Bush (London: Serpent's Tail, 2012), 21.

60. As we will see in Chapter 3, Badiou's conception of the "Pau-line" event, in contrast to his conception of love, is more congenial to Shakespeare's skepticism.

61. Barthes, *A Lover's Discourse*, 234.

62. Bersani, *Homos* (Cambridge, MA: Harvard University Press, 1995), 128–9.

63. Hardt points out that while we readily conceive of the politics of friendship, we tend not to think of a politics of love; "our intimate notions of love and our social notions," Hardt writes, "are generally held to be radically separate and even divergent." We think of love as inward-looking, acutely exclusive, dangerously volatile, unlike the more mea-sured, respectful, and moderate affects of friendship. In Hannah Arendt's famous distinction, love, unlike friendship, destroys the "in-between" that separates individuals and that, for Arendt, is a necessary constituent of the social. But if love is defined otherwise—as not so much destroying the in-between as being an excruciating in-between—then a politics of love becomes thinkable. Indeed, for those of us to whom self-sovereignty is neither an assumption of, nor an end for, politics, love could prove a rich resource for political thinking. Michael Hardt, "For Love or Money," *Cultural Anthropology* 26.4 (2011): 676–82, esp. 677.

64. Heather Davis and Paige Sarlin, "'On the Risk of a New Relationality': An Interview with Lauren Berlant and Michael Hardt," *Reviews in Cultural Theory* 2.3 (2012): 7–27, esp. 9.

65. Berlant, "A Properly Political Concept of Love: Three Approaches in Ten Pages," *Cultural Anthropology* 26.4 (2011): 683–91, esp. 685.

66. Berlant, "On the Risk of a New Relationality," 16.

67. Berlant, "A Properly Political Concept of Love," 685.

68. Philip C. McGuire reads the scene in the Senate Chamber as already positive in that there we see accurate "sifting and interpreting of divergent testimony." "*Othello* as an 'Assay of Reason,'" *Shakespeare Quarterly* 24.2 (1973): 198–209, esp. 200.

69. For an interesting account of how Othello works in this speech "to respond to a desire to ground the passage, to produce a sense of agency in a scene of seduction without cause, without seducer or seduced," see Christopher Pye, "'To throw out our eyes for brave Othello': Shakespeare and Aesthetic Ideology," *Shakespeare Quarterly* 60.4 (2009): 425–447, esp. 436.

70. Rabkin, for example, argues that "Shakespeare wants us to understand that his love and Desdemona's, like Romeo's and Juliet's, Demetrius' and Helen's, Ferdinand's and Miranda's, has, in a rational sense, no cause." Rabkin, *Shakespeare and the Common Understanding*, 65.

71. Were issues in political fora approached with a humility like that urged by *Othello*, politics might well become a branch of disability studies, as Bruno Latour would like it to be. See Latour, "Introduction" to *Making Things Public: Atmospheres of Democracy* (Cambridge: MIT Press, 2005), 31.

3. *THE WINTER'S TALE*: FAITH IN LAW AND THE LAW OF FAITH

1. *The Trew Law of Free Monarchies*, in *Political Writings*, ed. Johann P. Sommerville (Cambridge: Cambridge University Press, 1994), 62–84, esp. 76.

2. "Speech to Parliament, 9 November 1605," and "Speech to Parliament, 21 March 1610," both in *Political Writings*, 155 and 186.

3. *Trew Law of Free Monarchies*, 77.

4. For example, Lynn Enterline reads that skepticism as coterminous with its misogyny, tracing a "disquieting gap between language and world" that leads to various male anxieties about female speech and about male possession of women. See Enterline, "'You Speak a Language

That I Understand Not': The Rhetoric of Animation in *The Winter's Tale*," *Shakespeare Quarterly* 48.1 (1997): 17–44. See also Howard Felperin's "'Tongue-Tied, Our Queen?': The Deconstruction of Presence in *The Winter's Tale*," in *Shakespeare: The Last Plays* (London: Longman, 1999), 187–205.

5. Cavell, "Recounting Gains, Showing Losses: Reading *The Winter's Tale*," in *Disowning Knowledge*, 193–221.

6. Hillman, *Shakespeare's Entrails*, 153–70, and Sherman, *Skepticism and Memory in Shakespeare and Donne*, 65–88. Hillman focuses on skepticism's somatic dimensions, which spur "an attempt to deny the susceptibility of one's interior to external influence" (27–28). Cavell and Hillman present skepticism as a problem, a disease to be struggled against and, to some extent, overcome. Sherman, by contrast, focuses on skepticism's therapeutic possibilities, by contrasting Leontes's early doubt with what we encounter at the end. "While the beginning of *The Winter's Tale* shows that skepticism can give rise to a reactionary agenda," Sherman writes, "the end of the play suggests that Hermione will usher in a new era for Sicilia, where the likes of Leontes will learn to listen and to live with the imponderables of uncertainty in a spirit of trust and cooperation" (85).

7. See Knight, "'Great Creating Nature': An Essay on *The Winter's Tale*," in *The Crown of Life: Essays in Interpretation of Shakespeare's Final Plays* (London: Methuen, 1958). Knight's Pauline context is that of resurrection. For Battenhouse's and Diehl's arguments, see Battenhouse, "Theme and Structure in *The Winter's Tale*," in *Shakespeare Survey* 33, ed. Kenneth Muir (Cambridge: Cambridge University Press, 1980), 123–38; and Diehl, "'Does not the stone rebuke me?': The Pauline Rebuke and Paulina's Lawful Magic in *The Winter's Tale*," in *Shakespeare and the Cultures of Performance* (Burlington: Ashgate, 2008), 69–82. Battenhouse argues that in Paulina, Shakespeare depicts "a spiritual progress from an initially moralistic rigidity to a more gracious shepherding, analogous perhaps to the growth of the biblical Saul of Tarsus into a St Paul" (137).

8. In terms of recent criticism, see especially Lupton, *Afterlives of the Saints: Hagiography, Typology, and Renaissance Literature* (Stanford: Stanford University Press, 1996), 175–218. Lupton, in contrast to more straightforward readings such as Diehl's, argues that the play is neither Protestant nor Catholic. I address her argument below. Numerous other articles have also attempted to position the play in terms of Protestantism and Catholicism. See David N. Beauregard's "Nature and Grace in *The Winter's Tale*," in *Catholic Theology in Shakespeare's Plays* (Newark: University of Delaware Press, 2008), 109–23; Richard Wilson's *Secret*

Shakespeare: Studies in Theatre, Religion, and Resistance (New York: Manchester University Press, 2004), 246–70; and James Ellison's "*The Winter's Tale* and the Religious Politics of Europe," in *Shakespeare's Romances: Contemporary Critical Essays*, ed. Alison Thorne (New York: Palgrave Macmillan, 2003), 171–204.

9. Diehl, "'Does not the stone rebuke me?,'" passim.

10. Lupton, *Thinking with Shakespeare*, 240.

11. Badiou, *Saint Paul: The Foundation of Universalism*, trans. Ray Brassier (Stanford: Stanford University Press, 2003), 1.

12. Badiou, *Ethics: An Essay on the Understanding of Evil*, trans. Peter Hallward (New York: Verso, 2002), 43. For Badiou, to be a subject is not a function of possessing psychological depth or the capacity for self-reflection. To be a subject is simply to be "the bearer of a fidelity" (43).

13. Badiou, *Saint Paul*, 28, 31. Fidelity to the event, fidelity that Othello fails to sustain in the event of love, takes the form of the following wager: "'This event has taken place, it is something which I can neither evaluate, nor demonstrate, but to which I shall be faithful.'" Badiou, *Infinite Thought: Truth and the Return to Philosophy*, trans. Oliver Feltham and Justin Clemens (New York: Continuum, 2005), 46–7.

14. For Badiou's Paul, the event of Christ's Resurrection destroys the systems of Jewish law and Greek wisdom alike; thus the project of Badiou's Paul is that of "intervening *ouk en sophiai logou*, 'without the wisdom of language.'" See Badiou, *Saint Paul*, 28.

15. Agamben, *The Time That Remains: A Commentary on the Letter to the Romans*, trans. Patricia Dailey (Stanford: Stanford University Press, 2005), 129.

16. For a preliminary sense of this, see the collection *St. Paul Among the Philosophers*, ed. John D. Caputo and Linda Martin Alcoff (Bloomington and Indianapolis: Indiana University Press, 2009).

17. Agamben, *Time That Remains*, 95.

18. For Badiou as for many radical theorists, such irony has dreadful consequences, making individuals into automatons of an especially perverse sort. "The law," Badiou writes, "is required in order to unleash the automatic life of desire, the automatism of repetition" (*Saint Paul*, 79). Slavoj Žižek thus writes that the Pauline project is "not the standard morbid moralistic one (how to crush transgressive impulses)" but rather is to "break out of this vicious cycle of the Law and desire, of the Prohibition and its transgression." See Žižek, *The Ticklish Subject: The Absent Centre of Political Ontology* (New York: Verso, 1999), 149.

19. Agamben, *Time That Remains*, 106, 119, 107.

20. Ibid., 44–58, esp. 47.

21. Ibid., 52, details Agamben's greatest disagreement with Badiou.

22. Badiou, *Saint Paul*, 109.

23. Agamben, *Time That Remains*, 52. Because he finds identity so dangerous, Agamben dreams of a world in which, "instead of continuing to search for a proper identity," humans seek instead to become "a singularity without identity, a common and absolutely exposed singularity"; in such a world we would "not be-thus in this or that particular biography" but would "be only *the* thus, their singular exteriority and their face," forming "a community without presuppositions and without subjects." Agamben, *The Coming Community*, trans. Michael Hardt (Minneapolis: University of Minnesota Press, 1993), 65.

24. Such perseverance, Badiou remarks, "presumes a genuine subversion [*détournement*] of the 'perseverance in being,' " of the self in its given state. *Ethics*, 47, 53.

25. My reading of the play might thus be said to build on one of Lupton's recent accounts of Shakespeare's Pauline quality, which details the presence in his work of a "death into citizenship." See *Citizen-Saints*, 21, and Chapter 1 generally.

26. It is not possible, here, to cite the voluminous output on Shakespeare and Montaigne, but for an excellent preliminary sense of how scholars have tended to think the two together, see Bradshaw, Bishop, and Holbrook, eds., *The Shakespearean International Yearbook 6: Special Section, Shakespeare and Montaigne Revisited* (Aldershot: Ashgate, 2006). Scholars often focus on Montaigne's Pyrrhonism and its links with antimonarchical, liberal ideals of pluralism and toleration, or on his adjudication of confessional questions.

27. Raising the possibility that there are "as many Pauls as there are readers of the New Testament," Julia Reinhard Lupton argues that the Pauline renaissance in literary studies ought, in part, to place Shakespeare's works "in a broader, more mobile, and more layered Scriptural tradition whose coordinates are existential rather than confessional." Lupton, *Thinking with Shakespeare*, 220, 230.

28. *The Complete Works*, trans. Donald Frame (New York: Alfred A. Knopf, 2003), 401.

29. The translation I use is that of the 1568 *Bishop's Bible*.

30. "Apology for Raymond Sebond," 509.

31. In Greene's tale, at least, there is genuine intensity, and even some concealment, in the relationship between Egistus (a basis for Polixenes) and Bellaria (a basis for Hermione): "there grew such a secret uniting of their affections, that the one could not well be without the other." P. G. Thomas, ed., *Pandosto or Dorastus and Fawnia* (London: Chatto & Windus, 1907), 5.

32. I cite *The Winter's Tale*, ed. Frances E. Dolan (New York: Penguin, 1999).

33. Cavell, *Disowning Knowledge*, 179.

34. "Apology for Raymond Sebond," 513.

35. "Of the power of the imagination," in *The Complete Works*, 82.

36. "Apology for Raymond Sebond," 547–8.

37. For an account of how Leontes acts despite his detachment, how he "sees himself as both ruler and instrument, both on stage and remote manipulator / observer," see T. G. Bishop, *Shakespeare and the Theatre of Wonder*, 144.

38. Hutson, *The Invention of Suspicion: Law and Mimesis in Shakespeare and Renaissance Drama* (New York: Oxford University Press, 2007), 1–63.

39. "Apology for Raymond Sebond," 424.

40. For a perceptive account of the oracle's function, one which ultimately finds in *The Winter's Tale* what I cannot ("an accommodation of royal and common law ideologies"), see Virginia Lee Strain, "*The Winter's Tale* and the Oracle of Law," *ELH* 78.3 (2011): 557–84, esp. 580.

41. Leontes declares Hermione an adulteress and a traitor in the same breath (2.1.88–9). For more on treason and adultery, see Karen Cunningham, *Imaginary Betrayals: Subjectivity and the Discourses of Treason in Early Modern England* (Philadelphia: University of Pennsylvania Press, 2002), 40–76; and John Bellamy, *The Tudor Law of Treason: An Introduction* (Buffalo: University of Toronto Press, 1979).

42. Lemon, *Treason by Words: Literature, Law, and Rebellion in Shakespeare's England* (Ithaca: Cornell University Press, 2006), 137–59.

43. "Speech to Parliament, 31 March 1607," in *Political Writings*, 159–78, esp. 161.

44. *The Trew Law of Free Monarchies*, in *Political Writings*, 62–84, esp. 76–7.

45. Fortescue, *On the Laws and Governance of England*, ed. Shelley Lockwood (Cambridge: Cambridge University Press, 1997), 5.

46. Smith, *De Republica Anglorum*, ed. Leonard Alston (Cambridge: Cambridge University Press, 1906), 10.

47. *Trew Law of Free Monarchies*, 78–81.

48. As Strier points out, Camillo—rightly—believes transgression to be more loyal than obedience. See "Faithful Servants: Shakespeare's Praise of Disobedience," in *The Historical Renaissance: New Essays on Tudor and Stuart Literature and Culture*, ed. Heather Dubrow and Richard Strier (Chicago: University of Chicago Press, 1988), 104–33, esp. 124–5.

49. Consider Fortescue: a king being "free to do wrong does not increase his freedom, just as to be able to be ill or to die is not power, but is rather to be deemed impotency because of the deprivation involved. For, as Boethius said, 'There is no power unless for good,' so that to be able to do evil, as the king reigning royally can more freely do than the king ruling his people politically, diminishes rather than increases his power" (23–4).

50. See Kuzner, "Unbuilding the City."

51. In his speech to parliament of 21 March 1610, James avers that he "wil not be content that my power be disputed vpon" and is "accomptable to none but God onely." See *Political Writings*, 184, 181.

52. Buchanan, to cite just one example, writes that monarchs, because of their passions, need "the Law, as it were a Colleague, or rather a bridler of his lusts." *De jure regni apud Scotos*, 1680, 22. I take up this idea later, in considering self-governing states in the context of *The Tempest*.

53. This is not to say that Montaigne uniformly opposes emergency power. In "Of custom," he writes, "it is true that Fortune, always reserving her authority above our reasonings, sometimes presents us with such an urgent necessity that the laws must needs give some place to it." See Montaigne, "Of custom and not easily changing an accepted law," in *The Complete Works*, 106–7.

54. Montaigne, "Of Presumption" in *The Complete Works*, 583.

55. Janet Adelman puts the point in terms of gender: "If Leontes founds his masculine identity on separation from the female," she writes, "Florizel embraces the female." See Adelman, "Masculine Authority and the Maternal Body in *The Winter's Tale*," in *Shakespeare's Romances*, ed. Alison Thorne (New York: Palgrave Macmillan, 2003), 145–70, esp.156.

56. This embrace of dependence makes love for Florizel what Paul says it ought to be: that which "suffreth all thynges, beleveth all thynges, hopeth all thynges, endureth all thynges" (1 Cor. 13:7). Whereas Leontes initially does none of these and Othello briefly does only some of them, Florizel arguably does a modest version of them all. Heir to his affection for Perdita, he is happy to bear a lost succession, to believe Perdita will love him nevertheless, and to hope that in dedicating himself to "unpathed waters" and "undreamed shores," he and Perdita will find a haven (4.4.566). Florizel believes in the value of hazarding all that he has and can only do so by having faith in humility.

57. *The Complete Works*, 397.

58. Here, Montaigne repeats Galatians 6:3: "for if any man seeme to himselfe that he is somewhat, when he is nothing, the same deceaveth hymselfe in his own fansie."

59. Cavell, *Disowning Knowledge*, 208.

60. *The Complete Works*, 448–9.

61. Bishop, *Shakespeare and the Theatre of Wonder*, 148.

62. Sherman, *Skepticism and Memory in Shakespeare and Donne*, 71, 73.

63. Lim, "Knowledge and Belief in *The Winter's Tale*," *SEL* 41.2 (2001): 317–34, esp. 330–31.

64. Lupton, *Afterlives of the Saints*, 216.

65. Adelman describes this as a faith in theater: "Shakespeare requires us to give up our position as knowing audience . . . asking that we recreate Leontes's faith in ourselves by our own willingness to believe in what we know cannot be happening" ("Masculine Authority," 162–63).

66. Gross, *The Dream of the Moving Statue* (Ithaca: Cornell University Press, 1992), 109.

67. Bishop, *Shakespeare and the Theatre of Wonder*, 170, 167.

68. Charles Altieri, similarly, reads the play as advancing "a grace whose value exists beyond any epistemic judgments." See Altieri, "Wonder in *The Winter's Tale*: a cautionary account of epistemic criticism," in *A Sense of the World: Essays on Fiction, Narrative, and Knowledge*, ed. John Gibson, Wolfgang Huemer, and Luca Pocci (New York: Routledge, 2007), 266–86, esp. 282.

69. Battenhouse, "Theme and Structure," 134.

70. Barkan explores Hermione's seeming double nature in the context of sculpture, noting that Shakespeare "does not let us in on the secret" of whether Hermione ever was literal marble. See Leonard Barkan, "'Living Sculptures': Ovid, Michelangelo, and *The Winter's Tale*," *ELH* 48.4 (1981): 639–67, esp. 663.

71. Agamben, *Time That Remains*, 129.

72. Such strangeness and unknowability help distinguish the reading proposed here and that is sometimes offered in certain psycho-analytical readings. According to Janet Adelman, for instance, *The Winter's Tale* is a play that moves toward a salutary certainty, from "the anguish of a masculinity that conceives of itself as betrayed at its point of origin" to "a pastoral richly identified with the generative potential of the female body" (*Suffocating Mothers*, 222). In the play's early acts, Leontes exorcises female generativity only to realize that the exorcism generates only "the landscape of tragedy, an endless winter of barrenness and deprivation" (228). The remainder of the play represents the return of female generativity, "the return of the world to him and his capacity to tolerate and participate in its aliveness" (232). Adelman sees the world returning through the process of doubt being replaced by faith: "in this play's gendering of doubt and faith," Adelman writes, "faith means willingness to submit to unknown processes outside the self, processes

registered as female" (232). Adelman acknowledges that this faith is incomplete, arguing that "Leontes is fully restored to personal and political potency at the end" and that "the female agents of restoration turn out to have been good patriarchalists all along" (235). I, like Adelman, read the play as critical of Leontes's absolutist presumption (though less in terms of gender). I also agree that the play is about submitting "to unknown processes outside the self, processes registered as female." On the other hand, as suggested above, I do not see Leontes at the end as "fully restored to personal and political potency." Rather, I see him as divided and undefined, his fantasies of absolute control—not to mention a clear, patriarchal self-conception—well behind him.

73. Boyarin, *A Radical Jew: Paul and the Politics of Identity* (Berkeley and Los Angeles: University of California Press, 1994), 235.

74. Hutson, *The Invention of Suspicion*; and Kahn, *Wayward Contracts: The Crisis of Political Obligation in England, 1640–1674* (Princeton: Princeton University Press, 2004).

75. Cicero, *On the Commonwealth*, 30.

76. Smith, *De Republica Anglorum*, 12.

77. As Sherman puts it, if anything, the play's end "demands that we be accountable for our lapses" (*Skepticism and Memory in Shakespeare and Donne*, 79).

78. Engle, "*Measure for Measure* and Modernity: The Problem of the Sceptic's Authority," in *Shakespeare and Modernity: Early Modern to Millennium*, ed. Hugh Grady (London: Routledge, 2000), 85–104, esp. 86.

79. Jeffrey S. Shoulson, *Fictions of Conversion: Jews, Christians, and Cultures of Change in Early Modern England* (Philadelphia: University of Pennsylvania Press, 2013), 14.

80. For a fascinating account of Pauline conversion, of how it is "less like decisive change" and much more an unstable, uncertain state in which "opposition ceases to be opposition," see Jonathan Goldberg, *The Seeds of Things: Theorizing Sexuality and Materiality in Renaissance Representations* (New York: Fordham University Press, 2009), 23. Goldberg writes, for instance, that Paul's conversion "functions to slaughter flesh" but also "is delivered in the flesh and to the flesh."

81. Sarah Beckwith puts this point differently, but brilliantly, remarking that "Leontes is transformed in his understanding of himself—sinful and redeemed from sin in one and the same moment." See Beckwith, *Shakespeare and the Grammar of Forgiveness* (Ithaca: Cornell University Press, 2011), 142.

82. This position can be found in Johnson's folk theory of the moral law in *Moral Imagination*, 1–50. See also Lakoff and Johnson, *Philosophy in the Flesh*, 290–336, as well as Johnson's more recent *Morality for*

Humans: Ethical Understanding from the Perspective of Cognitive Science (Chicago: University of Chicago Press, 2014).

83. Johnson calls for a new form of moral theory, "one in which laws and formal decision procedures do not play the central role," one that takes into account conflicting goods, narrative contexts, and the self's contingent, ever-transforming character (*Moral Imagination*, 77).

84. Strier, *Resistant Structures: Particularity, Radicalism, and Renaissance Texts* (Berkeley and Los Angeles: University of California Press, 1995), 4–5.

85. Thorne, *The Dialectic of Counter-Enlightenment*, 84.

86. Popkin, *The History of Scepticism: From Savonarola to Bayle*, xxi, 3–16, 44–63.

87. Thorne, *The Dialectic of Counter-Enlightenment*, 11.

88. Calvin, *Institutes of the Christian Religion*, trans. Henry Beveridge (Peabody, MA: Hendrickson Publishers, 2008), 222.

89. Luther, *Only the Decalogue Is Eternal*, trans. Holger Sonntag (Minneapolis: Lutheran Press, 2008), 34.

90. Holbrook, *Shakespeare's Individualism*, 143–44.

4. DOUBTFUL FREEDOM IN *THE TEMPEST*

1. Norbrook, "'What cares these roarers for the name of king?': Language and Utopia in *The Tempest*," in *The Politics of Tragicomedy: Shakespeare and After*, ed. Gordon McMullan and Jonathan Hope (London: Routledge, 1992), 21–54, esp. 25.

2. All references are to *The Tempest*, ed. Peter Holland (New York: Penguin, 1999).

3. See Peter Holbrook, *Shakespeare's Individualism*, especially Chapter 11, "Libertarian Shakespeare: Mill, Bradley."

4. See Lakoff and Johnson, *Philosophy in the Flesh*, 329.

5. Lakoff, *Whose Freedom?*, 29.

6. As Paul Kottman remarks, such absolute freedom comes to look like radical abandonment. See Kottman, *Tragic Conditions in Shakespeare: Disinheriting the Globe* (Baltimore: The Johns Hopkins University Press, 2009), 147.

7. Kottman puts the point somewhat differently: that Ariel "is subjected to, and by, the promise of freedom" (147).

8. Nancy, *The Experience of Freedom*, trans. Bridget McDonald (Stanford: Stanford University Press, 1993), 2.

9. Greenblatt, *Shakespeare's Freedom* (Chicago: University of Chicago Press, 2010), 1.

10. Holbrook, *Shakespeare's Individualism*, 1.

11. Greenblatt, *Shakespeare's Freedom*, 14.

12. Holbrook, *Shakespeare's Individualism*, 29.

13. In exploring the theme of dependence, Kottman focuses on the issue of recognition. He argues that although freedom in *Romeo and Juliet* is a question of claiming separate individuality—of establishing their lives as their own—the only way to lodge the claim is through another. For Kottman, freedom arises in acts of mutual self-recognition, so freedom cannot be claimed by autonomous agents, as Greenblatt and Holbrook claim Barnardine does. But Kottman's nuanced model also cannot capture what is at work in *The Tempest*. Freedom in the play is not always autonomy and does, as Kottman suggests, often only come to be through forces beyond those at the self's disposal. Yet as I have suggested and as we will see, freedom in the play emerges in acts not of recognition but of transformation, in separateness not from other people but from the self as it is given. See Kottman, "Defying the Stars: Tragic Love as the Struggle for Freedom in *Romeo and Juliet*," passim.

14. Scodel focuses on Shakespeare's syncretic use of two ideas of freedom: the Stoic, defined as "obedience to one's reason, free of enslaving passions," and the Christian, defined as "obedience to God, freed by grace from sin." Scodel, "Finding Freedom in *Hamlet*," *MLQ* 72.2 (2011): 163–200, esp. 164.

15. In one sense, Scodel makes an argument about *Hamlet* that resembles Greenblatt's: namely, that "social and political freedom" is an "ability to act freely toward other human beings and political authorities," an ability that "depends on attaining freedom from thoughts and feelings that block free action" (164).

16. Holbrook, "Freedom and self-government: *The Tempest*," in *Shakespeare's Individualism*.

17. Montaigne, "Of anger," 655, 658.

18. See Orgel, "New Uses of Adversity: Tragic Experience in *The Tempest*," in *In Defense of Reading: A Reader's Approach to Literary Criticism*, ed. Reuben A. Brower and Richard Poirier (New York: E.P. Dutton & Co, 1962), 110–32, esp. 114.

19. See Berger, Jr., "Miraculous Harp: A Reading of Shakespeare's *Tempest*," in *Second World and Green World: Studies in Renaissance Fiction-Making* (London: University of California Press, 1988), 147–85, esp. 178–81, and Holbrook, 206. Cantor, for his part, argues that Prospero cultivates ideals of wisdom and moderation in his rule. See Cantor, "Prospero's Republic: The Politics of Shakespeare's *The Tempest*," in *Shakespeare as Political Thinker*, ed. John E. Alvis and Thomas G. West (Wilmington, DE: ISI Books, 2000), 241–59.

20. *Sextus Empiricus: Selections from the Major Writings on Scepticism, Man & God*, ed. Philip P. Hallie, trans. Sanford G. Etheridge (Indianapolis: Hackett, 1985), 41.

21. Montaigne, "Of sadness," 9.

22. I will cite a range of works, but see especially Foucault, *The History of Sexuality, vol. 3: The Care of the Self*, trans. Robert Hurley (New York: Vintage, 1988); "The Ethics of the Concern of the Self as a Practice of Freedom," in *The Essential Works of Foucault, vol. 1: Ethics: Subjectivity and Truth*, ed. Paul Rabinow, trans. Robert Hurley and others (New York: the New Press, 1998), 281–301; and *The Hermeneutics of the Subject: Lectures at the College de France, 1981–1982*, ed. Frédéric Gros, trans. Graham Burchell (New York: Palgrave Macmillan, 2005).

23. For more on this, see, for instance, Foucault, "Self Writing," in *Ethics: Subjectivity and Truth*.

24. Marcus Aurelius, *Meditations*, 4, 17, 23.

25. Seneca, *Anger, Mercy, Revenge*, 29.

26. Montaigne, "Of anger," 661.

27. Foucault, *Ethics: Subjectivity and Truth*, 210.

28. Seneca, *Anger, Mercy, Revenge*, 14.

29. Foucault, *The Hermeneutics of the Subject*, 212.

30. Montaigne, "Of solitude," 214.

31. See "On solitude," 214, for Montaigne's metaphor of the self's back shop.

32. For an argument to this effect about Shakespeare generally, see A. D. Nuttall, "Stoics and Sceptics," in *Shakespeare the Thinker*, 171–220.

33. Foucault, *The Hermeneutics of the Subject*, 207.

34. Aurelius, *Meditations*, 23, 32.

35. Orgel, "New Uses of Adversity," 111.

36. Writing of *Hamlet*, Scodel argues similarly, insofar as he contends that Hamlet "radically deflates a Stoic and Neostoic view of reason's liberatory power." See "Finding Freedom in *Hamlet*," 181.

37. Montaigne, "Apology for Raymond Sebond," 399, 401.

38. Jordan, *Shakespeare's Monarchies: Ruler and Subject in the Romances* (Ithaca: Cornell University Press, 1997), 147–209, esp. 177.

39. Richard Strier, along similar lines, has argued that the play's critique of magic implies not only a critique of colonial enterprises but also of the mystical dimensions of absolute sovereignty. See "'I am Power': Normal and Magical Politics in *The Tempest*," in *Writing and Political Engagement in Seventeenth-Century England*, ed. Derek Hirst and Richard Strier (Cambridge: Cambridge University Press, 1999), 10–30, esp. 30.

40. Harrington, *The Commonwealth of Oceana and a System of Politics*, ed. J. G. A. Pocock (Cambridge: Cambridge University Press, 2001), 64.

41. Buchanan, *De jure regni apud Scotos*, 1680, 22.

42. Visconsi, "*Vinculum Fidei: The Tempest* and the Law of Allegiance," *Law & Literature* 20.1 (2008): 1–20, esp. 3. Julia Reinhard Lupton, to cite another example, focuses on Caliban and on the category of minority, one that, if acknowledged by Prospero, ought to have incorporated care *and* autonomy; minority, for Lupton, represents "an unrealized capacity for independence," one that, Shakespeare suggests, ought to be fostered by family life and protected by law. See Lupton, "The Minority of Caliban," in *Thinking with Shakespeare*, 188.

43. As has long been recognized, difficulty and obscurity are staples of Shakespeare's late style. See, for instance, Russ McDonald, *Shakespeare's Late Style* (Cambridge: Cambridge University Press, 2006), esp. 30–7. The difficulty of Ferdinand's speech, though, seems purposeful.

44. Evett, *Discourses of Service in Shakespeare's England* (New York: Palgrave Macmillan, 2005), 14. See also Schalkwyk, "Between Historicism and Presentism: Love and Service in *Antony and Cleopatra* and *The Tempest*," *Shakespeare in Southern Africa* 17 (2005): 1–17.

45. Schalkwyk, 14.

46. See Evett, 7.

47. Luther, "A Treatise on Christian Liberty," in *Works of Martin Luther*, trans. W. A. Lambert (Philadelphia: A. J. Holman Company, 1915), 2:312–48, esp. 312.

48. For a brilliant consideration of consent as an "event," see Lupton's reading of *All's Well That Ends Well* in *Thinking with Shakespeare*, esp. 127.

49. For a consideration of this sort of Christian liberty in the context of metaphysical poetry, see my essay, "Metaphysical Freedom," *MLQ* 74.4 (2013): 465–92.

50. Berger, "Miraculous Harp," 179.

51. For an argument that *The Tempest* is, nevertheless, a Christian play that champions virtues such as forgiveness, justice, and perseverance, see John D. Cox, "Recovering Something Christian About *The Tempest*," in *Christianity and Literature* 50.1 (2000): 31–51.

52. Praising *philia* rather than *eros*, Montaigne declares that "our free will has no product more properly its own than affection and friendship" ("Of friendship," 166). Yet in this essay Montaigne again is anti-Stoic; he contends that the act of supreme free will, by which true friendship forms, leads to the dissolution of discrete individual will. True

friends' "souls mingle and blend with each other so completely that they efface the seam that joined them, and cannot find it again" (169). Boundaries blur to the point that "this mixture . . . having seized my whole will, led it to plunge and lose itself in his," and "having seized his whole will, led it to plunge and lose itself in mine" (169–70). Such blurring, for Montaigne, is an extreme rarity between friends and an outright impossibility between lovers. Montaigne arguably adopts an even more skeptical view about human capacity to employ free will for its dissolution than he does about our capacity to strengthen the will toward the goal of Stoic self-sufficiency. Through Ferdinand, Shakespeare seems to ratify these claims about rarity and impossibility. No one in the play, let alone Ferdinand, achieves what Montaigne would deem genuine friendship. Ferdinand and Miranda's love is, as Montaigne remarks of *eros*, "more active, more scorching, and more intense" than any other form of affection in the play (167).

53. Norbrook, "'What cares these roarers for the name of king?'," 41.

54. Hill, *The most pleasuante arte of the interpretacion of dreames*, 1576, dedicatory epistle.

55. See, for instance, "New Uses of Adversity," where Orgel writes that "Caliban is the mind that cannot learn, that will not impose controls on its passion" (124).

56. Hill, *The most pleasuante arte*, 1576.

57. Montaigne, "Of prognostications," 32.

58. Montaigne, "That the taste of good and evil depends in large part on the opinion we have of them," 46.

59. Strier made this remark in a conference paper called "When Is Bondage Freedom?," given at the 2014 meeting of the Renaissance Society of America.

60. Longinus, *On the Sublime*, trans. Thomas R. R. Stebbing (Oxford: T. & G. Shrimpton, 1867), 23–4.

61. Lewin, "'Your Actions Are My Dreams': Sleepy Minds in Shakespeare's Last Plays," *Shakespeare Studies* 31 (2003): 184–204, esp. 193. For a different account of how the dream "typifies the island's permissions regarding subjectivity and power," see Simon Palfrey, *Late Shakespeare: A New World of Words* (Oxford: Oxford University Press, 1997), 184.

62. Longinus's *On the Sublime* is a manual that advises how to mold one's speech so that it will seem unpracticed and the speaker will seem as surprised by his words as he hopes his audience will be. But we have no reason to think that Caliban's speech merely seems unpracticed; the suggestion, rather, is that it really is unpracticed.

63. In the hands of early modern republicans, Patrick Cheney argues, the practice of sublime utterance can be a way of seizing liberty

out of defeat: of creating an imaginative domain of liberty and thereby drawing a limit beyond which sovereign power cannot pass. For Cheney, when republics dissolve or are otherwise out of grasp, republican culture persists in practices of the self. Caliban's utterance draws a limit not unlike that described by Cheney, but unlike Cheney's republican heroes, we have no sense that Caliban draws the limit deliberately. Cheney, *Marlowe's Republican Authorship: Lucan, Liberty, and the Sublime* (New York: Palgrave, 2009).

64. Montaigne, "Of prompt or slow speech," 31.

65. Orgel, "New Uses of Adversity," 116.

66. Arendt, "What Is Freedom?," passim.

67. Foucault, *The Hermeneutics of the Subject*, 210–23.

68. For an excellent account of "white cannibalism" in the play, see Richard Halpern, " 'The Picture of Nobody': White Cannibalism in *The Tempest*," in *The Production of English Renaissance Culture*, ed. David Lee Miller, Sharon O'Dair, and Harold Weber (Ithaca: Cornell University Press, 1994), 262–92.

69. Montaigne, "Of idleness," 24–5.

70. Montaigne, "Apology for Raymond Sebond," 408.

71. *An Apology for Poetry (or The Defence of Poesy)*, ed. R. W. Maslen (Manchester: Manchester University Press, 2002), 85.

5. LOOKING TWO WAYS AT ONCE IN *TIMON OF ATHENS*

1. Empson, "Timon's Dog," in *The Structure of Complex Words* (London: Chatto & Windus, 1951), 175–84, esp. 180.

2. Most but not all scholars are in accord with Empson, G. Wilson Knight being the most prominent counterexample. Knight writes that "this play is *Hamlet, Troilus and Cressida, Othello, King Lear*, become self-conscious and universal; it includes and transcends them all." Knight, "The Pilgrimage of Hate: An Essay on *Timon of Athens*," in *The Wheel of Fire*, 207–39, esp. 236.

3. Dawson, "Is Timon a Character?" in *Shakespeare and Character: Theory, History, Performance, and Theatrical Persons*, ed. Paul Yachnin and Jessica Slights (New York: Palgrave, 2009), 197–213, esp. 197. A. D. Nuttall suggests that many of the play's characters, aside from Timon, are presented even more "colourlessly," "as in some ancient frieze." Nuttall, *Timon of Athens* (Hertfordshire: Harvester Wheatsheaf, 1989), 4.

4. See Kahn's essay in *Timon of Athens*, ed. Barbara Mowat and Paul Werstine (New York: Simon & Schuster, 2006), 217.

5. *Timon of Athens*, xxii.

6. For a contrasting viewpoint, see Harold Bloom, who finds that "the play stages better than it reads; it is intensely dramatic, but very unevenly expressed." Bloom, *Shakespeare: The Invention of the Human*, 588.

7. See Lukas Erne, *Shakespeare as Literary Dramatist* (Cambridge: Cambridge University Press, 2003), for an argument that Shakespeare wrote texts not only for the audience and the stage but also, specifically, for the reader and the page. In a sense, Erne stands at the end of a tradition of a "literary" or "cerebral" Shakespeare at least as old as Charles Lamb.

8. All references are to *Timon of Athens*, ed. Barbara Mowat and Paul Werstine.

9. Greene, "'You Must Eat Men': The Sodomitic Economy of Renaissance Patronage," *GLQ* 1.2 (1994): 163–97, esp. 175. Greene reads the play in the context of sodomy, as I do elsewhere. See "Skepticism, Sovereignty, Sodomy," in *ShakesQueer*, ed. Madhavi Menon (Durham: Duke University Press, 2010), 361–8.

10. Greene calls this an "insatiability," "which constantly but never adequately feeds the appetite of 'covetous men'" (174).

11. Bevington and Smith, "James I and *Timon of Athens*," *Comparative Drama* 33.1 (1999): 56–87, esp. 57.

12. Leinwand, *Theatre, Finance, and Society in Early Modern England* (Cambridge: Cambridge University Press, 1999), 35.

13. Hadfield, "*Timon of Athens* and Jacobean Politics," *Shakespeare Survey* 56 (2003): 215–26, esp. 226.

14. See, for example, Hadfield, 219–20.

15. For some examples of James's calls for economy, as well as an important exchange with Carr, see *Letters of King James VI & I*, ed. G. P. V. Akrigg (Berkeley and Los Angeles: University of California Press, 1984), 261, 291, and 336–39.

16. The tradition of reading *Timon* as a moralistic play in this sense is quite long. For one recent example, see Daryl Kaytor, "Shakespeare's Political Philosophy: A Debt to Plato in *Timon of Athens*," *Philosophy and Literature* 36 (2012): 136–52. Kaytor argues that Timon falls because of his susceptibility to flattery and his supreme overconfidence in others.

17. Lakoff and Johnson, *Philosophy in the Flesh*, 48.

18. As Amanda Bailey puts it, "*Timon* indexes its own historical moment at which a bewildering variety [of monies] jostled for recognition," rendering money an unstable fiscal and social phenomenon. Bailey, "*Timon of Athens*, Forms of Payback, and the Genre of Debt," *ELR* 41.2 (2011): 375–400, esp. 377.

19. For another account of how Timon strains toward the impossible, see Ken Jackson, " 'One Wish' or the Possibility of the Impossible: Derrida, the Gift, and God in *Timon of Athens*," *Shakespeare Quarterly* 52.1 (2001): 34–66.

20. Knight argues that this is actually Timon's aim, not a symptom of his disease. According to Knight, Timon "would break down with conviviality, music, art, the barriers that sever consciousness from consciousness." See Knight, "The Pilgrimage of Hate," 211.

21. Zunshine, *Why We Read Fiction: Theory of Mind and the Novel* (Columbus: Ohio State University Press, 2006).

22. Bataille, *The Accursed Share: An Essay on General Economy*, 3 vols., trans. Robert Hurley (New York: Zone Books, 1988).

23. There we might also find Bersani's gay outlaw. See *Homos*, which in many ways develops the earlier "Is the Rectum a Grave?," *October* 43 (Winter 1987): 197–222.

24. Bataille, *The Accursed Share*, vol. 3, 221.

25. Ibid., vol. 3, 203.

26. Ibid., vol. 3, 242.

27. Dawson, "Is Timon a Character?," 197, 210.

28. Bersani, "Psychoanalysis and the Aesthetic Subject," *Critical Inquiry* 32.2 (2006): 161–74, esp. 170.

29. Bataille, *The Accursed Share*, vol. 3, 219.

30. Bersani, *Homos*, 129.

31. Grady, "*Timon of Athens*: The Dialectic of Usury, Nihilism, and Art," in *A Companion to Shakespeare's Works, vol. 1: The Tragedies*, ed. Richard Dutton and Jean E. Howard (Oxford: Blackwell, 2003), 430–51. "Timon," Grady writes, "reconciles his impulses by aestheticizing his hate and leaving it as a gift within a work of environmental art" (448–9).

32. This emergence of a protected interior space, supposedly in early modernity, is much commented upon. For an account drawn from the perspective of intellectual history, see Charles Taylor, *Sources of the Self: The Making of the Modern Identity*; for one focused on the domain of literary studies, see Anne Ferry, *The "Inward" Language: Sonnets of Wyatt, Sidney, Shakespeare, Donne* (Chicago: University of Chicago Press, 1983).

33. See Lucian, *Selected Dialogues*, trans. C. D. N. Costa (New York: Oxford University Press, 2005), 26–44.

34. *Sextus Empiricus: Selections from the Major Writings on Scepticism, Man & God*, 33.

35. For two recent accounts that link Shakespeare to Sextus Empiricus, though in very different terms than the ones set out here, see Anita Gilman Sherman, *Skepticism and Memory in Shakespeare and Donne*, and William M. Hamlin, *Tragedy and Scepticism in Shakespeare's England*.

36. *Sextus Empiricus,* 64.

37. *Sextus Empiricus,* 63.

38. Coleridge, *Biographia Literaria,* 151.

39. Eliot, "Shakespeare and the Stoicism of Seneca," in *T. S. Eliot: Selected Essays* (London, 1951), 126.

40. Greenblatt, *Renaissance Self-Fashioning: From More to Shakespeare,* 254.

41. See the entire introduction to Bloom's *Shakespeare: The Invention of the Human,* but especially 8–10.

42. Carey, *What Good Are the Arts?* (London: Faber and Faber, 2005), 177.

43. Bloom, *How to Read and Why* (New York: Touchstone, 2001), 22.

44. Carey, *What Good Are the Arts?,* 213.

45. Bloom, *How to Read and Why,* 25.

46. Wolfgang Iser argues that literary texts can generate interest only when authors leave room for readers to employ imagination. A literary text must "be conceived in such a way that it will engage the reader's imagination in the task of working things out for himself, for reading is only a pleasure when it is active and creative." Iser, "The Reading Process: A Phenomenological Approach," *New Literary History* 3.2 (1972): 279–99, esp. 280.

47. Carey, *What Good Are the Arts?,* 214.

48. Bloom, *How to Read and Why,* 22.

49. Carey concludes his chapter on literature and critical intelligence by relating how a number of young offenders, exposed to Golding's *Lord of the Flies,* found that they could "manage and respond to literature," which in turn helped them "repair their crushingly low self-esteem." *What Good Are the Arts?,* 212.

50. What the impoverished Copperfield gets from them, Carroll writes, "is lively and powerful images of human life suffused with the feeling and understanding of the astonishingly capable and complete human beings who wrote them. It is through this kind of contact with a sense of human possibility that he is enabled to escape from the degrading limitations of his own local environment. He is not escaping from reality; he is escaping from an impoverished reality into the larger world of healthy human possibility. By nurturing and cultivating his own individual identity through his literary imagination, he enables himself to adapt successfully to this world. He directly enhances his own fitness as a human being, and in doing so he demonstrates the kind of adaptive advantage that can be conferred by literature." Carroll, *Literary Darwinism: Evolution, Human Nature, and Literature* (New York: Routledge, 2004), 68.

51. Neither Bloom nor Carey thinks that literature makes readers more ethical, but they do believe it improves our comprehension of ourselves and our worlds. Bloom writes that we read first for what he calls "difficult pleasure," but also because "we cannot know enough people profoundly enough; that we need to know ourselves better; that we require knowledge, not just of self and others, but of the way things are." Bloom, *How to Read and Why*, 29.

52. Dutton, *The Art Instinct: Beauty, Pleasure, and Human Evolution* (London: Bloomsbury, 2009), 110.

53. As noted in my introduction, in *Timon* Shakespeare discourages choosing between opposed worlds, and so is not amenable to the importance of choice that both Norman Rabkin and Graham Bradshaw ascribe to Shakespeare's program of opposition.

54. *Sextus Empiricus*, 93.

55. *Sextus Empiricus*, 35.

56. To be so stretched is, in Deborah P. Britzman's words, "[t]o engage the limit of thought—where thought stops, what it cannot bear to know, what it must shut out to think as it does," what I must shut out to read coherently. Britzman, "Is There a Queer Pedagogy? Or, Stop Reading Straight," *Educational Theory* 45.2 (1995): 151–65, esp. 156.

57. Thorne, *The Dialectic of Counter-Enlightenment*, esp. 1–116.

58. Cavell, *Disowning Knowledge*, 5.

59. One of the great virtues of Sherman's *Skepticism and Memory in Shakespeare and Donne* and Spolsky's *Satisfying Skepticism: Embodied Knowledge in the Early Modern World* (Aldershot: Ashgate, 2001) is the careful attention that both books pay to therapeutic dimensions of the skeptical outlook, even though Spolsky attaches evolutionary value to skepticism in a way that I would not.

60. Here is a point where we do well not to equate Timon's perspective with that evinced by the play. In her otherwise brilliant reading of *Timon*, Janet Adelman does just this. She insightfully describes how "Timon transfers to himself the nurturant qualities of the female body" early in the play and how, when this fails—when he cannot equate "his bounty with the infinitely renewable female resource of breast milk"—he turns to misogynist invective (*Suffocating Mothers*, 167–8). I agree with Adelman here, but not with her conflation of Shakespeare's perspective with Timon's. Adelman writes that, "shrunk to the limits of Timon's masculine self, founded in scarcity, the play itself becomes parsimonious" (174). As I read it, Shakespeare puts readers in a situation where they cannot decide whether the world—or the self—is, or should be, founded in scarcity or surplus, and asks them to undergo and even embrace the exquisite cognitive disorientation that this requires. So while Timon is

amenable to the sort of psychoanalytical reading that Adelman proposes, *Timon* itself is not; *Timon's* Pyrrhonism, in a sense, is the antidote to Timon's absolutist fantasies.

61. For an excellent account of this strand of Cavell's thinking, see Gerald L. Bruns, "Stanley Cavell's Shakespeare," *Critical Inquiry* 16.3 (1990): 612–32.

62. Cavell, *Disowning Knowledge*, 5.

63. Sedgwick, *Touching Feeling: Affect, Pedagogy, Performativity* (Durham: Duke University Press, 2003), 130.

64. See Sedgwick, *Touching Feeling*, passim. For the conversation with Litvak, see 147.

65. Though not particularly focused on reading, some terms set out by Sarah Ahmed in *Queer Phenomenology: Orientations, Objects, Others* (Durham: Duke University Press) help capture what reading *Timon* does in these regards. "[P]henomenology," she writes, "is full of queer moments; as moments of disorientation that Maurice Merleau-Ponty suggests involve not only 'the intellectual experience of disorder, but the vital experience of giddiness and nausea, which is the awareness of our contingency, and the horror with which it fills us'" (4). Whereas Merleau-Ponty's *Phenomenology* accounts for how moments of disorientation are overcome and "bodies become reoriented," Ahmed urges us to "stay with such moments," those "where the world no longer appears 'the right way up,'" as they "may be the source of vitality as well as giddiness. We might," Ahmed speculates, "even find joy and excitement in the horror" (65, 4). Reorientation effects the "becoming vertical" of perspective and a triumph over queer effects, and in *Timon*, reorientation happens when I nominate one of its worlds as true (65). Ahmed counsels against the "straightening devices" that, in reorienting us, make following straight lines and seeing straight easy, so Ahmed might be heartened to know that the straightening devices I have brought to bear on *Timon* all have broken (72). The breakage, I think, results from the play being among what Ahmed calls "disorientation devices," which force us to view objects at different angles, bring new objects into view, and present the world "aslant," the change in perspective being so drastic as to mean dwelling in a different world (172).

EPILOGUE: SHAKESPEARE AS A WAY OF LIFE

1. Zunshine, *Why We Read Fiction*, 123.

2. Hadot, *What Is Ancient Philosophy?*, 189.

3. Foucault, "The Ethics of the Concern of the Self as a Practice of Freedom," 294–5.

4. Foucault, *The Hermeneutics of the Subject*, 251.

5. Bloom, *Shakespeare: The Invention of the Human*; and Emerson, *Journals and Miscellaneous Notebooks*, ed. Gilman and Allardt (Cambridge, MA: Harvard University Press, 1982), 57.

6. *Selected Letters of John Keats*, 24.

7. Foucault, "On the Genealogy of Ethics: An Overview of a Work in Progress," in *Ethics: Subjectivity and Truth*, 266.

8. For an account of how Pyrrhonism can be "an anti-systematic way of doing philosophy, an always-unfinished enquiry in which unforeseen shifts and reversals are programmatically allowed for," see Terence Cave, "Imagining Scepticism in the Sixteenth Century," in *Retrospectives: Essays in Literature, Poetics, and Cultural History* (London: Maney, 2009), 111.

9. *Sextus Empiricus*, 41–2.

10. Hadot, *Philosophy as a Way of Life*, 267.

11. Hadot, *What Is Ancient Philosophy?*, 123.

12. Bevington, *Shakespeare's Ideas*, 213–17.

Index